Abraham Kuenen

National religions and universal religions : lectures delivered at

Oxford and in London, in April and May, 1882

Abraham Kuenen

National religions and universal religions : lectures delivered at Oxford and in London, in April and May, 1882

ISBN/EAN: 9783337261610

Printed in Europe, USA, Canada, Australia, Japan

Cover: Foto ©Lupo / pixelio.de

More available books at **www.hansebooks.com**

THE HIBBERT LECTURES,
1882.

THE HIBBERT LECTURES, 1882.

NATIONAL RELIGIONS

AND

UNIVERSAL RELIGIONS.

LECTURES

DELIVERED AT OXFORD AND IN LONDON,

IN APRIL AND MAY, 1882,

BY

A. KUENEN, LL.D. D.D.

Professor of Theology at Leiden.

WILLIAMS AND NORGATE,
14, HENRIETTA STREET, COVENT GARDEN, LONDON;
AND 20, SOUTH FREDERICK STREET, EDINBURGH.

1882.

LONDON:
PRINTED BY C. GREEN AND SON,
178, STRAND.

PREFACE.

In offering this book to the English public, I have to discharge a two-fold duty. In the first place, I must thank my friend the Rev. Ph. H. Wicksteed, M.A., for his readiness to undertake the translation of my Lectures, and for the manner in which he performed his task. It was originally my intention to write the Lectures in English myself. But I was not long in perceiving that the execution of this plan would take more time than I could well spare, and that, after all, the product of my exertions would be unworthy to occupy its place in the Series for which it was destined. Under these circumstances, I considered it from the first as a great privilege that my friend Wicksteed was willing to come to my aid; but only when the work was going on and when we were constantly discussing it together, I became fully aware how much reason I had to congratulate myself upon the possession of such an interpreter. I must be allowed to offer him my sincere thanks, and also to extend them to the Hibbert Trustees for approving his co-operation and kindly furthering it.

Looking back from my quiet study at Leiden on the days—over-filled, but extremely interesting and pleasant—which I passed in England for the delivery of my Lectures, I must necessarily add another to this first tribute of gratitude. It is due to those whose friendly reception made me feel quite at home in the foreign country, both in London and at Oxford, more especially to the Hibbert Trustees and to the members of the Oxford Local Committee. Their kindness will be for ever stored up in my grateful memory.

A. KUENEN.

Leiden, *May* 13*th*, 1882.

CONTENTS.

LECTURE I.

INTRODUCTION. ISLAM.

	PAGE
National religions and universal religions	1
Division of religions into these two groups	3
Is Islam a universal religion?	5
The connection of the universal with the national religions the explanation and measure of their universalism	8
Islam. Sources of our knowledge of Islam	10
Representations of the Qorán as to the relation of Islam to "the religion of Abraham"	11
Criticism of these representations	14
Mohammed's precursors; the hanyfs	19
The real origin of Islam: Mohammed's personality	21
The influence of Judaism	25
Apparent in the representation of the Qorán as the book of Allah	26
And in the destination of Islam for all peoples	28
Want of correspondence to this destination in the intrinsic character of Islam	31
Spread of Islam as a proof of its universalism	34
Evidence of history on this point	36
a. Relation of Islam to the previous faith of its confessors	37
b. Adoration of Mohammed and the saints	41
c. Çufism	45
d. Moslem theology: the Mo'tazilites	47
e. Wahhábism	50
Conclusions as to Islam	52

Lecture II.

THE POPULAR RELIGION OF ISRAEL. PRIESTS AND PROPHETS OF YAHWEH.

	PAGE
Christianity and the religious development of Israel	55
Was Yahwism the national religion of Israel?	57
Yahwism not a foreign importation	58
The popular worship of Yahweh in Israel	61
Further proofs of the recognition of Yahweh as the god of Israel	65
Why this relation between Israel and Yahweh is disguised or ignored by the historical books of the Old Testament	69
The priests of Yahweh: their character and origin	77
Account of their functions: worship	80
Consultation of Yahweh by means of the priests	81
Their judicial function	82
Its great significance admitted by Hosea and Malachi	86
Yahweh's ethical character implied therein	90
The prophets of Yahweh: definition of the point at issue	91
The prophets generally recognized as organs of Yahweh	94
Their relation to the priests of Yahweh	96
Their activity in the spirit and after the heart of the people	98
Pre-eminent members of the prophetic order: their zeal for right and righteousness	100
The origin of written prophecies	103
The fundamental thought of the preaching of the canonical prophets	105
They, too, represent the national religion of Israel	109

Lecture III.

UNIVERSALISM OF THE PROPHETS. ESTABLISHMENT OF JUDAISM.

	PAGE
The conflict of the prophets with their people to be explained by the strongly ethical character of their preaching	111
Recognition of Yahweh's ethical character and its consequences	114
Prophetic monotheism a result of this conception	118
The popular religion and the prophetic Yahwism, as influenced by the events of the eighth century B.C.	120
Ethical monotheism	124
Anticipations of the prophets concerning the future of Yahwism	125
Universalism of the second Isaiah	128
His utterances concerning Cyrus considered in connection with this universalism	131
The prophetic Yahwism and the Israelitish nationality	137
Their mutual relation in Amos	138
,, ,, in Isaiah	141
,, ,, in Jeremiah	144
,, ,, in the second Isaiah	146
Establishment of Judaism. Prophetic Yahwism not at once taken up into the national consciousness	147
Enforcement of Deuteronomic thorah	149
Did not effect its purpose, and why	153
Priestly legislation enforced by Ezra and Nehemiah	156
Judaism becomes a national religion	156
Its relation to the prophetic preaching; the conception of God	158
Moral acceptation of Yahweh-worship	159
Holiness the demand of Yahweh	160
Public worship, ordained and regulated by Yahweh	162
The Jewish people identified with its religion	164
Prophetic universalism does not appear to pass over into Judaism	166

Lecture IV.

JUDAISM AND CHRISTIANITY.

	PAGE
Religion amongst the Jews an independent power	169
The Jews in the dispersion	171
The prophetic expectations live on in Judaism	174
The framework of the priestly law universalistic	178
Antinomy between strict monotheism and the limitation of the true religion to one people	180
Universalistic regulations concerning the "gêrîm;" their origin	182
Mode of development of Christianity out of existing universalistic germs remains to be indicated	187
Relation of this inquiry to Jesus and to the recognition of the significance of his personality	188
The assertion that Christianity did not spring out of Judaism rejected	191
Its origin to be sought in Palestinian, not in Hellenistic Judaism	193
Universalism of Christianity not the creation of Paul	196
The derivation of Christianity from Essenism considered and rejected	199
Significance of Essenism for the appreciation of Judaism	206
The Pharisees	208
Internal contradictions in Scribism	211
Its powerlessness to realize its ideal	215
Satisfaction for the religious needs sought and sometimes found by side paths	218
The Messianic expectation: its manifestation in zelotism, its effect on the inner life	222
Proselytism: its extent and the restrictions it had to remove	226
Retrospect and conclusion	229

CONTENTS. xi

LECTURE V.

BUDDHISM. RETROSPECT AND CONCLUSION.

	PAGE
Christianity independent of Buddhism in its origin	232
Indication of the point of view from which Buddhism is here regarded and of the limits to be observed	237
Opposition between Brahmanism and Buddhism	239
This opposition fictitious: Buddhism does not abrogate the castes	241
The Buddhistic metaphysic borrowed from Brahmanism	247
And so, too, the regulations of the Buddhistic order of monks	248
Alleged dependence of the Buddhists on the Jainas	253
Close relationship between Brahmanism and Buddhism now generally acknowledged, and abundantly confirmed by the Jâtakas	256
How Buddhism really rose: state of the question concerning the person of the Founder	258
Results, as affecting the prosecution of the inquiry	264
Buddhism originally an order of monks	264
Passes into a church: how is the transition to be explained?	268
Analogy of Christian mendicant orders	271
The Founder's personality an indispensable factor	273
Pre-Buddhistic asceticism in India and the modification introduced by the Buddha	277
The Buddha-legend and its moral influence	279
The origin of Buddhism is also the explanation of its character	280
Buddhism and Christianity: points of resemblance	285
The difference in principle between the two religions considered in connection with their origin	287
Retrospect and conclusion. The three religions of the world compared in respect of their universalism	292
The mutability of Christianity its commendation	294
The future of Christianity	297

NOTES.

		PAGE
I.	"The Rolls of Abraham and Moses" and "the Fables of the Ancients"	299
II.	The Hanyfs	303
III.	Did Mohammed place the Hajj amongst the Duties of the Moslem?	306
IV.	The Pronunciation of the Divine Name "Yahweh"	308
V.	Interpretation of Hosea ix. 3—5	312
VI.	The Egyptian Origin of Levi	314
VII.	The Antiquity of Israelitish Monotheism	317
VIII.	Inferences from the Inscription of Cyrus	320
IX.	Ezra and the Establishment of Judaism	323
X.	Explanation of Leviticus xxii. 25	327
XI.	Bruno Bauer and Ernest Havet	329
XII.	Explanation of Matthew xxiii. 15	333
XIII.	The Buddha-Legend and the Gospels	334
XIV.	The Founder of Jainism in the Buddha-Legend	337

ERRATA.

P. 13, n. 2, for "Ibn Isbák," read "Ibn Hishám."
P. 45, n. 2, for "pp. 45 sqq.," read "pp. 50 sqq."
P. 46, n. 1, for "Migmún," read "Mejmún."
P. 113, line 5, for "Beershebah," read "Beersheba."
P. 192, n. 1, for "Davet," read "Havet."
P. 202, n. 1, for "on the writers," read "and the writers."
P. 212, line 4, for "Sochoh," read "Socho."
P. 254, line 13, for "Buddha's converts," read "Buddha's defeated opponents."
P. 256, line 8, for "the last ten years," read "recent years."

I.

INTRODUCTION.—ISLAM.

ONE of the most striking features of the HIBBERT LECTURES is their international character; and none of my hearers will wonder that this is the special point which forces itself upon my attention at the present moment; for to this I owe the honour of now addressing you—an honour of which I am deeply sensible, and for which I cannot refrain from offering my sincerest acknowledgments, at the outset, to the Hibbert Trustees. A concomitant result, however, is that you are now addressed by one who is but imperfectly acquainted with your language, one whose utterance will declare only too plainly that he is a foreigner, and that in his youth he never had the privilege that was to fall to him in later years of observing and receiving from the lips of Englishmen the mysteries of English pronunciation. Why should I deny that this difficulty has more than once presented itself to my mind in alarming colours during the preparations for my task, and that it has lost none of its terrors now? But it is useless to expatiate on all this. The die is cast. The difficulty I must now encounter is one which most of you have doubtless experienced yourselves, and, mindful of this experience, you will extend your indulgent kindness to him who now addresses you. With no lack of confidence, therefore, I throw myself upon your mercy; and be assured that in extending it to me, so far from stimulating any pride on my part, you will but increase my sense of the obligation under which you have laid me.

The transition is easy from the Hibbert Lectures to their subject-matter, and so likewise from the difficulties of the present Hibbert Lecturer to the material which he has selected for treatment. For if there is no universal *language*, there certainly are universal *religions;* and it surely needs no proof that they are at least as worthy of our full attention as the national religions are. Apart from the personal concern that we have in one of these universal religions, the mere fact of their having overstepped the boundaries of nationality is itself a remarkable phenomenon, and presents a highly interesting problem. Why these forms of religion and no others? Are they of a special and peculiar nature, that they have spread their wings so much wider than all others? And yet are they not most closely connected with the national religions? Have they not their roots in them? Any attempt, however incomplete and defective, to throw light on these questions, may borrow from the importance of the subject a claim to a favourable reception and a candid judgment. It is this belief that encourages me to lay before you, in this and in the following Lectures, a few thoughts on *national religion* and *universal religion*.

You will readily understand, however, that this is a general heading, and not an exact description of a subject that can be dealt with in a few short hours; for the wealth of material would overwhelm us hopelessly unless we chose some single point of view and resisted all temptations to desert it. To justify the selection I have made, I must ask permission to delay you for a few moments in the ante-chamber of the science of religion.

In every branch of human science the phenomena are grouped in classes. In a certain sense this grouping is the beginning of the work, for it furnishes the indispensable clue to the study. And yet, on the other hand, a correct classification may be regarded as the final outcome of research, for it is built upon all that observation has taught us concerning the objects studied, their characteristics and their mutual relations. Regarded thus, as epitomizing the results of study, it has great and unmistakable importance. Although, in the age of Darwin, we can recognize no impassable barriers between the several species and genera, though the transitions are everywhere gradual, nowhere abrupt, we nevertheless seek orderly arrangement, and cannot rest till we find it. As the chronicle must yield to history, so must the bare enumeration of phenomena yield to classification.

If this is true in general, it is true likewise in its special application to one of the youngest in the rank of sciences—the science of religion. Classification as an instrument is indispensable here if anywhere; for the field is almost too wide for survey, and the diversity of the phenomena may well bewilder the student at the outset. And as the final outcome of its historical and psychological investigations likewise, this science attaches the utmost importance to the just grouping and arrangement of the phenomena studied. It may indeed be called the bridge that joins the descriptive to the philosophical portions of the science of religion. And accordingly we see that the pioneers in this field have bestowed great pains on classification.

It is not my intention, however, to expound or criticise the attempts that have already been made in this direction. Unanimity has not been reached, and no one had any right to expect it as yet. The important and in some respects fascinating task of conducting you through the wide domain of the science and, after due historical preparation, marshalling its phenomena in fitting ranks, is reserved for one of my successors in this chair. I now confine myself to a single point. The *universal religions* are, with fair unanimity, placed in one group, and opposed to the *national religions*. Nothing is more natural. The difference on which this division rests is sufficiently striking, and seems, moreover, to have its roots in the nature of the religions themselves. It is obvious that we cannot rest content with this one division. The national religions differ too widely from each other to be included in a single group. Take, for instance, the contrast between those forms of religion which seem as it were spontaneously to rise, to grow and to disappear with particular peoples, and those others, known as personal or historical religions, which have their special founders or at least their sacred literatures. Yet, important as this distinction may be, a national religion is in every case confined to a single people or to a group of nearly related peoples, whereas the universal religions seem to know no such limitations.

There is a general agreement, then, as to these two groups, but it is qualified by a divergency for which we should hardly have been prepared. It concerns the question: Which are the universal religions? Some will only admit Buddhism and Christianity to the title,[1] while others add Islam as a third.[2]

How is any difference of opinion on such a matter possible?

It can hardly be a mere question of millions! It is true that Islam has fewer professors than the others;

---

[1] E. g. O. Pfleiderer, Religionsphilosophie auf geschichtlicher Grundlage, S. 725 ff.

[2] E. g. C. P. Tiele, Outlines of the History of Religion, to the Spread of the Universal Religions, pp. ix and 91 ff.

according to one of the latest estimates,[1] a hundred and seventy-five millions against Christendom's four hundred and Buddhism's four hundred and fifty millions. But who would exclude Islam on that ground? We need not even reflect on the uncertainty of these numbers, especially in the case of Buddhism, or remind ourselves that Islam is still advancing, and spreads more rapidly than either Buddhism or Christianity; for how could a scientific classification be based in any case on simple numbers?

The ground of the difference of opinion lies deeper. The term "universal religion" is used in two senses: to signify either a *fact* or a *quality*. The fact is the spread of the religion in question, beyond the limits of a single people, over many and diverse nations. Now in this sense Islam is, beyond all question, a universal or— if you prefer the more modest designation which keeps closer to the truth—an international religion. Semites, Arians, Tartars, Malays and Negroes, bow down before Allah and recognize Mohammed as his apostle. Islam "still has its grip"—as one of its most talented defenders expresses it[2]—"on two continents, and a foothold, even if a precarious foothold, in a third. It extends from Morocco to the Malay peninsula, from Zanzibar to the Kirghis horde. . . . ." But enough.

---

[1] W. Seawen Blunt, in the Fortnightly Review, 1881, II. p. 208.

[2] R. Bosworth Smith, Mohammed and Mohammedanism. Second Edition, p. 27.

As long as we rely on the outward test of fact, Islam's right to take rank with the two other universal religions cannot be so much as questioned.

And yet, as already said, that right has not only been questioned but sometimes denied. It is urged—and who shall gainsay it?—that we cannot determine the character of this or of any other religion, or fix the place that should be assigned to it, simply by the success that it has met with in the world. The causes of the conquests of Islam unquestionably demand investigation; but it by no means follows that they lie in Islam itself and in its natural fitness for peoples and tribes that differ widely from each other,—in a word, in its universalistic nature. It is quite conceivable that it may have spread, not because of, but in spite of, its peculiar character; that the absence or the weakness of genuinely universal elements in it was counterbalanced or compensated by all manner of circumstances which cannot be taken into account in its ultimate characterization. I speak, as you will observe, hypothetically. We must not anticipate the results of our further investigation; but in principle it seems impossible to deny the right of applying this second test. In the study of nature we may rest content with establishing the phenomena and determining their connection; but in the case of man and the products of his self-conscious activity, we must go on to *estimate*—with impartial caution indeed, but with freedom likewise. Nowhere is this more true than in the study of religions and their history. He who banishes the thought of "higher" and "lower" from this study, degrades it into a mere means of gratifying curiosity, and disqualifies it for the lofty task which it is called on to perform for our modern society.

We shall have occasion to return to this hereafter. Let me now remark that the "genuine universalism" of which I have just been speaking is not external and accidental to the religions in which we observe it, but is very closely connected with their origin and the nature of their connection with those national religions out of which, or on the soil of which, they have been developed. This proposition will not seem strange. That which is destined to penetrate and inspire every nationality must not have been evolved in the study. It must have been tested and matured in the life of a people. But again: that which is to combine with every nationality, satisfying the special needs of each, must not be inseparably bound to any one nation. "Born of the nation and rising above it" —must not this be the formula of that which is destined for all nations? But I am myself the first to admit that such considerations as these are in no way conclusive. The true appeal lies to history; and to history, therefore, we will submit the question. The answer, as it seems to me, is clear enough; and with a view to it I may now describe the narrower limits of the subject I have already indicated in general terms. We are to examine, *The connection between the universal and the national religions as furnishing the explanation and the measure of their universalism.*

One more word of introduction. The complete treatment of my subject would require far more time than we have at our disposal and would quite exceed my powers. Every student of religious history is compelled by the nature of his studies sometimes to venture upon ground that he dare not exactly call his own; but naturally he makes such excursions as seldom as possible, and in any case hastens to return to his own household gods. You will, I am sure, permit me to observe this rule, with which, moreover, my personal inclinations are in harmony. The connection between Christianity and Israelitism will accordingly be my main subject, and will be set forth at length, while Buddhism and Islam will detain us only for a much shorter time, and we shall chiefly note those points from which, by resemblance or contrast, we may hope for some illustration of the origin of Christianity. I shall by this means also escape the danger of repeating what has already been said so admirably from this chair on Buddhism,[1] or of anticipating the future treatment of Mohammed and his religion.

The order I shall follow is that of reversed chronology. We shall thus be enabled to begin with Islam, concerning the origin of which we are best informed,

---

[1] Lectures on the Origin and Growth of Religion as illustrated by some Points in the History of Indian Buddhism. By T. W. Rhys-Davids. (The Hibbert Lectures, 1881.)

and our treatment of which may be linked on to the remarks already made on the difference of opinion as to the place that should be assigned to it.

How often has the wish been expressed that records of the rise of Buddhism and Christianity could have been preserved as certain and as accurate as those that relate to Mohammed and the origin of Islam! Renan's reference to "that strange spectacle of a religion coming into being in the clear light of day,"[1] is in every mouth. And we have in truth reason to be thankful. The authenticity of the Qorán, with a few trifling exceptions, is above suspicion. And by the side of Mohammed's preaching, preserved in the Qorán, we have the traditions about his person which have been handed down authenticated by the testimony on which they rest, and which go back to his own immediate surroundings. The biography of the prophet is later, but still it is relatively ancient, it rests upon materials yet older than itself, and, above all, it can be tested by the authentic documents. What more, in reason, can we require?

But, alas! the thirst for *certain* knowledge is not easily quenched. We know much, but we would fain know more. And the fact is, that our information is most defective just at the very points where it would

---

[1] Etudes d' Histoire Religieuse, p. 230.

be most valuable. The tradition is coloured throughout by the dogmatic convictions of the first believers, and is often open to the gravest suspicion. And the Qorán? Sprenger has called it "a book with seven seals."[1] As showing what Islam *is*, it may leave nothing to be desired in point of clearness, and may even suffer from over fulness; but as soon as we try to follow Mohammed in his development, the confused mass of revelations constantly fails us. This or that saying would give us the light we want, did we but know where to place it. Behind this or that passage an important fact obviously lies concealed, but who shall unveil it for us?

Our present task is to define the relation of Mohammed's preaching to the religion of the Arabs. Can we accomplish it with adequate certainty? Mohammed preached the *one* Allah, and in so doing combated the polytheism of the great majority of his people. So far of course all is clear. But no sooner do we pass beyond this generality than we are assailed by doubt, and find a wide diversity of opinion even amongst the historians of Mohammed.

Let us first listen to the prophet himself. More than once he declares that his object is simply to restore "the religion of Abraham," the father of Ishmael, and therefore the ancestor of the Arabs. "Believers! bow down and prostrate yourselves and worship

---

[1] Das Leben und die Lehre des Mohammed, Band I. S. xv.

your Lord, and work righteousness, that ye may fare well; and do valiantly in the cause of Allah as it behoveth you to do for Him. He hath elected you, and hath not laid on you any hardship in religion, (nothing but) the religion of your father Abraham. He hath named you the Moslems, heretofore and now, that the apostle (of Allah) may be a witness against you, and that ye may be witnesses against the rest of mankind."[1] Abraham, with Ishmael's assistance, had built the house of Allah, the Ka'ba, and had prayed to his Lord, even then, for such a prophet as afterwards appeared in Mohammed: "O our Lord! accept (this temple) from us, for thou art he who heareth and knoweth. O our Lord! make us Moslems (resigned) to thee, and our posterity a Moslem people; and teach us our holy rites, and turn to us, for thou art he that turneth, the merciful. O our Lord! raise up among them an apostle from their midst, who may rehearse thy signs unto them, and teach them in the book and wisdom, and purify them: of a truth thou art the mighty, the wise!"[2] Thus Mohammed appears as the vindicator of an age-old tradition. Arabia had strayed away from it; Jews and Christians had failed to keep it pure; Allah had sent him, Mohammed, to restore it to its original purity and to make all men Moslems even as Abraham was.

Without accepting this theory in its entirety, as set

---

[1] Sura xxii. 76—78; cf. ii. 124, 129; iii. 89; iv. 124; vi. 162; xiv. 40, 41; xvi. 124.

[2] Sura ii. 121—123.

forth in the Qorán, scholars are generally disposed to allow a considerable degree of truth to it. The recognition of Allah taäla, the one supremely exalted God, is supposed to lie at the basis of Arabian polytheism. In all that Mohammed says of Abraham, the friend of Allah,[1] the father of the Arabs, and the founder of the sanctuary of the Qoraishites, he reproduces (according to this theory) the beliefs of his contemporaries, amongst whom were some who had rejected the idolatry of the great mass of their countrymen even before Mohammed. Dissatisfied with Judaism and Christianity and seeking some better religion, these men are represented as having found what they sought in "the milla of Ibrahím." There is a well-known story, told by Mohammed's earliest biographer, Ibn Isháq, that in the days of ignorance four of the Qoraishites had withdrawn from participation in a feast in honour of the idols and agreed together that they would set off in search of the true faith. One of them, Waraqa, thought he had found it in Christianity; another, Zaid ibn Amr, recognized and preached, even before Mohammed, the religion of Abraham.[2] This story is admitted to have rather too romantic an air to pass for pure history; but it is true enough, we are told, that before the prophet came forward there were already *Hanyfs*, a word which the Qorán loves to employ with reference to Abraham, and which, accordingly, Mohammed also

---

[1] Sura iv. 124.
[2] Ibn Ishák ed. Wüstenfeld, p. 143; Sprenger, l.c. Band I. 81 ff.

applies to himself.¹ His religion, if this be true, was the natural product of Arab culture at the stage which it had now reached. It was the secret thought and wish of the best of his contemporaries to which he succeeded in giving expression. The immoral practices which he sternly forbad in the name of Allah—drunkenness, the ill-treatment of women, the slaughter of female children—had, accordingly, been combated by others already. Islam, then, was a moral as well as a religious reformation, and under either aspect alike it reveals its connection with the national life of the Arabs.²

Now, can this view be adopted? Its intrinsic probability might be matter for discussion; but there is one fact which imperatively forbids us to accept it as true. If the conception of Abraham, the monotheist, the father of Ishmael and the founder of the Ka'ba, had really been familiar to the Arabs at the beginning of the seventh century after Christ, then Mohammed would necessarily have proclaimed it from the first, or at any rate would not have contradicted it. But what are the facts? We can show from the Qorán itself that the prophet's ideas about Abraham underwent a remarkable change in the course of years, and that his theory of "the milla of Ibrahím" is of very late origin. Permit me to lay a few texts, which demonstrate this, before you. Observe, in the first place, that Ishmael,

---

[1] Sura iii. 89; iv. 124; vi. 162; vii. 79, &c.; cf. infra, p. 19.
[2] Bosworth Smith, l.c. p. 109; cf. 3 sqq.

as the eldest son of Abraham, is an essential element in the traditional conception. Now the *name* of Ishmael certainly occurs in the earlier Suras. But Mohammed does not know, at first, that he is a son of Abraham. He mentions him after Moses and before Idrís (i.e. Enoch) as "a prophet, true to his promise, who enjoined prayer and almsgiving on his people, and was well-pleasing to his Lord."[1] Elsewhere he is mentioned, with Job, Idrís and Dhu'l-Kefl—an unknown worthy—as a model of patience and perseverance.[2] In another place, Abraham, Isaac and Jacob are all named together, while Ishmael only comes afterwards and in conjunction with Elisha and Dhu'l-Kefl again.[3] It is still more significant that, in another passage, Isaac and Jacob are given as sons to Abraham, and are followed by a whole string of prophets, amongst whom Ishmael appears in the company of Elisha and Jonah.[4] Now if, after all this, we find Ishmael elsewhere mentioned as Isaac's elder brother,[5] we can only suppose that this represents a later conception in Mohammed's mind.

The inferences which these texts would in themselves justify find confirmation elsewhere, for the prophet is not consistent with himself in regard to Abraham either. It is a question whether, at first, he even

---

[1] Sura xix. 55, 56. [2] Sura xxi. 85.
[3] Sura xxxviii. 45, 48. [4] Sura vi. 84, 86.
[5] Sura ii. 127; xiv. 40, 41.

knew that Isaac was his son;¹ and when he had found this out, it is certain that for some time he regarded Jacob as Isaac's brother.² Abraham already occupied a high place in his estimation. More than once he mentions "the book-rolls of Abraham and Moses," or "of Moses and Abraham;"³ but what he meant by the expression is not clear. Sprenger's conjectures on the subject are extremely hazardous, and in some respects are certainly false.⁴ Probably we should simply infer that Mohammed had heard something of Abraham's preaching to his kinsfolk, and of the law of Moses, and that he conceived the former, after the analogy of the latter, as set down in writing. So much is certain, that he saw in Abraham a faithful servant of Allah, who bore witness to his faith in opposition to his relatives and in spite of the danger to which it exposed him, and who received glorious promises in reward.⁵ But however warmly Mohammed may speak of Abraham, he has, as yet, no notion of assigning a special place to him, or bringing him into a wholly exceptional relation either to the Arabs or to himself, the preacher. Abraham is *one* of the many

---

[1] Sura li. 24 sqq.; xv. 51 sqq.; cf. xxxvii. 11 sqq. See C. Snouck Hurgronje, Het Mekkaansche feest. bl. 31. This author's investigations form the basis of my own.

[2] Sura vi. 74 sqq.; xi. 72 sqq.; xix. 42 sqq.; xxi. 52 sqq.; xxix. 15 sqq.

[3] Sura lxxxvii. 19, liii. 37.

[4] See Note I. at the end of the volume.

[5] See the passages already cited.

prophets, one of the most eminent it is true, but nothing more. So far is he, as yet, from passing as the founder of that Islam which Mohammed proclaims, that on one occasion he is placed among the disciples of Noah.[1] So far is Mohammed, as yet, from regarding him as the preacher of monotheism to his Arabian posterity, that he more than once declares himself to be the first messenger of Allah to the Arabs.[2] Nay, his assurance, "We have given them no books in which to study deeply, nor have we sent any one to them before thee, charged with warnings," is preceded by the words: "When our distinct signs (i.e. the verses of the Qorán) are recited to them, they say, 'He (Mohammed) is merely a man who would fain pervert you from your fathers' religion.'"[3] "Your fathers' religion!"—but was not Mohammed come for the very purpose of restoring what Abraham and Ishmael had established? Unquestionably this is what he himself afterwards declared; but those whom he introduces as speaking in this passage have not the least suspicion, as yet, of anything of the kind. And this is equivalent to saying that he himself had not yet thought of it.[4]

Whence, then, "the milla of Ibrahím"? We have

---

[1] Sura xxxvii. 81: "of his (Nuh's) shí'a was Ibrahím."

[2] Sura xxxii. 2; xxxiv. 43; xxxvi. 5. Cf. Snouck Hurgronje, l. c. bl. 33.

[3] Sura xxxiv. 42, 43; cf. ii. 165.

[4] Observe also the *absolute* contradiction between Mohammed's religion and that of the "unbelievers" in Sura cix.

only to read with care the texts in which it is mentioned, and we shall find the answer to our question. It is well known that Mohammed kept the Christians, and still more the numerous Jews who were settled in his fatherland, steadily in view. For a long time he hoped that both, but especially the Jews, would recognize him. In this expectation he found himself at last disappointed; but even then he could not completely sever himself from them. He could not and would not deny that Allah had revealed himself to them too by Moses and other prophets. Thus he felt the need of a formula which would express what was common to himself and them on the one hand, and what severed him from them on the other. This formula he found in "the milla of Ibrahím," the great man of God who was reverenced by his opponents as well as himself, but who was not one of them, being rather, as Mohammed constantly reminds us,[1] "neither Jew nor Christian." As a preacher of this "milla," Mohammed could still recognize the divine origin of the sacred books of Jew and Christian, though he secured the right of rejecting whatever he disapproved of in them, or, as he prefers to put it, in the Jewish or Christian reading and interpretation of them.[2] The formula, then, answers so completely to the needs of

---

[1] Sura ii. 134; iii. 60, and elsewhere.

[2] Compare W. Muir, The Corân, its Composition and Teaching, and the Testimony it bears to the Holy Scriptures, pp. 229 sqq., with the texts there cited.

the time and its polemical exigencies, that we have no hesitation in deriving it from them, and have not the least occasion to look for its origin either in the actual history or in the Arabic conceptions of it. The fact that it is only in the later Suras that Ishmael appears as the ancestor of the Arabs and the joint founder of the Ka'ba can only confirm us in our judgment.

The opinion, then, that Mohammed came to re-awaken and to restore what already existed amongst his people, if only as a faint reminiscence of a distant past, finds no support in the Qorán, when read in the light of criticism. But it is another question whether —independently of him and indeed before him—a band of devout Arabs had been formed whose ideas he adopted, and, throwing the weight of his prophetic authority into the scale, succeeded in bringing home to his contemporaries. But who in the world were these "hanyfs" so often regarded as his teachers and predecessors? I dare not undertake to solve this riddle; but I do not shrink from saying that the answer most in favour at present is difficult, nay impossible, to reconcile with the use of the word "hanyf" in the Qorán. There Abraham is called a "hanyf,"[1] and—as we should expect after that—Mohammed also. Allah says to him: "Set thou thy face then, as a hanyf, towards the religion which Allah has made, and for which he has made mankind."[2] A sectarian name, as hanyf is commonly

---

[1] Sura ii. 129; iii. 60, 89; iv. 124; vi. 79, 162; xvi. 121, 124.
[2] Sura xxx. 29; cf. x. 105.

supposed to be, might conceivably have been adopted by the prophet himself, but that he should have applied it to Abraham is very hard to believe. The improbability becomes still greater if "hanyf" is rightly supposed to have been a name originally given in reproach, meaning "apostate" or "impious," and afterwards, like so many others, adopted as a title of honour by those against whom it was hurled. In this case how could Mohammed, when speaking of Abraham, describe him more closely and as it were commend him to his hearers, by declaring: "Verily he was a leader, obedient to Allah, *a hanyf*, not one of those who deny God's unity"?[1] Elsewhere too he describes the true religion as "the milla of Ibrahím, *the hanyf*, for he was not of them who deny God's unity."[2] Here at any rate no trace remains of the unfavourable signification the word is supposed originally to have had. For my own part, I cannot escape the suspicion that when we refer to the hanyfs of tradition in explanation of texts in the Qorán, we are guilty of a ὕστερον πρότερον, and that in reality the name assigned in the tradition to Mohammed's supposed predecessors is simply borrowed from the Qorán. They are called "hanyfs" because Abraham is so called in the Qorán, and because it is "the milla of Ibrahím" that they are represented as seeking, or even, like Zaid ibn Amr, as actually finding and openly pro-

---

[1] Sura xvi. 121; cf. 124. [2] Sura vi. 162.

fessing. When once Mohammed had identified his religion with the faith of the patriarch, was it not a historical necessity that pre-Mohammedans should conform in Moslem tradition to the type of Abraham? This explains the name they bear. We are certainly not justified in relegating these predecessors to the region of myth, or even in denying their influence on Mohammed's development. But whenever the records concerning them reflect the convictions of those to whom we owe them, we must set them aside as unhistorical.[1] What remains after this is certainly insufficient to make us regard Islam as the result of a national, though not universal, longing for something higher and better in the matter of religion. If such a need was felt at all, it was only in a very small circle and in a very small degree. In one word—remove Mohammed, and neither Islam, nor anything like it, comes into existence.

Perhaps this conclusion strikes some of my hearers as rather strange. Is not so high an estimate of Mohammed's personal contribution to the production of Islam inconsistent with the want of originality that we are accustomed, not unfairly, to ascribe to him? And yet you will readily grant that there is no necessary contradiction here. As for Mohammed, we can resolve him into his factors, so to speak, and thus explain him; but we cannot explain Islam without him. If I might

---

[1] Cf. Note II.

for a moment separate those elements which in reality never appear except in combination, I should say: Islam is in a high degree, and far more than most other religions, the product not of the time or of the people, but of the personality of its founder. But for all that, the founder was not a creative genius, or at least was so in a much less degree than others who were yet supported and driven on by their surroundings far more than he. Permit me to work out this thought in greater detail. But do not expect more than a rapid sketch, simply intended to place the well-known facts in what appears to me to be their true light.

Let us begin by laying down what must furnish the point of departure in every attempt at an explanation: Mohammed's nature was truly religious. To deny, or even occasionally to forget, that the deity was to him the supreme reality, under the power of which and in communion with which he was conscious of standing,—this appears to me the grossest injustice. No researches as to his physical constitution or his human teachers must tempt us to lose sight of this fact. It beams forth from his life-history, especially in the years before the flight. On more than one right royal passage of the Qorán it stands visibly impressed. He who—to take one instance out of many—could thus describe the faithful and put these words into their mouths, was in truth a genuine child of religion himself: "To Allah belongs the dominion over the heaven and the earth, and Allah hath power over all things.

Verily, in the creation of heaven and earth, and in the succession of night and day, are signs to them who have a heart; who standing, sitting and reclining, bear God in mind, and muse on the creation of heaven and earth (and say), 'O our Lord! thou hast not created this in vain. Thine be the glory! Keep us from the torment of the Fire! O our Lord! thou shalt surely put them to shame whom thou dost cast into the Fire, and the wrong-doers have none to help them. O our Lord! we have heard the voice of one calling, who called us to the faith, 'Believe ye on your Lord!' and we have believed. O our Lord! forgive us then our sins, and hide our transgressions for us and let us die with the righteous! O our Lord! give us then what thou hast promised us by thine apostles, and put us not to shame on the day of the resurrection! Verily thou wilt not fail in thy promise!'"[1]

There were other religious natures in Arabia in the last years of the sixth century, but amongst them all there was but the one Mohammed who rose up as a preacher and reformer of religion. What was it that stirred him to the task? If we are to accept the testimony of the Qorán, the answer is not doubtful. It was the grief and indignation aroused by the religious condition of his contemporaries, their polytheism, their superstition, their often sceptical and irreverent attitude towards the higher powers which they professed

---

[1] Sura iii. 186—192.

to recognize. Others might be religious without breaking with these forms of their times, inspiring them by their own devoutness or letting them pass for just what they were; but to him they were a thorn in the flesh, a blasphemy against God that roused his whole soul to protest. The rise of this feeling is the mystery of his individuality, and as such cannot be wholly unveiled. But how it *may* have sprung up and been stimulated can be pointed out readily enough. Even before any impulse came from without, dissatisfaction with the religion of the people may have been seated in his soul. Mohammed was a Semite of the Semites. And this implies, not indeed, as some have maintained, that he was a monotheist by nature and as it were by instinct, but that he was predisposed to become a monotheist. The fundamental thought of all Semitic religions is the recognition of the Lord and Ruler of nature and all her phenomena; the key-note of Semitic piety is submission to the divine power, bowing itself in awe to the very dust. In the one no less than in the other lies the germ of a protest against that multiplicity of the gods which is necessarily accompanied by a limitation of the dominion of each, and which divides and therefore weakens the dread they inspire. It remains questionable, however, whether this Semitic predisposition alone would have enabled Mohammed to discern with perfect clearness the shortcomings of the popular religion. But he was not left to himself. In his own land and on his mercantile expeditions he came into contact with Christians and Jews, whose faith challenged the national tradition by the very fact of differing from it. Moreover the Jews, especially, offered Mohammed, in their monotheism, the very thing after which his soul was thirsting. Yes! the Lord whom they worshipped was worthy of his and of all men's adoration. The worship of other powers in place of Him was an infringement of his majesty, a national sin which would be punished here and hereafter!

Thus, we may suppose, the impulse was given. Amidst dire struggles, overstraining his nervous system and breaking into visions and other delusions of the senses, the conviction ripened within him that he was called to bear witness, at Mecca in the first instance, to the Only One who has no other at his side. In its further development, his preaching was still determined both in matter and form by Judaism, or rather by the little which he knew of it at first and only gradually supplemented. To Judaism we may trace the main features of his eschatology. It was under Jewish influence that he framed the moral demands which he pressed on his hearers in the name of Allah with an emphasis and zeal that command our admiration. Indeed, his whole mission was really a copy of the past revelation to the Jewish people, to which the sacred books bore witness. The apostle, the prophet of Allah, is a reproduction of Israel's great leaders, and the Qorán which he produces is a counterpart of "the Book" which Jews and Christians alike recognized and reverenced as the foundation of their religion, and which indeed they almost deified. This last point we must especially keep in view. What a large place is occupied in the Qorán by praise of the Qorán itself! How often and how emphatically are the Arabs reminded of their privilege in now possessing, in "the signs" which are shown them, that is in the verses of the Qorán, the word of Allah himself, yielding no whit to the sacred books of those who profess other religions, nay, exalted high above them! From the beginning, and with unabated vigour throughout, the attention is fixed upon this. In one of the earliest Suras the question is asked:

> "What hath come to them (the opponents) that they believe not?
> And that, when the Qorán is recited to them, they adore not?
> Nay, the unbelievers dare to call it a lie!
> But Allah knoweth their concealed hatred:
> Bring thou them the tidings of woful punishment!"[1]

And elsewhere, in a passage dating from the same period:

> "Nay, I swear it by the setting of the stars,—
> And that, if ye will but know it, is a mighty oath,—
> That this is the exalted Qorán,
> Written in the book that is hidden (with Allah):
> Let none touch it but the purified;
> It is a revelation of the Lord of the worlds."[2]

---

[1] Sura lxxxiv. 20—24. [2] Sura lvi. 74—79.

No less a one than Allah himself declares: "We have made the Qorán come down to you as a revelation from on high."[1] Nay, he swears "by the glorious Qorán."[2] Frequent allusions are likewise made to the language, of which Allah now for the first time avails himself.[3] Nothing is clearer, therefore, than that Mohammed himself assigns to the Qorán its place in the list of sacred books. It is true that he did not reduce it in its entirety to writing, that he took no steps to make others do so, and did not even approve of its being done at all. One of his biographers turns it thus: It was his desire that the word of Allah should live in the hearts of men.[4] Doubtless it was. But we must not suppose from this that he was content with the mere upholding of his principles, and gladly left it to the heart and head of the believers to work them out and apply them. Such reliance on the independence of his followers is inconsistent with the place which he assigns to himself and his revelations. It was to their memory that he trusted, and this he might safely do. Perhaps, too, he was not without fear that the written Qorán might become the subject of contention and so lead to disunion. But nevertheless the Qorán was and continued to be the word of Allah in

---

[1] Sura lxxvi. 23.   [2] Sura l. 1.

[3] Sura xliv. 58, "in your language;" xii. 2; xiii. 87; xx. 121, and elsewhere, "an Arabic Qorán."

[4] Sprenger, l.c. III. S. xxxiii. xlii.

the strictest sense, and was intended to exercise all the authority with which its origin clothed it.

"The kernel of Judaism, transplanted to Arabian soil"—such a description of Islam, considered in its essence, would not be far from the truth. Yet in one respect the definition would be incomplete and would give a wrong impression; for it would make it seem as though Mohammed had his eye exclusively on his own people and was contented with the rôle of prophet of the Arabs. Originally he may really have aimed at nothing more. There are places in the Qorán which confine his activity within these limits, which represent him as the first apostle of Allah to the people of Arabia, as one in whom that people had at last obtained what had long ago been granted to other nations—a prophet out of its midst.[1] But these texts are thrown into the shadow by a number of utterances which extend his mission to all men without distinction. "The Qorán," we read, "of a truth is no other than a warning to all creatures."[2] And elsewhere: "We have not sent thee to mankind at large otherwise than to preach and warn; but most men understand not."[3] We shall presently meet with other passages equally clear; but meanwhile we may remember that the literal acceptance of this "mission to all mankind" is absolutely demanded by Mohammed's deeds, which are

---

[1] See the passages cited on p. 17, note 2.
[2] Sura xxxviii. 87, literally, "for the worlds."
[3] Sura xxxiv. 27.

surely the best commentary on his words. In the seventh year of the Hejra (628 A.D.) he despatched six emissaries with six almost identical letters directed to as many princes, inviting them to recognize him as a prophet and to embrace Islam. "Become a Moslem and thou art saved. Become a Moslem and Allah giveth thee a two-fold reward." Thus he wrote to the Byzantine emperor Heraclius, amongst others, and to the king of Persia.[1] We can hardly imagine that he expected any practical result from this step. It was probably taken with a view to its effect on the Arabs rather than for the conversion of these foreign princes. But in any case this action testifies to a universalism as complete and conscious as we could well imagine. It was the whole world known to him which he claimed for Islam by his messengers. As a prophecy of what was actually to take place within a few years, this deed is remarkable enough, but no less so as revealing what he himself intended, and considered feasible.

These far-reaching claims, however, were in reality less strange than they seem at first. When we become acquainted with Mohammed's conceptions of the history of the past, we soon perceive that he could not well have given himself any lower position or assigned any more contracted destination to his religion. His horizon is anything but extended. The Bible and the Jewish haggada are his authorities for universal

---

[1] W. Muir, The Life of Mahomet, IV. 49—60; Sprenger, l.c. III. 261 ff.

history; and that history consists essentially in the preaching of Allah's apostles, its rejection by those to whom it is directed, and Allah's chastisements of the stubborn ones. "One family and one religion" might have been the epitome of Mohammed's view of history. *One family*, or if you will *one people* ("ommah"):—that was his point of departure, and it never ceased to be his ideal. The splitting up into nations was falling away from Allah's original ordinance.[1] *One religion* ("dín") had therefore existed originally, had been preached by each successive prophet to his own people,[2] and was now proclaimed anew by Mohammed in all its purity, in opposition to the errors of "the people of the book."[3] Mohammed himself, according to the well-known expression of the Qorán, is "the apostle of Allah, *the seal of the prophets.*"[4] But this implies that he has a message for all men without distinction. The limitation of his mission to the Arabian tribes would have been, under such a conception of history, equivalent to the renunciation of his prophetic self-consciousness.

A message to all without distinction. But how ill do the contents of Islam answer to such a destiny! We shall not make it a reproach to Mohammed that he never deliberated with himself as to what could meet

---

[1] Sura ii. 209, x. 20.
[2] Sura x. 48; xxx. 46, and elsewhere.
[3] Sura xxi. 92; xxxiii. 54.   [4] Sura xxxiii. 40.

the wants of all, and what might therefore prove acceptable to all. What religious founder ever went so to work? But this we may lay to his account—less as a fault than as a striking evidence of spiritual immaturity—that the difference between the national and the universal had never entered into his mind, so that he could see no difficulty in laying upon Persians and Greeks what was exclusively adapted for Arabs. And this, again, is connected with what I might call the *artificial origin of Islam*. Mohammed *made* Islam out of elements which were supplied to him very largely from outside, and which had a whole history behind them already, so that he could take them up as they were without further elaboration. The sifting of the national from the universal, which was accomplished in other instances in and by the life of the people, had not taken place in the preparation of Islam. Inasmuch as Mohammed places himself in the line of God's previous revelations to Israel and to the Christians, and appears as completing them and setting the seal upon them, nothing is wanting to the universalism of his own prophetic consciousness; and yet in his religion itself—just because of its origin—we miss the true character of universalism.

But we must go still further. It is not only Mohammed's person in its entirety, not only his antecedents and general culture, that are reflected in the religion thus put together and determine its special character. Beyond all this, there is something in Islam—nay, there is much—that is simply arbitrary. The unforeseen and intrinsically incalculable plays no small part in it. The changing political relations, the circumstances of the prophet's life, and, alas! his passions also, his vengeance and his sensual desires, leave their mark on the word of Allah that he preaches,—the word which, when once it is spoken, he will lay not only upon Arabia, but upon all the world! Examples, it is notorious, meet us everywhere. Perhaps the clearest, and certainly the most important for the later development of Islam, is the exalting of the Ka'ba to the position of the central sanctuary, and the assumption of pilgrimages to it and to the other sacred places at Mekka amongst the religious duties of the Moslem.[1] It need hardly be said that the usages of the hajj stand in no real connection with Islam, or rather that they are in direct contradiction with it. It has been truly said: "The veneration of the black stone is in such glaring contradiction with the Moslem's otherwise pure conceptions of God, that a reconciliation can only be effected by the most far-fetched theories, and even then imperfectly."[2] We must not insist upon our own ideas of decency, beauty and harmoniousness, as the only standard. We do not forget the words with which Burton closes his account of the last scene of the pilgrimage: "I have seen the religious ceremonies of many lands, but never—nowhere—aught so

---

[1] See Note III.   [2] Sprenger, l.c. II. 346.

solemn, so impressive, as this spectacle."[1] We heartily assent when he forbids us to pronounce a harsh judgment on the pilgrimage, and shows us how the devout feelings of the heart find satisfaction in its ceremonies.[2] The religious disposition is indeed ineradicable. It can give its consecration to all that is frivolous, and can find nourishment in all that is incomprehensible. But none the less it remains a fact that the hajj, as celebrated by Mohammed himself in the tenth year of the Hejra, and as kept up to this day, was from the first, and is now yet more conspicuously, a fragment of incomprehensible heathenism taken up undigested into Islam. You may tell me that Mohammed could not help it; that he himself was too deeply attached to the Ka'ba and its belongings to be able to relinquish them; that he could not be expected to rob his followers of what they had held dear and sacred from their childhood. I shall not contradict you. But that is not the matter at issue. Why should he not seek satisfaction for his own and his followers' religious needs wherever he thought he could find it? But when he exalts the impulse of his own heart into a duty for all mankind, we can hardly acquiesce. This is the caprice of the religious founder. It is individuality erecting itself as universality, and claiming to rule where it ought to serve.

---

[1] Personal Narrative of a Pilgrimage to Mecca and Medina, Vol. III. p. 316.

[2] l. c. III. 332 sqq.

These criticisms may perhaps strike you as theories affecting superiority to facts. What signifies all this carping at the universalism of Islam, when weighed against the fact of its spread, first over all Arabia, then over a territory that soon equalled the Roman empire in extent, and presently far surpassed it? I will not deny that this triumphal march through the world impresses the spectator. But, on the other hand, its amazing rapidity must itself excite our suspicion. And when we go into details, we see at once that, here as elsewhere, mere success is far from establishing the merits of a cause. The first converts, in this case, are an exception. It is impossible to doubt their sincerity. It is no mean testimony to Mohammed's character that so many of his earliest followers came from the circle of his immediate friends and relations. To Chadija, who shared his life for so many years, he was, and continued to be till her death, the apostle of Allah. But the number of believers long remained extremely small. Even in the year of the flight there was no sign as yet of the future triumph of Islam. There is nothing whatever to show that Mohammed met an existing want or satisfied the longings of his people. It is true that from the settlement at Medina onwards his following gradually increases. But how? There is not a trace of enthusiasm or of spiritual awakening. It is a matter for consideration and negotiation. It is a bargain—sometimes struck, moreover, under pressure of violence and the instinct of self-preservation. True believers were not wanting. They were the cement that held the structure together. It was they who supported or restored it when it threatened to collapse. But the great mass remained strangers at heart to the new religion. It was the prospect of plunder and conquest—a prospect which could only be realized if all the tribes united under one banner—that made them embrace Islam. No doubt the character of Mohammed's religion not only made this result possible, but actually provoked and stimulated it. Its sobriety and simplicity recommended it to the practical and sceptical Arab. It could be summed up in one brief formula—the two-fold confession, "No god but Allah" and "Mohammed his prophet." And even when accepted more seriously and expanded more fully, Islam retained the same character of conciseness and definiteness. Every one knew what it meant. Religious duties were soon clearly defined and reduced to the well-known five—the pillars of Islam. The Qorán, only extant in one text after Othman's redaction, was the complete and exclusive book of Allah. The consecration of a whole people to such a system is no more surprising than the rapidity with which it spread. If you would win the great masses, give them the truth in rounded form, neat and clear, in visible and tangible guise. This lesson is taught by all history, and not least by the first century of Islam. And if this be so, then Islam's victories, apart from the fact that they were prepared and partly carried out by force of arms, cannot be urged in proof of its universalism.

But at this point we are assailed by the fear that we may have been dealing unfairly after all. We remember that the defenders of Christianity are never weary of appealing to "the simplicity of the Gospel." Is it fair, while admitting this appeal, to reproach Islam with what we call its meagreness? Must we require it absolutely and from the outset to embrace everything? Is it not the highest praise that can be given to any form of religion to say that it is marked at once by simplicity and definiteness? Yes! but under one condition: It must further, or if this is too much to require, at least it must not hinder, the free spiritual development of man, in those directions in which it makes no direct provision for his wants. Then, but then only, it may be universal in spite of its limitations, and may prove a true blessing to mankind.

Does Islam comply with this condition?

A first glance leaves the impression that Mohammed's creation need not shrink from this test. It seems to respect the characteristics of race and nationality, and to possess the power of adapting its development to special social and national peculiarities. For instance, do we not find (confining ourselves to incontestable cases) a Persian, a Hindoo, a Javanese variety of Islam? And again, such a glance at the Mohammedan world appears to show us that it has freely sought and found satisfaction for those needs which were only half recognized, if recognized at all, by the primitive Islam. If the mystic element was almost entirely wanting at first, and if the pressure of the sense of sin was left unrelieved, Çufism and the belief in the mediation of Mohammed himself and of the saints so assiduously honoured, filled up the gap. And lastly, Moslem theology seems to bear witness to Islam's capacity for development; for it has been asserted, not unreasonably, that the Moslem theology will bear comparison with the Christian, and need not yield to it either in boldness or in acumen. Is not all this a speaking proof that the original poverty of Islam needed but the magic touch of more favourable surroundings and a higher intellectual development in order to be transformed into wealth?

I have said that this is the impression the Moslem world produces upon the superficial observer. And by putting it so, I have already implied my belief that closer inspection dissipates this first impression. It remains for me to attempt to justify this opinion, and to this attempt I must strictly confine myself. I have not the most distant intention of giving a history of Islam. In what relation does its later development stand to its primitive character as already expounded? Such is the single question to which we must now direct our attention.

The religious faith that has once struck root in the

heart of a people never dies. Other conceptions that are at war with it find entrance, and seem as though they must cast it out. But even under their dominion the old faith lives on, transformed indeed, subordinated to the higher conception and assimilated by it, but by this very means preserved from complete extinction.

This proposition, which is supported by so many and such striking examples that it may almost be called a law of religious development, seems at first to find its full confirmation in the Moslem world. Islam, alike in its first establishment and in its permanent influence, has failed, like every other religion, to root out all that its converts had previously believed, and all that, in accordance with their beliefs, they had taken up into their manners and customs. All this is in strict conformity with the general rule. It is the most natural thing in the world that in Persia, for instance, the old Zoroastrian faith, and in Hindustan the ideas native to the country, should gleam through the doctrine and the life of Moslems. But is this all? The truth is, that in these and other countries where Islam has been introduced, it has *not* succeeded in assimilating these incongruous convictions and usages, in taking them up into its own sphere, in penetrating them with its own spirit. They live on, preserving their original character, at most with a Moslem tinge cast over them, but for the most part not even reduced to a show of consistency with the system to which they theoretically belong. De Gobineau—and we may admit him as a competent witness to the present state of the East, without accepting his views as to the origin of Mohammed's conceptions[1]—calls Islam "ce voile très léger, sous la garde duquel les opinions, les doctrines, les théories anciennes se sont très-aisément maintenues et n'ont absolument rien perdu ni de leur force, ni de leur crédit."[2] And elsewhere, "Comme l'islam, avec ses formules vagues et inconsistantes, semblait inviter tout le monde à le reconnaître, sans forcer personne à abandonner rien de ce qu'il pensait, il est devenu ce que nous le voyons, le manteau commode, sous lequel s'abrite, en se cachant à peine, tout le passé."[3] And all this holds good in countries of which de Gobineau can hardly have been thinking when he wrote these words. My own countryman, Veth, with his intimate knowledge of the East-Indian Archipelago, speaks of Islam, in his fine review of the religious condition of Java, as "the official cloak that is stretched over native society."[4] If a flap of this cloak be lifted here and there, the Buddhism brought to Java long ago by missionaries from Hindustan is revealed; and side by side, often in grotesque confusion with it, the Siwaïsm brought by the Hindu colonists from their fatherland;[5] and beneath it all lies the

---

[1] Les religions et les philosophies dans l'Asie Centrale (2e éd. 1866), p. 41 svv.
[2] l.c. p. 26.   [3] l.c. p. 54.
[4] Java, geographisch, ethnologisch, historisch, I. 340.
[5] Ibid. I. 332 vv., II. 149 vv.

old popular animistic belief that has really lost none of its force for the masses.[1] Nature-worship and spirit-worship are still *the* religion of the Javanese. Hindu and Mohammedan elements have linked themselves to them, and so that strange compound has been formed which is not inappropriately called "Javanism." It would be a complete mistake to regard this Javanism as a variety of Islam, with a national colouring. No doubt there are in Java sincere believers in Islam, men who are Mohammedans in heart and soul, and who therefore detest the yoke of a Christian people. Their fanaticism, constantly fired by colonists from Arabia and by pilgrims returning from Mekka, infectious too, like all fanaticism, by its very nature, might easily lay hold of the masses of the population, and certainly makes them very dangerous subjects.[2] But this infectiousness of the political idea of Islam is no proof of its spiritual supremacy; and emphatic evidence against that supremacy is supplied by the want of assimilating power of which Javanism is a striking but far from a solitary instance. It is true that no candid judge of Islam will cite as a proof of its weakness its inability to regulate land tenure in Java by Mohammedan law,[3] although Islam itself no doubt claims supremacy over all civil matters; but when we see that on its own

---

[1] Java, &c. I. 314 vv. [2] Ibid. I. 399 vv.

[3] Ibid. I. 349 vv. Neither would it be fair to cite the degeneration of the "five pillars" as a proof that Islam has not attained supremacy in Java.

field of the spiritual life and the religious convictions it has to be content to play the part of a mantle that covers all unrighteousness, and by that very means sustains and defends it, then surely we have found a sign of poverty and feebleness that deprives the spread of Islam in the Indian Archipelago of all value as a proof of its universalism.

Amid the many forms under which Islam has developed itself in widely severed localities, we note a phenomenon that presents itself so systematically and persistently that it may well be reckoned amongst its essential and permanent characteristics. The whole Moslem world pays honours to Mohammed, not merely as the incomparable founder of its religion, but as still living and pleading on its behalf with Allah. Very high, though lower than Mohammed, stand the *walis* or saints, with their magnificent tombs, the goal of constant pilgrimages. We can hardly exaggerate the place occupied by this adoration of the prophet and the saints in the life of the Moslem peoples. It is to this that Medina owes its rank next to Mekka and hardly inferior to it.[1] As to the worship of the saints, open the first book of travels in any Moslem country on which you chance to lay your hand, and you will instantly come upon numerous and striking proofs of

---

[1] Burton, l. c. Vol. II. ch. i.—viii.

its extent and of the significance it has acquired in the life of the people.¹

To pronounce any judgment on the adoration of saints in the abstract would of course be out of place here. For ourselves, I suppose, there are serious objections which would prevent our taking part in it. But this does not preclude us from admitting that amongst the Moslems it evidently satisfies deeply rooted wants and possesses a genuinely religious significance. No doubt many a wali failed to deserve when living the reverence which has been paid him since his death; many of the graves owe their supposed sanctity to simple misapprehension; here and there old heathen gods still receive their honours under the new names of saints; and, worst of all, the adoration of the saints furnishes a mantle under cover of which immoral practices, surviving from the days of the deification of the powers of nature, are shamelessly perpetuated.² But all this does not prevent the adoration of the saints, taken all in all, from being an encouraging phenomenon. Here the sense of dependence and the need of redemption assert their claims. The faculty of admiration is not dead. True merits are

---

[1] That Java forms no exception to this rule may be seen in Veth, ibid.

[2] The proofs of this are collected in an interesting treatise by Ignace Goldziher, Le culte des saints chez les Muselmans (Revue de l'hist. des religions, 1ère année, Tome I. pp. 257—351).

recognized by the contemporary, and continue to be reverenced by a thankful posterity. As the expression of these emotions, and no less as a protest against the vices of those who have succeeded the pious men of a former age in the seat of honour,[1] the adoration of saints has genuine claims on our sympathy.

But the real question is not whether we find the phenomenon easy to explain, or can even rejoice in it up to a certain point. The adoration of the walis must not only be considered as evidence of what goes on in the heart of the Moslems, but must also be examined in its relation to Islam. Its general prevalence might lead us to regard it as a product of Islam itself. But as a fact it is far from being so. It is rather a protest against the very religion in which it occupies so prominent a place. The Moslem seeks what his faith withholds from him, and seeks it where the authority which he himself recognizes forbids him to look.

Far be it from us to condemn Islam for not satisfying all the demands its confessors think fit to make on it! It is indeed its merit to receive many a complaint in silence and to reject many a prayer. A religion which formally granted all that the Moslem desires to obtain at the graves of his different saints, would present a singular spectacle indeed. Sobriety may not always appear attractive or winning, but it remains a virtue none the less. We must further acknowledge

---

[1] Cf. A. von Kremer, Geschichte der herrschenden Ideen des Islams, S. 180 f.

that it is not always easy to draw the line between the unlawful and fanciful and the genuine and ineradicable needs of the pious soul. But this at least may be laid down, that "to be near God" and to feel God near us is no exaggerated demand and need not remain an unsatisfied longing. Now it is just this that Islam does not give, either in the conception of Allah's nature and attributes which it preaches, or in the worship which it has introduced. Though Allah is called by preference "ar-rahmáno'r-rahímo," the Compassionate and Merciful, yet he is "a god afar off." The people knows no other than Him, and therefore observes the religious duties imposed by Him, and appears at the stated time in His house of prayer; but this does not satisfy the wants of the heart, and the people therefore makes itself a new religion.[1] At the graves of its saints it seeks compensation for the dryness of the official doctrine and worship.

But the pious do this in spite of the faith that they profess. Mohammed rejected as emphatically as he possibly could the supernatural rank and mediatorial office that has been forced upon him.[2] There is no room in his religion anywhere for adoration of the saints. The orthodox Mohammedan theology has been compelled to admit it, and has taken the "kerámát," the miracles of the saints, under its protection against

---

[1] Von Kremer, l.c. S. 165 f.
[2] Goldziher, following others, has shown this, l.c. pp. 259—265.

the scepticism that assailed them.[1] But those who have held closest by the prophet have never been able to acquiesce in this popular enrichment of Islam, against which they have repeatedly raised their protest.[2] And even if they had held their peace, the Qorán itself would have spoken loud enough. We are far indeed from grudging the Moslem the satisfaction of his religious needs. But such an extension as Islam has received in the adoration of the saints cannot be put down to its credit. When an unmistakable want, because it can get no satisfaction legitimately, seeks and finds it illegitimately, we are surely in the presence of a weighty testimony against the religion within which this phenomenon has presented itself from the earliest times up to the present day. If it is only in this form that Islam can satisfy the demands of the pious soul, then it has become a religion of the world in the teeth of its own proper nature.

Precisely the same judgment must be pronounced on Çufism. There are some who build their favourable forecasts of Islam's future upon it.[3] Their admiration of the marvellously profound mysticism of the Çufis, expressed in such beautiful forms by the Çufi

---

[1] To the evidence collected by Goldziher, l.c. pp. 335 svv., may be added that of Sha'ráni, cited by Flügel in Zeitschr. der deutschen morgenl. Gesellschaft, XX. 18.

[2] Goldziher, l.c. pp. 330 svv., infra, pp. 45 sqq.

[3] "L'unique voie qui, dans l'Islam, puisse conduire à la réforme, c'est la doctrine du mysticisme:" Mirza Kasem Beg, in Journal Asiatique, 1866, p. 381.

poets, is easy enough to understand; but so also is the disgust with which others mention both the godless doctrine of many Çufis, and the lives of their followers who "go idle in the name of Allah." For Çufism is a motley phenomenon, and cannot be delineated by a single stroke. But let us assume that its purely religious elements maintain the ascendant, and let us take them alone into consideration. What promise for the future *of Islam* is contained in Çufism? It came into the Moslem world from without, perhaps from Buddhism. It made great way from first to last. Was this because it agreed in principle with Islam, or at any rate might serve as a complement to it? No! It was rather because it gave what Islam by its very nature could not give. Deism and mysticism cannot really go together. No doubt the Mohammedan theology has taken up Çufite elements, here more and there less, and has worked them up with sayings of the Qorán and the tradition into a so-called whole. Nor was it at all rare, at any rate in former times, for lines of Çufite poetry to make their appearance in the Friday chotba or sermon.[1] But this only shows that the religious leaders of the Moslems, when endeavouring to establish the reasonableness of their faith or to edify their brethren, borrow from any quarter where they can find what they want. The conflict of principle is thus disguised but not removed. The Moslem

---

[1] Goldziher, from Ali ben Migmún al-Maghribí in Zeitschr., d. d. M. G. XXVIII. 321.

who makes terms with Çufism thereby gives his own religion a certificate of poverty, and the true Çufite is a Moslem no more.

There is much more reason in the plea that Islam's capacity for development is evinced by the activity of *the Mo'tazilites*, under which name I include, as others have done before me, the theologians who, from the second century of the Hejra onwards, distinguished themselves in the head-quarters of Islam, Baçra first and afterwards Bagdad, by their liberal tendencies.[1] They were produced by Islam itself, though perhaps they early felt the influence of Greek philosophy and had their thoughts brought to maturity by it.[2] Their importance rests on the earnestness with which they maintained the ethical aspects of the conception of God. This gave its significance to their polemic in favour of free-will and against the doctrine of predestination. The name "ahlo't-tauhíd w'al-adl," upholders of God's unity and righteousness, with which they designated themselves by preference, points in the same direction; and if we did but know them by the writings of their own best representatives instead

---

[1] H. Steiner, die Mu'taziliten oder die Freidenker in Islam. Ein Beitrag zur allgemein Culturgeschichte (1865); M. Th. Houtsma, de strijd over het dogma in den Islam tot op al-Asha'rî (1875), bl. 42 vv. and elsewhere. On the orthography of the name, cf. Flügel and Fleischer in Zeitschr. d. d. M. G. XX. 32 f.

[2] W. Spitta, zur Geschichte Abu'l-Hasan al-Ash'arî's, S. 2 ff., 51 ff., at variance with Houtsma, l. c. bl. 87 v.

of through their opponents only, it is highly probable that this tendency of their doctrine would come out still more clearly. It was in the service of this ethical conception likewise that they developed the rationalism —no unwonted ally of great zeal for morality—that has earned them the name of "the free-thinkers of Islam." Their thesis that the Qorán was *created* gives striking expression, under the forms of the age, to their aspiration after independence and reasonableness. For some little time they might flatter themselves with the hope that their bold attempt would succeed. More than one of the Abbasidæ, especially al-Mamún (813—833 A.D.), favoured them, protected their freedom, or kept them in the ascendant by his authority. But the disenchantment was soon to follow. Under al-Motawakkel (847—861 A.D.) the Mo'tazilites lost the favour of the court, and the dogma of the uncreated Qorán was first officially proclaimed and afterwards enforced. Were we to regard this revolution as produced simply by the spiritual supremacy of the caliph, and capable of being subsequently reversed by himself or one of his successors, we could but bewail the lot of its victims. But the matter was far more serious. The caprice of a tyrant may have been the occasion of the overthrow of the Mo'tazilites, but its real cause lay deeper, in the essence of Islam which the popular instinct had apprehended justly.[1] The masses were not competent to

---

[1] Houtsma, l. c. bl. 110 v.

follow the discussions of the scholars, but they felt that the defenders of the uncreated Qorán were upholding the absolute claims of their religion and must therefore be right. It was not in the God of the Mo'tazilites, whose essence was righteousness, but in the God of orthodoxy, the Almighty, subject to no other rule than his own caprice, that they recognized their own and Mohammed's Allah.[1] Alas! they were in the right. The law of Islam contains admirable moral precepts, and, what is more, succeeds in bringing them into practice and powerfully supporting their observance. But this is not enough to make it an *ethical* religion. It is the glory of the Mo'tazilites that they endeavoured to raise it to this character. But their effort struck at once upon the rock that must ultimately wreck it—the fixed character of Islam, fixed even then, nay fixed from the very outset. Hence, too, the fact that their fall was followed by no resurrection. More than one of their theses was adopted by al-Ash'arí, the father of Mohammedan scholasticism, who had formerly been of their number,[2] but only when so modified as to be made harmless; and henceforth they did but serve to give a show of reason to the

---

[1] "Allah der willkürliche tyrannische Herrscher, nach persönlichem Gutdünken, nach Belieben und Gewohnheit die Welt regierend, ohne ewiges Gesetz und ohne Zweckursachen, die reine Abstraction, in der alles individuelle Geistesleben, selbst der Unterschied von gut und böse verschwand, *der Gott der flachen Wüste*" (Steiner, l.c. S. 86).

[2] See Spitta, l.c. S. 36 ff., 50 ff.

system, instead of working as the leaven which leavens the whole lump. It is a spectacle that may well sadden us. But to the historian it is in the highest degree instructive. The men of the uncreated Qorán sincerely believed themselves to be maintaining the dignity and the sublime destiny of Islam. In truth, they were damming up against their religion the one channel that leads to true universalism. For the ethical is the universally human.

The conclusion to which we are led by a consideration of the development of Islam, is confirmed in the most striking manner by that remarkable movement—Arabian to the core and Moslemite without adulteration—which is known as Wahhábism. Its fame has been widely spread by the romantic appendix to de Lamartine's "Voyage en Orient,"[1] and subsequently by Palgrave's "Narrative."[2] If I were compelled to pronounce an opinion on the future of this movement, I should be sorely puzzled. In the peninsula itself, the supremacy of Wahhábism, which Palgrave found

---

[1] Récit du sejour de Fatallah Sayeghir chez les Arabes errants du grand désert, rapporté et traduit par les soins de M. de Lamartine (Œuvres, Bruxelles, 1840, pp. 679—759). The notes of de Lascaris, the agent of Napoleon I., in whose service Fatallah was at the time, appear still to be in existence. Cf. W. Scawen Blunt, in the Fortnightly Review, 1881, II. 326, *note*.

[2] Narrative of a Year's Journey through Central and Eastern Arabia (1862-63); cf. M. J. De Goeje's criticism in de Gids, 1866, IV. 261 vv.

at its culminating point, appears quite recently to have sustained a very sensible shock.[1] Whether it will ever recover from it is at least doubtful. But in any case, Wahhábism, as a conception of Islam, remains a most formidable power, with a centre of its own in the school at Derajah, and with its numerous and zealous missionaries who find the ears of many open wherever they present themselves in Moslem lands.[2] And no wonder! For, as the Ulema at Damascus declared, Wahhábism is *the true Islam*. Its founder, Ibn Abdo'l-Wahháb (about 1745 A.D.), simply intended to root out the heathenism that still survives in Arabia, and to restore Mohammed's religion in its original purity. These are likewise the ideas that inspire his true followers and which constitute their strength. Accordingly, we see that the Wahhábites are always zealous in word and deed against those elements of the faith and practice of the Moslems which we too have been compelled to note as foreign to Islam and as imported into it from without. Where Islam is professed according to the Wahhábite conception of it, it allows no adoration of saints and no Çufites. It casts them out as energetically as it banishes wine and tobacco, and secures the strict observance of religious duties, if need

---

[1] W. Scawen Blunt, Recent Events in Arabia, Fortnightly Review, 1880, I. 707 vv.

[2] Cf. C. N. Pischon, der Einfluss des Islâms auf das häusliche, sociale und politische Leben seiner Bekenner, S. 132—138, and the accounts of Dr. Mordtmann and others there cited.

be, by the lash.[1] The Wahhábites have been called the Puritans of Islam. The comparison is not unjust. But whereas no serious historian would ever dream of simply identifying Puritanism and Christianity, Wahhábism really is Islam itself—Islam, the whole of Islam, and nothing but Islam. And this is the very reason why it bears such strong evidence against the universalism of Islam. A religion which can be restored in such a shape, with a well-founded appeal to its genuine sources, may meet the wants of the inhabitants of the desert which witnessed its birth— but there are other and higher demands which it cannot satisfy.

The latter portion of our review seems almost like an indictment of Islam. And yet I trust that I have not been unjust, and I am certainly far from intending to deny the relative value of Mohammed's institution, or the salutary effect which it has produced or still produces in sundry regions. But the real question we have had under discussion has not been this, so much as what I may call the *compass* of Islam, the possible extension marked out for it by its character. This examination necessarily brought to light the narrow

---

[1] See the original documents—letters of Sa'ud ibn Abdo'l-Azíz and his commander, Uljan ad-Dabíbí—translated by Fleischer in Zeitschrift, d. d. M. G. XI. 427 ff., and especially S. 435, on the opposition to innovations; S. 431, 437, on the rejection of the adoration of saints, the dervishes, &c.

limits within which its influence is necessarily bounded, and the way in which its founder himself cut it off from the possibility of true development, and therefore from the widest measure of extension. This fact, I hope, now stands clearly before us. May I not also assume that we need make no further search for its cause, inasmuch as we have already found it in the special origin of Islam?

The Arabic nationality was not the cradle but the boundary-wall of Islam. We may, if we will, give rein to the imagination, and think of the possibility of the Arabs having made a different contribution to the religious development of mankind. The religion of the Arab race, so highly gifted in many ways, in full possession of the energy of its first confessors, freed from childish superstition, bursting through the limits of nationality and rising above time and space—what a future might not have been in store for such a creation! But this is pure speculation, and moves beyond the realm of facts. Dante, long ago, sketched the character of the historical Islam in nearer accordance with the truth, when he assigned a place to Mohammed, the arch-heretic, in one of the lowest circles of the Inferno.[1] For it was thus that he expressed, under current forms, the fact that Islam is a side branch of Christianity,

---

[1] Canto xxviii. On earlier and later Christian writers who have taken the same view, cf. Ed. Sayous, Jésus-Christ d'après Mahomet, ou les notions et les doctrines musulmanes sur le Christianisme, pp. 90—92.

or better still, as we should now say, of Judaism: a selection as it were from Law and Gospel, made by an Arab and for Arabs, levelled to their capacity, and further supplemented—or must we say adulterated?—by national elements calculated to facilitate their reception of it. Thus derived from the long acknowledged documents of God's revelation, and presently entering the lists against them, Islam was destined, after a very brief period of growth and development, to stereotype itself once for all and assume its unalterable shape. Succeeding generations, and nations with other mental equipment, might add to it from their own stores, and might attempt to modify and expand its rigid form. Only for a time, and indeed only in appearance, could these attempts succeed. Almost as old as Islam itself and destined to last as long, there stood and there stand immovable the Qorán and the tradition. The better they were fitted partly to inspire and partly to subdue Mohammed's fellow-countrymen, and so in the first period to work marvels, the more uncompromisingly do they bar the way to the realization of their own ideal—the spread of Islam amongst all the children of men. True universalism is to Islam, in virtue of its very origin, unattainable.

II.

THE POPULAR RELIGION OF ISRAEL.
PRIESTS AND PROPHETS OF YAHWEH.

CHRISTIANITY is the second of the universal religions which we are to examine in connection with the national religions from which they have sprung. Now the period at which Christianity rose is known, and you might naturally expect me to transport you to Palestine at about the beginning of our era. But before I realize this expectation, I must allow myself, nay I am compelled, to make a long détour with you. What Judaism was at the time of Jesus, and what germs it contained within itself, we can only understand when acquainted with its past, for there we discover the cause of its really being so much more than it seemed to be. Cut loose from its antecedents it impresses us as something very different from what it turns out to be when regarded in its true light as the lawful heir of its own past. We have reason therefore to begin with a retrospect. And, moreover, the spectacle of Israel's past is in itself of an interest that chains our attention, while it contains—and that is my present point—the prophecy of the wonderful development that took place eighteen centuries ago. In a certain sense this is the view that has always been taken by Christians. The Church dates her origins from the creation itself, and regards the fates of Israel as an express portion of her own history. To the prophets, especially, she assigns a place amongst her founders, inasmuch as they beheld her glory in the spirit and rejoiced in her salvation in hope. I must not let it seem, even for a moment, as though I were intending to maintain or confirm this idea in its true and uncorrupted sense. Our point of view is not that of the Church, and our conclusions accordingly differ essentially from hers. But in recognizing the close connection between the Judaism out of which Christianity sprang, and the whole of the preceding spiritual conflict in Israel, I join in hearty agreement with the Christianity of all ages. We have therefore no choice but to study the character and motives of this conflict. The antithesis of "national" and "universal" will serve as our clue, and by following it I may perhaps succeed in placing facts with which none of you are unacquainted in such a light that they will not altogether lack the charm of novelty.

When we speak of the antecedents of Judaism, we can only mean the recognition and worship of that god whose proper name our translations of the Old Testament interpret by *the Lord*,—a name which we have good grounds for pronouncing *Yahweh*.[1] You will understand what I mean, then, if I begin by propounding the question: Was the worship of Yahweh amongst the pre-exilian Israelites national? And, if so, in what sense?

At first the question seems likely to prove a very perplexing one. If we follow the traditional view, which, as we shall presently see, is rooted in the Old Testament itself, we shall be ready enough to answer: Previous to the Babylonian captivity, Yahwism was the religion of a minority, and the worship of other gods had a better claim to be called national; for the prophets, Yahweh's representatives, *opposed* themselves to the great masses of their people. This last fact is certainly undeniable. And yet the answer, however natural it may seem, does not satisfy us. We could point to other instances in which a genuinely national conception is represented by a comparatively small number of chosen spirits. And apart from this, we must ask whether the mass of the people really was hostile to Yahwism. This at least is certain, that they themselves would never have admitted as much. Many of those whom we cannot but reckon as belonging to this majority were devoted with all their hearts to Yahweh, and threw all their zeal into his cause. Was there more than one Yah-

---

[1] Cf. Note IV.

wism? And, if so, in what relation did the one stand to the other? We are evidently dealing with a singularly complex phenomenon, the various factors of which we must duly separate in our study if we are to form a true conception of the whole.

It is in this study that I now offer myself as your guide. In dealing with such a question, every simplification must be welcome; and I may therefore begin by reminding you that the hypothesis of the *introduction of Yahwism from without* must be definitely abandoned at the stage which scholarship has now reached. I am not speaking of foreign *influence* on the development of Israel and the consequent development of its religion. The possibility of such influence cannot be denied. Even in the ages of which we are now speaking, Canaan, so far from being a secluded country, was the battle-ground of the peoples and tribes of Asia. So far was Israel from standing outside the turmoil of conflicting nations, that the idea has been suggested of assigning it that central place on the stage of the earliest history which is taken in succeeding ages first by the Greeks and then by the Romans; and this not only in virtue of the place of honour to which Israel itself has claims, but also and yet more because all the civilized nations of Asia came successively into contact with it, and thus take their places, so to speak, each in its turn, upon the field of the history and give the historian occasion to sketch their special characteristics,—first the Egyptians, then the Assyrians, then the Babylonians, and lastly the Medo-Persians.[1] It would indeed be more than strange if Israel, while capable of lending itself to such a historical purpose, nevertheless bore no traces in its own development of the influence of all these peoples. Such traces are indeed easy to discern. But the introduction of Yahwism from abroad, which I have called a hypothesis now antiquated, is a very different matter. Its advocates are necessarily restricted to a narrow circle. Unless their procedure is to be altogether capricious, if they are to take any account at all of the evidence of the historical documents, then the Egyptians are really the only people that can come into consideration; and accordingly it is to them, and specifically to the Egyptian priests, that the establishment of Yahwism in Israel has been assigned, and is here and there still assigned, with a perseverance worthy of a better cause. In 1841, Auguste Comte pronounced the "little Jewish theocracy to be a 'dérivation accessoire' from the Egyptian, and perhaps also the Chaldean, theocracy, from which it very probably emanated by a kind of colonization, of an exceptional nature, effected by the priestly caste, the superior classes of which, having long arrived at monotheism by their own mental development, may have been led to found a purely monotheistic colony, by way of an asylum or as an experi-

---

[1] P. J. Veth, in *de Gids*, 1864, I. 619—625.

ment. And there, in spite of the permanent antipathy of the lower population to so premature an institution, monotheism must have preserved its existence, though not without difficulty, in a pure and openly avowed form, at any rate after having consented to the loss of the greater number of its elect by the famous secession of the Ten Tribes."[1] The father of Positivism expressed his belief that a closer analysis of "this strange anomaly" would confirm his own views, as soon as it should be undertaken by a philosopher who should place himself at the "rational" point of view which he had indicated. Since that time forty years and more have passed, and the prophesied confirmation is still to be looked for. Amongst students of Israelite religion, there is not, as far as I know, a single one who derives Yahwism from Egypt, either in the strange manner hit upon by Comte or in any other. The documents which form the basis of their studies favour the idea that Yahwism was roused from its slumbers by the Egyptian religion, and was made conscious of its own characteristics by its conflict with it, rather than that it sprang out of a faith from which it is seen to be radically different. Certain Egyptologists, however, still show a not unnatural disposition to seek the cradle of Yahwism on the Nile; but their attempts to point it out have failed one after another. Instead of dilating on this subject, I prefer to appeal to the

---

[1] Cours de Philos. Posit., Tom. v. 206 (2e éd.).

testimony of one who, himself an Egyptologist, is also one of my predecessors in this chair. "It may be confidently asserted," he says, "that neither Hebrews nor Greeks borrowed any of their ideas from Egypt." He holds that the agreement between Israelite and Egyptian ideas, as far as it is not delusive, is confined to those conceptions which are common to all religion. "I have looked through a number of works," he declares, "professing to discover Egyptian influences in Hebrew institutions, but have not even found anything worth controverting."[1]

Setting aside this hypothesis, therefore, we recognize the fact that, from the earliest period down to the Babylonian captivity, Israel had its own national religion, which we can only call "Yahwism." Regal temples were consecrated to Yahweh, not only at Jerusalem, but at Dan and Bethel[2] likewise; and the same may be said of the sanctuary at Shiloh during the period of the Judges.[3] The "bamôth" also, though the prophet Ezekiel is very probably correct in supposing them to be of Canaanitish origin,[4] were employed by the inhabitants of the cities where they stood and of

---

[1] P. le Page Renouf, Lectures on the Origin and Growth of Religion, as illustrated by the Religion of Ancient Egypt (The Hibbert Lectures, 1879), pp. 243—245.

[2] 1 Kings xii. 26 sqq.; Amos vii. 10 sqq.

[3] Judges xxi. 19—23; 1 Sam. i. sqq.; Jer. vii. 12—14; xxvi. 6, 9.

[4] Ezekiel xx. 27—29.

the surrounding localities in the service of Yahweh.[1] The number of these "bamôth" was very great, I had almost said unlimited. Even at Jerusalem, although the temple stood there, they were not wanting.[2] Most of them were doubtless very simple. Natural or artificial mounds were provided with an altar to do service as occasion required; or in some cases a chapel or even a temple was added, designed and adapted for regular worship.[3] We can hardly suppose that any fixed rules obtained either in the choice or the structure of the "bamôth." Everything was left to the devotion and zeal of the people of the cities and villages in which the want of a sanctuary made itself felt. As a rule, every one would repair to the high place that lay nearest to him; but there were also "great bamôth," which were considered specially sacred on account of their antiquity or some other circumstance, and these were sought by pilgrims from more distant regions.[4]

Corresponding to the many sanctuaries of Yahweh are the numerous offerings made to him and the feasts celebrated in his honour by the great masses. Even those who in other respects find most to object to in the popular worship, do not deny that it is intended as a tribute of reverence to Yahweh. Amos, for instance, is not contemplating the worship of other gods when

---

[1] 1 Sam. ix. 12 sqq., &c. [2] 2 Kings xxiii. 8.
[3] 1 Kings xii. 31; xiii. 32.
[4] 1 Kings iii. 4; cf. Amos iv. 4; v. 5; viii. 14.

he makes Yahweh declare, "I hate, I despise your feasts, and cannot endure your assemblies."[1] It was to Yahweh himself that the sacrifices and gifts were offered, and in his honour that those oxen were slain which he would not accept or regard. It was of him that those hymns were sung which he would not hear.[2] Equally explicit on this point is the unimpeachable evidence of Hosea[3] and Isaiah.[4]

Now when we hear of temples, high places, altars, feasts and sacrifices, the terms might well suggest a clearly defined sacred territory trodden by the Israelite only now and then and on exceptional occasions. But this idea would be quite mistaken. The same unexceptionable witnesses whom we have already consulted may teach us how the worship of Yahweh penetrated and hallowed the personal, the domestic and the family life of ancient Israel. The prophet Hosea gives us an idea of this when he describes the existence of the Israelites in a foreign land, where they "sit down for many days without king and without prince, without sacrifice and without maççebah, without ephod and teraphím."[5] There, he declares, "they shall eat unclean food, for they pour out no wine to Yahweh and lay not their sacrifices before him (on the altar); as food eaten in time of mourning is their food; he who

---

[1] Amos v. 21.
[2] Amos v. 22, 23.
[3] Hos. ii. 13 (11 in the A.V.).
[4] Is. i. 11—17, and elsewhere.
[5] Hos. iii. 4.

eats thereof is made unclean; for their food serves only to still their hunger; it comes not into Yahweh's house."[1] This implies that in ordinary times Yahweh received his portion of whatever the Israelite ate, especially the meat. It was at the sanctuary (for there was always one in the immediate neighbourhood) that his ox or his sheep was slaughtered; and a portion was either offered upon the altar or granted to the priest. When this was rendered impossible by expulsion from "the land" or "the heritage" of Yahweh,[2] then he could only eat "unclean food." So closely was Yahwism interwoven with the ordinary life of the Israelite! It follows of itself that his feast days were holy days. Not without reason does Hosea place "the rejoicing" of Israel in the same line with his "feasts (i.e. pilgrimages to one of the sanctuaries), new moons, sabbaths and all appointed times."[3] What an important place in life must these ever-returning days have taken! The sabbath, on which all ordinary work stood still, and a visit was made to the sanctuary or the representative of Yahweh;[4] the new moon, which was celebrated in the same fashion,[5] and on which, moreover, the united members of one household joined in the festive meal, which must have borne a religious character, inasmuch as none who were unclean might

---

[1] Hos. ix. 3 b, 4; cf. Note V.
[2] Hos. ix. 3; 1 Sam. xxvi. 19.   [3] Hos. ii. 13 (11).
[4] Amos viii. 5; Isaiah i. 13; 2 Kings iv. 23.
[5] See the passages referred to in note 4.

share it.¹ Then "the rejoicing of the harvest" mentioned by Isaiah² was undoubtedly consecrated to Yahweh from the earliest times downward. Finally, there was the feast with which the shearing of the sheep was associated;³ and this too was a religious solemnity, for a portion of the wool was granted to the priest.⁴ And as these annually returning events in the life of the farmer or the cattle-feeder were sanctified by religion, so likewise was the bond encircling the members of a single family. At any rate the mishphachah, to which David belonged, held a sacrificial feast every year at Bethlehem,⁵ and there is not the smallest reason why we should not ascribe the same usage to other families also.

If we weigh these facts, taken in their mutual connection, we shall find it extremely natural that the people should trust in Yahweh their god, should look for help from him in times of peril, and expect his succour when their enemies prevailed against them. "Is not Yahweh in our midst? No harm will befall us!"—so speak the contemporaries of Micah.⁶ Amos refers to Israelites who long for "the day of Yahweh,"⁷ that is to say, the time when he shall make his might felt by Israel's opponents. In the time of Jeremiah the possession of Yahweh's temple serves the

---

[1] 1 Sam. xx. 5, 18, 25.　　[2] Isaiah ix. 2 (3).
[3] 1 Sam. xxv. 4 sqq.; 2 Sam. xiii. 23 sqq.
[4] Deut. xviii. 4.　　[5] 1 Sam. xx. 6, 28 sq.
[6] Mic. iii. 11.　　[7] Amos v. 18.

men of Jerusalem and the inhabitants of Judæa as a pledge that their god will remain with them;[1] and they are zealous to vindicate its honour. The prophet had been bold enough to foretell its devastation in the near future; and the people, stirred up by the priests and prophets, laid hold of him and cried threateningly, "Thou shalt die! Why hast thou prophesied in the name of Yahweh: This temple shall become like the temple of Shiloh, and this city shall be bereft of her inhabitants?" Jeremiah barely escaped with his life from the fury of the fanatical populace.[2]

In accordance with all this we find that, before the exile, nothing of any consequence was undertaken in Israel without the leaders of the people consulting Yahweh about it, and satisfying themselves of his approval. Barak, the son of Abinoam, engages in the unequal strife with Sisera, because Deborah, the prophetess of Yahweh, has roused him to it, and when she herself has promised to accompany him to the battle.[3] After a first defeat in the war with the Philistines, in the time of Eli, the Israelites send for the ark of Yahweh to their camp; and when it comes, under the escort of Hophni and Phineas, they greet it with loud acclamations.[4] Ere Saul ventures to follow in Jonathan's footsteps to improve the advantage gained by the latter, and again ere he pursues the fleeing foe by night, he consults Yahweh.[5] David, during his

---

[1] Jer. vii. 4. [2] Jer. xxvi. [3] Judges iv.
[4] 1 Sam. iv. [5] 1 Sam. xiv. 18 sqq., 36 sq.

flight from Saul, is guided once and again by the oracle announced by the priest Abiathar.[1] And after his exaltation to the throne of all Israel, when the land was visited by dire famine in three successive years, he consulted Yahweh, whether through a priest or a prophet, and acted on the response that was given him[2]—let us hope that he did so against his will, and that he only surrendered Saul's descendants to the vengeance of the Gibeonites because he could not answer to the sorely afflicted people for disregarding the utterance of Yahweh. But is there any need that I should cite more examples? If the assistance of Yahweh's interpreter was called in for the occasions of daily life—(remember how Saul consults Samuel about his father's lost asses,[3] and how Jeroboam's wife visits Ahijah[4])—what is more natural than that Jehoshaphat and Ahab, before their expedition to recover Ramôth in Gilead,[5] and Hezekiah, when Sennacherib is threatening his capital,[6] and Josiah, before he carries out the precepts of the book of law found in the temple,[7] should consult Yahweh's representatives?

One trait is still wanting to this rapid sketch of Yahwism in the people's life in Israel. Yahweh's mark was, so to speak, stamped upon many of the Israelites in the very names they bore. About a hundred and ninety personal names which appear in

---

[1] 1 Sam. xxiii. 1 sqq., 9—11, &c.   [2] 2 Sam. xxi. 1—14.
[3] 1 Sam. ix.   [4] 1 Kings xiv.   [5] 1 Kings xxii.
[6] 2 Kings xix. 1—7, 20 sqq.   [7] 2 Kings xxii. 11—20.

the Old Testament are compounded with "Yahweh."[1] From Jehoshaphat downwards, all the kings of Judah but three were named in some way after him. This is not accidental, and it is not without significance. As in later times,[2] so doubtless amongst the earlier Israelites, the name-giving was the solemn act of the father, or, if the mother had anticipated him, was at least dependent on his sanction. The thing was not done thoughtlessly, and names were never mere conventional sounds. We see this clearly enough from the explanations of names so constantly given in the Old Testament, explanations which have sorely perplexed the commentators of later ages with stricter notions of etymology. Compound names such as "Sheár-jashúb" and "Mahér-shalál chaz-baz" are exceptional; but what Isaiah says of these two sons of his, "they are signs and warnings from Yahweh Zebaôth, who dwells on Zion," he testifies of himself also, in allusion to the "salvation of Yahweh" that was proclaimed in his own name "Isaiah."[3] It deserves notice, too, that both Nechoh and Nebucadrezar gave fresh names to the sons of Josiah whom they set upon the throne,[4]—names compounded with "Yahweh" which they borrowed from the common usage, without perhaps troubling themselves about their meaning.

---

[1] Cf. E. Nestle, die israel. Eigennamen nach ihrer religionsgeschichtlichen Bedeutung (Haarlem, 1876), S. 68 ff.

[2] Luke i. 59—63.   [3] Is. viii. 18.

[4] 2 Kings xxiii. 34, xxiv. 17.

This changing of the names was a symbolic act. It served to show that Jehoiakim and Zedekiah were their creatures, or, if you will, that they themselves—Nechoh and Nebucadrezar—were their fathers. The same idea appears in the message of Ahaz to Tiglath-Pilezer: "I am thy slave and thy son."[1] Did the two conquerors further signify, by the choice of these special names, that they owed their victory to the god of Israel himself, and that it would therefore be mere folly for the people of Yahweh to offer any further resistance? It is not impossible.[2] But even those who think the supposition too far-fetched will readily acknowledge our right to take the Israelitish proper names, in so far as they are connected with religion, as a veritable confession of faith, and to mark their derivation from "Yahweh" as an expression of the very special relationship in which Israel stood to this deity.

Everything that I have laid before you so far is taken from the Old Testament; and indeed I have not been free from the fear that I might seem to fall short of your just expectations, in doing no more than collect the information given by authorities accessible to every one. But how is it that the picture of ancient Israel which we have thus recovered differs so very widely from the current conception of its religious condition?

---

[1] 2 Kings xvi. 7.
[2] So J. L. S. Lutz, Biblische Dogmatik, S. 30.

The reason is not far to seek. The current conception is not derived from the special traits of which I have reminded you, but from the general reviews of the popular religion which the Israelitish historians lay before us—the introduction to the book of Judges,[1] and the retrospect of the fates of the kingdom of the ten tribes.[2] Their contents may be briefly summarized. According to the author of Judges, the generation that had conquered Canaan under Joshua's lead remained faithful to Yahweh.[3] Then began the apostasy. "The sons of Israel did what was evil in Yahweh's eyes, and served the Baals. They *forsook* Yahweh, the god of their fathers, who had brought them out of Egypt, and went after other gods."[4] When the well-deserved punishment came upon them, then indeed they returned to Yahweh. But it was only for a time, so long as the judge that had been raised up for them stood at their head; and on his death Yahweh was again forgotten, until another chastisement brought them back to his ways.[5] The state of things in the kingdom of Ephraim, according to the Second Book of Kings, was still more deplorable. There other gods were served, and the ways of the people which Yahweh had cast out before Israel were followed.[6] They bowed down before the dung-gods.[7] Yahweh, on his side,

---

[1] Judges ii. 6—iii. 6. [2] 2 Kings xvii. 7—23, 34—41.
[3] Judges ii. 7. [4] vv. 11, 12.
[5] vv. 14—19. [6] 2 Kings xvii. 7, 8.
[7] v. 12.

never ceased to warn them by his servants the prophets; but it was of no avail, for "they would not hear, but hardened their necks, like to the neck of their fathers, who had not faith in Yahweh, their god;"[1] they despised all his commandments, and "following after *nothings*—(i.e. the idols)—they came to *nought;*"[2] "all the commandments of Yahweh, their god, they broke, and they made themselves two molten calves, and made an Ashérah and worshipped all the host of heaven and served Baal,"[3] and offered their sons and daughters to Molech.[4] In Judah things were no better, for this tribe also "observed not the commandments of Yahweh and walked after the ordinances of Israel."[5] A dark picture in truth! Nor does the Chronicler lighten its colours. On the contrary, his judgment on the ten tribes and their religion is more unfavourable yet, and he cannot even find room for them in his review of the fates of the chosen people before the Babylonian captivity. This may be partly explained by his devotion to the house of David, and yet more to Jerusalem and the temple, but it is also connected with the abomination in which he held the ten tribes as idolaters.[6] Such being the judgments

---

[1] v. 14.

[2] v. 15. The play upon words is borrowed from Jeremiah (ii. 5), and is thus rendered in the A.V., "they followed vanity, and became vain."

[3] v. 16.   [4] v. 17.   [5] v. 19.

[6] 2 Chron. xi. 13—16; xiii. 3—18.

under the influence of which the current conception of Israel's early religion has been formed, is it surprising that the character of a national religion has been denied to Yahwism? According to this view, it was (at any rate before the exile) the opposition to Yahweh and his interpreters that better deserved to be called national.

But it is not enough to know the source from which the traditional view is drawn. We must also know *why* the Israelitish historians pass such a very unfavourable judgment upon the antecedents of their own people, and especially why they throw into the shadow a fact which even their own narratives reveal, and which in any case would be clear from the testimony of contemporaries. Even when writers simply tell us what occurred in the past, we must always bear in mind who they were, from what suppositions they started and for whom they were writing. But far more, nay everything, depends upon these considerations when the problem is to determine the value of such introductory or comprehensive surveys as we are now dealing with. Here the author's personality exercises a decisive influence. If he allows the events themselves to speak elsewhere, and often adopts unaltered what he finds in one of his precursors, here in these general surveys he comes forward in his own person to interpret the lessons of history for us,—or rather, not for *us*, whose only concern is to get at what actually happened, but for his own contemporaries, whose special requirements are never out of his mind.

It is to them that he looks. It is to them that he holds up the mirror of the past, that they may learn to be on their guard against the errors of a former generation, and to escape the judgment which will strike them too if they fail to walk in the ways of Yahweh. This admonishing and warning tendency is no incidental accompaniment, but the main purpose of the composition, and we must constantly keep it in view, on pain of utterly mistaking the drift of the writers.

The application of this general rule to the special case is not difficult. We must remember, in the first place, that the prophets themselves, while admitting the national worship of Yahweh as a fact, nevertheless condemn it from time to time in the strongest terms. It answers in no degree to their ideal. We shall return to this fact presently, and may now content ourselves with pointing it out, for no one will deny it. But whereas the prophets declare that the people serves Yahweh in its own way (i.e. in the wrong way), the historians give us the impression that Israel, either now and then or continuously, deserts and forsakes him altogether. It is this difference that we have to explain. Nor is it hard to do so. The Mosaic law is the standard of the historians—the book of Deuteronomy for the author of Judges and Kings (one person in all probability), and the whole Pentateuch for the Chronicler. Tried by this test, the popular religion was far indeed from deserving the name of "Yahwism." Only bear in mind that Deuteronomy confines the offerings and feasts in honour of Yahweh to the one temple of Jerusalem, and that the priestly law makes access to him dependent upon a host of conditions, not one of which had been observed by even his most zealous servants! What the people therefore had done in all sincerity to the glory of Yahweh, the later historians could only regard as opposition to him, could only brand as contempt for his commandments. In their eyes it was as abominable as idolatry itself—nay, even more so, inasmuch as it falsely declared itself to be the worship of Yahweh. Is it surprising that in their general surveys they do not so much as mention this pretext, but include everything—the building of bamôth, the sacrificing "on every high hill and under every green tree," the images of Yahweh, and the service of other gods—under one sweeping condemnation as apostasy from Yahweh? It was thus that our authors saw the past, and it was thus that they were compelled to judge it. Did a stray doubt ever rise in their minds whether they were really quite fair to the generations that had gone before them? Their zeal for Yahweh either never suffered such a thought to rise, or instantly repressed it. Was it not unconditional submission to his will that they themselves aspired to, and that they strove to quicken in their first readers? Obedience to all the regulations of the law was as yet by no means a second nature to their contemporaries. The danger of their going their own way was still imminent. Let there be no hesitation, then; for "if the trumpet gave forth an uncertain sound, who should prepare himself for the battle?"[1] And indeed how could they doubt what the fathers had really been? Yahweh himself had given sentence by the event. "Thus did the sons of Israel walk in all the sins of Jeroboam, which he had done; they departed not from them; until Yahweh put away Israel out of his sight, as he had said by means of all his servants the prophets. Thus was Israel carried away out of his own land to Assyria, unto this day."[2] Such is the goal towards which the whole history of the ten tribes moves. "Thus was Judah carried away out of his land."[3] So ends the story of the sister kingdom. The pious Israelite might hope for the repeal of that sentence of banishment, but as a testimony to the past it was in his eyes as unequivocal as it was irreversible. The fathers upon whom it had fallen had not served Yahweh!

So we must not allow the Israelitish historians to shake the conclusion to which our investigations had led us. So far as their judgment rests upon a basis of fact, it has every claim to our respect; but that does not necessitate our concurrence in their condemnation of the popular religion before the exile. Of course it is not the question whether the usages of the popular Yahwism secure our sympathy. Presumably neither you nor I should find them attractive. The images of

---

[1] 1 Cor. xiv. 8. [2] 2 Kings xvii. 22, 23.
[3] 2 Kings xxv. 21 b.

Yahweh which adorned most of the bamôth as well as the temples at Dan and Beth-el, imply that the ideas men had of him were crude and material in the extreme. Of the religious solemnities we know little, but enough to assert with confidence that they embodied anything but spiritual conceptions. Wanton licence on the one hand, and the terror-stricken attempt to propitiate the deity with human sacrifices on the other, were the two extremes into which the worshippers of Yahweh appear by no means exceptionally to have fallen. No one will undertake to defend all this, especially as at that very time there was already another and a higher standard in ancient Israel opposed to the lower and judging it. But yet we are not justified in denying all worth to the popular religion of Israel, and reckoning the participation in it as a grievous sin on the part of the masses. "The chosen people" may claim the same candour, the same unprejudiced breadth of judgment, which we are in the habit of extending to others. All sincere religion is true religion, and must secure its beneficent result. Even apart from the higher elements in this worship, which, as we shall soon see, were by no means wanting, we must avow that without its popular religion Israel would have been poorer—poorer in the wealth that uplifts, consoles and strengthens. Not in vain did men thank Yahweh for the blessing of harvest, perform their work with eyes fixed upon him, trust in his help under afflictions, and turn to him for succour in times of peril.

In describing the popular religion of Israel, I have more than once mentioned *the priests of Yahweh*. But you will hardly expect me to be content with such incidental references. For the just appreciation of Yahwism, a closer study of the activity of the priesthood is absolutely essential. It was with Israel, as with almost all the nations of antiquity: the priest had his special function to fulfil in the life of the people, whether in their worship or in their other affairs, which no one else could fulfil for him. It is true that during the first centuries after the settlement in Canaan the competency of every Israelite to offer sacrifices to Yahweh was recognized, and that in later times the privilege was still exercised by the kings, and probably also by the heads of the tribes and families; but this notwithstanding Yahweh had his priests from the first, and no sanctuary of any importance could have been without one. Even in sacrificing and in regulating the solemnities of worship generally, the priest's guidance was constantly and increasingly appreciated, and, moreover, he was the indispensable medium in "seeking" or consulting Yahweh.

But before we inquire how he acquitted himself of this task and of his other duties, we must fix our attention upon his person. Who were the priests of Yahweh? You are all aware that very different answers have been given to this apparently simple question. "The descendants of Aaron" is the most common. But some declare this limitation to be of later origin and say, "Before the Babylonian captivity all the Levites were qualified to assume the priestly functions." Yet others limit even this restriction to the very latest period of the kingdom of Judah, and say that in earlier times the Levites shared their priestly employments with men of other tribes, very possibly laying claim to exclusive rights in the matter, but certainly not establishing them. And, finally, yet others maintain that by putting the question in these terms we make the answer impossible. "Levites or non-Levites," they say, can have no meaning in this connection, inasmuch as the very name itself originally meant neither more nor less than the servants of Yahweh's sanctuaries, whoever they might be; and the idea of their all being related, in accordance with which they were provided with a tribal ancestor, Levi ben Jacob, only sprang up afterwards. You will readily conceive that I have formed my own opinion in this matter, and imagine myself to be in a position to defend it.[1] On this occasion, however, I need not make a choice. One hypothesis only I must exclude, viz. that of the descent of all the priests from Aaron; for it rests exclusively on the witness of the priestly legislation, and to accept it would be tantamount to acknowledging the pre-exilian origin of this legislation

---

[1] Cf. Religion of Israel, Vol. II. pp. 298—303, and Theol. Tijdschrift, VI. 628—670. Wellhausen, Gesch. Israels, I. 145 ff., has not convinced me of the soundness of his views, which differ to some extent from those I have myself put forward.

—an admission which, to my mind, makes any rational conception of Israel's religious development impossible. But in other respects I think we may arrive at certainty concerning the work of the priests and their relation to the popular religion, without being obliged to determine anything about their origin. The prophets, on whose intimations we shall rely by preference, make no distinction between Levitical and non-Levitical priests, and most of them never so much as mention Levi at all.

The question would assume a somewhat different aspect were there any reason to assign a foreign, and specifically an Egyptian, origin to the tribe of Levi. The share of this tribe in the direction of the worship would then no longer be a matter of indifference, and we should find ourselves once more faced by a new form of the problem of the foreign origin of Yahwism which we thought was already behind us.[1] But the sum of all that can be urged in favour of this Egyptian descent is very weak and insignificant. A few proper names—against which, moreover, others of undoubted Hebrew origin must be weighed—are surely insufficient to support such a hypothesis as this. And even if it were otherwise, we should still have to distinguish between Egyptian extraction and Egyptian modes of thought. If historical criticism has proved anything at all, it has proved that the Israelite people of the

---

[1] See above, pp. 58 sqq.

regal period had arisen out of the fusion of very heterogeneous elements.[1] Not only the earlier inhabitants of Canaan, but the bordering tribes also, had made their contribution. The incorporation of a few families partly or wholly Egyptian is far from improbable. But what gave the resulting aggregate not only its name but its character was undoubtedly the Israelite element, and to it rather than to any conquered or assimilated race we must ascribe the force and the initiative especially in the field of religion.[2]

So nothing hinders us from proceeding at once to observe the priests of Yahweh at work. As to their care of the ritual, only a single word. If we had to confess our ignorance with regard to the worship of Yahweh in general, still more must we despair of ascertaining its detailed regulations. It is certain, however, that even at the bamôth fixed observances were followed. When—as we read in the Second Book of Kings[3]— the Assyrian colonists were distressed by lions, they recognized in this fact a proof of the resentment of the god of the land, i.e. Yahweh, whose right to the name we see they did not question. The king of Assyria, when informed of this, sent them one of the priests who had been carried away captive, "that he might teach them the ordinance ('mishphat') of the god of the land;" i.e. the way in which he desired to be served. "And there came one of the priests whom they had

---

[1] See Religion of Israel, Vol. I. pp. 135—138, 146 sq., 176—183.
[2] Cf. Note VI.   [3] Chap. xvii. 25—28.

carried away out of Samaria, and he settled at Beth-el and taught them how they should fear Yahweh." An important part in the redaction of the books of Moses was ascribed, oddly enough, to this priest, when the criticism of the Pentateuch was in its infancy.[1] The solitary record which we possess concerning him assuredly fails to give the smallest countenance to this idea. "The ordinance of the god of the land" which he taught was evidently not yet reduced to writing, and presumably it bore small resemblance to the regulations concerning worship which we now possess in the central books of the Pentateuch. But this "ordinance" existed; the priest was in charge of it, and it was his duty to "teach" it.

Not less important—far more so, indeed, in the eyes of the masses—was the interpretation by the priest of Yahweh's will. The very name which he bears, "cohén," designates him as the man whose answer unlocks the secrets of the unknown, as a soothsayer or wizard; and in the ancient narratives, accordingly, he constantly appears in that character, as we saw but now.[2] Thanks to the number and variety of these narratives, the priest's *modus operandi* may be, to some extent at least, recovered. *The ephod* was indispensable in consulting Yahweh, and *the teraphim* are not unfre-

---

[1] (J. Clericus) Sentiments de quelques théologiens de Hollande sur l'histoire critique du Père R. Simon (Amst. 1685, p. 129 sv.); cf. Défense des Sentiments, &c. (ibid. 1686), p. 167 svv.

[2] See above, pp. 66 sq.

quently associated with it. Yahweh makes his decision known by the lot, or, as is sometimes the case, declares that he will not give any answer at all.¹ What we are to understand by this "ephod" is not yet clearly ascertained. The later usage would lead us to think of a cape which the priest assumed when he approached the deity to learn his will. But the old records themselves make it probable that the ephod was an *image of Yahweh*, silvered or gilt over, and perhaps so constructed that the lots could be concealed within it.² However this may be, it was the priest who applied the ephod to its use, and who had always been, or gradually came to be, regarded as exclusively qualified to employ it. This gave the priestly office a significance in the national life which we can hardly exaggerate.

Nothing that I have said about the priests and their activity so far takes us outside the field of popular religion, or exalts the priests themselves above it. If this were all we knew about them, we should have to assume that they stood upon the same level as the great masses, and followed rather than led them. But their function and their influence upon the national

---

¹ Cf. my note in the Religion of Israel, Vol. I. pp. 96—100.

² This opinion is rejected in the note cited above. But I cannot deny that it finds support in Judges viii. 27; xvii. xviii.; 1 Sam. xiv. 3, 18 (emended after LXX.); and is not contradicted by 1 Sam. xxi. 9; xxiii. 6, 9; xxx. 7; cf. Wellhausen, Gesch. Israels, I. 133, note 1.

life did, as a matter of fact, include something more than we have spoken of as yet. We are told of the priest who settled amongst the Assyrian colonists at Beth-el that he "taught" or "instructed" them. The Hebrew verb which we thus translate, together with the noun derived from it, is constantly employed with reference to the priest. He is the teacher, the *moréh*, of his people; and one of his standing attributes is that he gives instruction or teaching, *thorah*. It is not his own personal opinion that he puts forward under this title, but the revelation of Yahweh's will. This makes it all the more interesting to inquire what subjects were embraced in "the thorah of Yahweh" which the priest announced. In the first place, as we have just heard, the thorah expounded "how they should fear Yahweh"—with what conditions, for instance, the sacrificial beast must comply, and how it must be offered. Following the later priestly legislation we should come next to the distinction between "clean" and "unclean," for it is just in this connection that constant reference is made to the thorah of the priests;[1] nor is there the smallest doubt that these references correspond to the actual fact. Before the captivity the distinction in question was already recognized,[2] and it necessarily involved appeals to the priest's opinion, and even to his active intervention, whenever unclean-

---

[1] Deut. xxiv. 8; Lev. xiv. 54—57, &c.
[2] 1 Sam. xx. 26; xxi. 5, 6, &c.

ness had to be removed. But if we go by the older documents, we must attach still more importance to a third aspect of the priestly function, viz. *the pronouncing of judgment.* I should call this the spiritual, the ideal, element in the activity of the priest; and on that very account it now deserves our fullest attention.

The fact that Yahweh's priest pronounced judgment cannot be doubted. The Deuteronomist assures us in so many words that "Yahweh had chosen the priests, the sons of Levi, to serve him and to bless in his name," and that "*by their sentence every strife and every offence should be decided.*"[1] Does this mean that they were the sole judges? The expressions used are unqualified, and might therefore seem to sanction this interpretation. Possibly Ezekiel may have desired to see such a state of things actually brought about, for he writes concerning the priests, "Over disputes shall they stand in judgment. They shall decide them according to Yahweh's ordinance."[2] But the Deuteronomist does not really go so far as this. He himself speaks of judges, who probably belong to the "elders of the city," and at any rate are not priests.[3] His "every strife and every offence" must therefore be taken to imply more especially that the final decision in important cases depended on the priests. He speaks, indeed, of a high

---

[1] Deut. xxi. 5.   [2] Ez. xliv. 24 a.
[3] Deut. xvi. 18—20; xix. 12; xxi. 2 sqq., 19 sq.; xxii. 15 sqq.; xxv. 7 sqq.

court of justice at Jerusalem, in which priests and laymen are associated together, and over which, according to the nature of the case, the priest or the "judge" presides, the latter being a distinguished citizen.[1] Something of the same kind may have been established in the northern kingdom likewise, at Samaria or at one of the national temples of Dan or Beth-el. But it was not only as members of this court of appeal that the priests "taught the ordinances of Yahweh to Jacob."[2] There were matters which had to be referred to them in the first instance. We may learn their nature from the Book of the Covenant (Exod. xxi.—xxiii.), which does not, it is true, ever mention the priest expressly, but which nevertheless assumes his existence and his influence throughout. When the Hebrew slave has no desire for freedom after six years' service, but prefers to bind himself to his master for good, the two go together to "the deity," i.e. to the nearest bamah of Yahweh, where they ratify their agreement by a symbolical transaction,[3] superintended, naturally, by the priest, who must satisfy himself, as Yahweh's representative, that the slave really does voluntarily surrender the freedom to which he is entitled. Whenever property left in a man's charge has disappeared and the thief cannot be traced, then the man must "draw near to the deity" and declare on his oath "that he

---

[1] Deut. xvii. 8—13; xix. 17, 18; cf. 2 Chron. xix. 8—11.
[2] Deut. xxxiii. 10 a (presumably from the 8th century B.C.).
[3] Exod. xxi. 5, 6.

has not laid hand on his neighbour's goods."[1] If a man is accused of having possessed himself unlawfully of another's property, he likewise must appear, together with his accuser, before "the deity," and if proved guilty must make two-fold restitution.[2] In both these cases also the co-operation of the priest is indispensable. And no less so, it would appear, when the regulations as to places of refuge, given in the same book, come into play. Yahweh will appoint a place whither the unintentional homicide may flee.[3] But "if any man have risen up against his neighbour of set purpose, to slay him with guile, thou shalt drag him away from my altar, that he may die."[4] How could these rules be observed unless the priest who served at the altar pronounced judgment as to the guilt of the suppliant?

Perhaps there were other cases in which the priest was the natural judge, and at any time the parties to a dispute might voluntarily submit their difference to him for decision. But even if this was not so, the judicial functions of the priest still constitute a most important part of his task. Could we still doubt it, then all hesitation would be removed by the complaints of the prophets concerning the shortcomings of the priests in the performance of their judicial functions.

---

[1] Exod. xxii. 7 (8).

[2] Exod. xxii. 8 (9); cf. also vv. 9, 10 (10, 11) ("the oath of Yahweh"), and Dillmann's note on the passage.

[3] Exod. xxi. 12, 13.   [4] Exod. xxi. 14.

When Micah reproaches them with "giving thorah for money;"[1] Zephaniah with "soiling what is holy and making the thorah unrighteousness;"[2] or when Jeremiah accuses them of sordid avarice and untruthfulness,[3] the reference can only be to the abuse of judicial powers. Isaiah expressly formulates the complaint that they are guilty of unfairness in "the decision,"[4] i.e. in the exercise of their function as judges. Far more clearly yet appears the great significance of the thorah of the priests in the two severest denunciations of their doings which the Old Testament contains. The one is in Hosea,[5] the other in Malachi.[6] It is true that the latter passage does not belong to the pre-exilian period with which we are now dealing, but still the prophet bears testimony concerning that period when he holds up to the priest of his own day the ideal conception of his office which had been sketched already before the captivity.[7] "An upright thorah was in his mouth, and no iniquity was found on his lips; in peace and integrity he walked with Yahweh, and he brought back many from sin. For the lips of the priest preserved knowledge, and thorah was sought at his mouth; for is he not the messenger of Yahweh Zebaôth?" "But ye"—continues the prophet—"have departed

---

[1] Micah iii. 11 b.
[2] Zeph. iii. 4 b.
[3] Jer. vi. 13; viii. 10.
[4] Isaiah xxviii. 7.
[5] Hos. iv. 1—9.
[6] Mal. ii. 1—9.
[7] Cf. Deut. xxxiii. 8—11.

from the path, have brought many to their fall by the thorah, have corrupted the covenant with Levi, says Yahweh Zebaôth. So will I also bring you to contempt, and shame you before all the people, because ye have paid no heed to my ways and have had respect unto persons in the thorah." A more exalted conception of the moral task of Yahweh's priest there can hardly be. But as long as Malachi is our only witness, we may be inclined to doubt whether this ideal, though transporting us to the pre-exilian period, has really anything in common with the facts as they then were. All the more value, then, must we assign to Hosea's utterances concerning Yahweh's priests in the kingdom of Ephraim during the first half of the eighth century B.C. It is in truth a sombre picture of their work, or rather of their transgressions, that he paints. But would he have held them responsible in no small degree for the many evils which he perceived about him, had not their office conferred upon them that great influence which he complains of their not duly utilizing? It is time, however, to let the prophet speak for himself.

Yahweh has a controversy with the dwellers in the land, for there is no truth and no piety and no knowledge of God in the land.[1] Perjury, murder, theft and adultery are general.[2] Therefore the land pines, and all that dwells therein mourns, even down to the sense-

---

[1] Hos. iv. 1.   [2] v. 2.

less beasts.[1] And yet—thus Hosea interrupts himself —it is not really the people who should be contended with or rebuked, for with the priests themselves it is no better than with the people.[2] And therefore they too shall fall, and the prophets with them.[3] "My people is falling for want of knowledge, for ye (the priesthood) have cast knowledge away. And so will I cast you aside as my priests! And since ye have forgotten the thorah of your god, I too will forget your sons.[4] The more they have increased in number, the more have they sinned against me. Their glory (Yahweh) have they changed for shame (the idols).[5] They feed themselves fat on the sin of my people, and their longings go out after its trespasses.[6] Therefore it shall be with the priest as with the people, and I will visit their deeds upon them and repay them for their doings."[7]—The man who so speaks will hardly be suspected of partiality towards the priests. All the more weighty, then, is his judgment as to what they might and ought to have been. Israel is hastening to moral ruin, bereft of "the knowledge of God," which the priest of Yahweh possesses, but which at the dictate of interest and self-indulgence he fails to

---

[1] v. 3.

[2] v. 4, according to Wellhausen's emendation. See Gesch. Israels, I. 141, note.

[3] v. 5.   [4] v. 6.

[5] v. 7, with the amended reading ("hemíru").

[6] v. 8.   [7] v. 9.

communicate to the people. It cannot be more unequivocally stated that, as Yahweh's interpreter, he is the bearer and appointed upholder of *right*. Alas! he fails to fulfil so fair a task. He himself is absorbed in the mechanical duties of his office and urges the people to display their zeal for Yahweh in sacrifices and feasts. Still worse, he degrades himself into a servant of unrighteousness, and suffers himself to be bought by the strong who oppress the weak and defenceless. But the ideal of his calling, which Hosea holds up to him in reproof, still remains; and with it remains *the ethical character of Yahweh* to which it bears witness. I am not speaking, as yet, of the Yahweh whose word the prophets proclaimed, but of the god of Israel whom the people acknowledged and served. For it was to him that those priests belonged who were consulted by the masses, and who directed their sacrifices and feasts: Hosea unites them, and we must not separate them. Now this is enough to show that however great the outward resemblance may have been between this Yahweh of the people and the gods who were worshipped at his side or by Israel's neighbours, yet he was not one of them. Unless the prophet completely lost sight of the reality when he uttered his denunciation, Yahweh is distinguished from the others and towers above them as the god in whose name justice was administered, and of whom it could be said that he was not known where the laws of honour and of good faith were violated. We must therefore enrich our conception of the popular Israelitish belief by this trait. All the rest remains, but we must add this one point to it, *the ethical character of Yahweh.* And to this one trait belongs the future.

What I have advanced so far need hardly fear contradiction. The popular Israelitish religion, including the place taken by the priests of Yahweh in it, is very generally allowed to be national. If any objection were raised, it would be to my description of this religion itself, not to the national character I have assigned it. But at this point we are met by a "hitherto, and no farther!" We are told that the religion embraced and taught by the *prophets* can no longer be regarded as national. By the prophets, in this connection, are meant of course the men so designated whose writings are preserved to us in the Old Testament, and whom we shall henceforth call "the canonical prophets." It is from the books of these men that the proofs of the position we are discussing are derived. What can be clearer, it is urged, than that these prophets, so far from representing the spirit of the people, protest against it with all their might? Their judgment on the nation from which they have sprung is most unfavourable. The sentence rests upon religious grounds, and has special reference to the manner in which their contemporaries, and—for this is frequently added—the former generations also, had served

Yahweh. The contrast seems to be absolute. What the people regard as a duty, the prophets hold to be sinful and abominable; and, on the other hand, what they praise and support is rejected by the people. This relation between prophets and people, we are told, is so unmistakable that it would have to be admitted as a fact even if we were entirely unable to explain it. But this is far from being the case. The explanation, it is urged, may be found at once in the evidence given by the prophets (not here and there, but throughout their writings) as to the *origin* of the convictions which they proclaim and defend against the people. *Yahweh himself speaks through them.* They simply reproduce what he has shown them or caused them to hear. Is it any wonder, then, that they rise high above the popular conception? And does it not follow that their religion, great as its significance is to Israel and to all mankind, can by no means be called national? It was far more than national. It was not of Israel, but *of God*.

Perhaps, as I have spoken, the fear has laid hold of you that we are about to tread that ground of theological controversy from which we are so anxious to preserve our feet! The alarm is needless. I could not omit to indicate how belief in the divine inspiration of prophecy influences the conception formed of the religious strife in ancient Israel. But there is no necessity that we should enter upon an examination of that belief itself. In one possible case it would have been otherwise. If, namely, the canonical prophets had been alone in professing to derive their utterances direct from Yahweh, then the claim to a divine origin would have been the exclusive mark of their preaching, and the first and supreme question before us would have been, "Are we to acknowledge this claim? Yes or no?" But this possible case is remote from the actual one. The priest of Yahweh also came forward in Israel as the interpreter of the god he revered. So too did the prophets in general, including the very ones against whom the denunciations of the canonical prophets are hurled. If, then, we are to endorse the prophetic consciousness of the latter and to reject that of all others, we can only reasonably do so *a posteriori;* on the ground, that is, of what we learn from a study of their writings concerning their mode of thought and their character. This study itself, then, must not submit to any antecedent restrictions, least of all to any restrictions imposed by the prophets themselves with reference to the source of their conceptions—for this is the very point that has to be determined.

We may therefore pursue our historical investigation undisturbed. The necessity of carrying it further, or, in other words, the impossibility of resting in the sharp contrast between Yahweh's prophets and the Israelitish people, must have been evident to us from the moment that our attention was called to it. Unquestionably we have a difference, nay, a deep-rooted antagonism, before us. But we must not let it make us blind to all else. How many an antithesis that at first presents itself as absolute and irreconcilable, loses this character as soon as we turn our attention from one prominent contrast to a general view of the whole matter, and no longer neglect those finer shades in which, according to Renan's well-known saying, the truth lies! No doubt it seems to simplify matters first to sever the canonical prophets from their historical environment, and then to confine our attention to the points of their hostility towards the popular religion; but a true insight into the real state of things, and a fair estimate of the religious convictions of the prophets as a whole, will never be reached by such a method. Let us try, then, to supply what is wanting in the current conception. The facts of which I shall have to remind you are well known, and a reference rather than an exposition is all that is needed.

We must note, to begin with, that for many successive centuries "the prophets of Yahweh" constituted a special and recognized social order. There were "priests" and there were likewise "prophets" of Yahweh. When Josiah, in the eighteenth year of his reign, was about to give effect to the book of law which Hilkiah had discovered, he assembled "the prophets," with others, in the temple.[1] His contemporary Jeremiah speaks of "the prophets"—to cite a single instance —in the superscription of the letter which he addresses to the exiles in Babylon.[2] Isaiah[3] and Micah[4] adopt

---

[1] 2 Kings xxiii. 2.
[2] Jer. xxix. 1.
[3] Isaiah xxviii. 7; xxx. 10; iii. 1, 2.
[4] Micah iii. 5, 7.

THE PROPHETIC ORDER. 95

the same usage. A century or two earlier, Ahab and Jehoshaphat, before entering upon a war with the Syrians, consult "the prophets of Yahweh."[1] It is quite in accordance with all this that we should find prophecy referred to as a national institution in the proverb which Jeremiah[2] and Ezekiel[3] have preserved for us, and which we may paraphrase thus: "Never shall thorah fail the priest, nor counsel fail the sage, nor a word (a revelation of Yahweh) fail the prophet."

This had not been so always. The *name* "nabí" did not come into common use in Israel all at once. In the time of Samuel, people still said, "Let us go to the seer!" for "he who was afterwards called a 'prophet' was then called a 'seer.'" This we know from a note in the First Book of Samuel,[4] the accuracy of which will hardly be questioned. But even *the persons* who were afterwards known as "the nebiím" appear for the first time in the narratives concerning the close of the period of the Judges—doubtless because they did not exist before then. How interesting it would be could we give a historical sketch and explanation of their rise! But the rule that "all origins are obscure" asserts itself here too. It is only a conjecture, then, though it is one that has strong probability on its side, that the phenomena of inspiration and extasy which had long been native to the wor-

---

[1] 1 Kings xxii. 6 sqq. [2] Jer. xviii. 18.
[3] Ez. vii. 26   [4] 1 Sam. ix. 9.

shippers of the Canaanite deities, passed over at this period to the worshippers of Yahweh likewise. The "prophets of Yahweh" who thus rose up joined themselves together, and formed unions or colonies,[1] which gradually assumed a settled form under the guidance of Samuel, and thereby assured themselves a continued existence.

Are we to add that the prophets originally stood in the closest connection with the priests? It was so amongst the Canaanites. Baal's prophets offer him sacrifices on Mount Carmel,[2] and are mentioned on another occasion in conjunction with his priests,[3] just as the Philistine "priests and soothsayers" appear together.[4] And in the same way Samuel unites in his person the priestly with the prophetic function.[5] On the strength of these phenomena it has been supposed that the prophets of Yahweh were originally priests, and only gradually separated themselves and acquired more independence.[6] But there are no real grounds for this supposition. There is not a trace to be found in the Old Testament of any connection of the prophets with the altars or temples of Yahweh, and

---

[1] 1 Sam. x. 5, 10—12; xix. 18 sqq., &c.

[2] 1 Kings xviii. 19 sqq.   [3] 2 Kings x. 19.   [4] 1 Sam. vi. 2.

[5] 1 Sam. vii. 9, 17; xiii. 8 sqq.; xv. 33; xvi. 2.

[6] Cf. Wellhausen, l.c. I. 412; S. Maybaum, die Entwickelung des altisrael. Priesterthums, S. 12. A different view is supported by E. von Hartmann, das relig. Bewusstsein der Menscheit im Stufengang seiner Entwickelung, S. 389 f.

this would hardly be the case if they had originally been amongst the servants of the sanctuaries. The old relation, had it existed, would have been preserved here and there even when it had ceased to be normal. Neither, so far as we can tell, was the prophetic office ever regarded as hereditary, whilst from the earliest times the sons of priests were priests themselves.[1] This is a difference which has its grounds in the nature of the two offices, and one which marks so profound a separation between them that we must hesitate to connect them with each other in their origin more closely than our narratives require.

But when all is said, points of contact between prophet and priest remain. Both passed in the eyes of the people for the trusted interpreters of the deity. But whereas the priest was thus gifted in virtue of his office and as the bearer of a consecrated tradition, and was accordingly referred to on the ordinary occasions of life, such as the administration of justice, the privileges of the prophet were more personal and, if I may so express it, momentary and intermittent. The prophet is the *organ extraordinary* of Yahweh, and as such the natural counsellor in the perplexities which the oscillations of fortune or the uncertainties of the future bring upon Israel. Of course the contrast is not absolute. There were doubtless circumstances under which the prophet or the priest might be consulted

---

[1] Judges xviii. 30; 1 Sam. i. sq.

with equal propriety. If the special circumstances occasionally determined the choice, there were likewise times when no choice was open; for the prophet—not the priest, with whose office it would have been far less consonant—often came forward unasked to declare "the word of Yahweh," or sometimes, we may safely assume, at the head of a "company of prophets,"[1] to solve the problem himself—and not always by moral suasion!

Enough has been said to give us an idea of what prophecy as a social institution, and "the prophets of Yahweh," viewed and judged in the mass, must have been in Israel. So far we have met with nothing that could suggest our removing them from the sphere of the national religion. The Israelites themselves did nothing of the kind, and neither must we. Whatever the origin of prophecy may have been, and however strange the first impression it produced on the earlier generations of nomads, their amazement gradually disappeared, and they came to regard it as an integral part of their national life and as one of the proofs of the favour of their national god. There would be no lack of incidents to confirm them in this conception. When, in the presence of Ahab and Jehoshaphat, the four hundred prophets of Yahweh testified, as one man, their zeal for the campaign against the Syrians, and animated the two kings by the prospect of certain triumph,[2] how the hearts of true Israelites must have

---

[1] 1 Sam. x. 5, 10.   [2] 1 Kings xxii. 5 sqq.

glowed with sympathy! And are we not to suppose that, during the same period, many an one applauded, albeit in secret, that son of the prophets who dared to protest against Ahab's generosity towards Israel's hereditary foe? You remember the story.[1] The king of Israel had been moved to spare Benhadad of Damascus, whose life was in his hand, and had granted very favourable terms of peace to him, though he had defeated him utterly. As he was returning home he was hailed and stopped by a stranger, who told him that in the tumult of the battle one of his friends had entrusted a prisoner to him, and he had pledged his own life for his safety. Now the prisoner had escaped. .... But here Ahab interrupted him, saying it was useless to proceed. He had pledged himself to his friend, and must now make good his loss or must himself serve him as a slave. The prophet at once applied the principle to Ahab: "Thus saith Yahweh, Since thou hast let the man whom I had condemned go free, thy soul shall be in the place of his soul, and thy people in the place of his." We have little sympathy with the policy of blood and iron which this prophet upholds; but we shall none of us deny that he was actuated by patriotic motives, and that both he and the whole class to which he belonged could calculate upon the support of the most zealous servants of Yahweh when they came forward in defence of such principles. With such an

---

[1] 1 Kings xx. 35—43.

example before us, we can understand how the Israelite nation was comforted and encouraged in times of gloom by the thought that "the word of Yahweh would never fail the prophet."

Let us suppose for a moment that we knew nothing of the prophets of Yahweh beyond these general traits, and that we had nothing more to go upon in forming our ideas of the position they took and the spiritual development they attained. Judging by analogy, we should regard it as probable that the level of their average development would not stand high, but at the same time we should suspect that there must have been some who rose above it. On the first point I need not enlarge. The consciousness of standing in connection with a higher world, of being inspired or impelled by the spirit of God, is in itself glorious and exalting. In spite of the aberrations to which it is exposed and the abuses to which it too readily lends itself, we may yet aver that *power* goes forth from this consciousness— power for the cleansing of the inner man, for the support of self-sacrifice and heroism. But if it is artificially excited and cultivated, if there is a premium, so to speak, on extasy, and its absence makes a man unfit for the chosen task of his life, then it becomes a very different matter. *Corruptio optimi pessima.* What is more miserable than assumed transport of spirit and pretended divine inspiration? The application of this to the prophetic *order* is too obvious to need pointing out. Taken as a whole, it cannot have stood much above the soothsayers and wizards amongst other ancient peoples. But—and here we come to the second point—might we not expect *a priori* that some few eminent personalities would rise up from the order itself, or would be fired by the example of its members, and would realize the idea of prophecy? The conception of a close and trusted intercourse with Israel's mighty protecting deity, which is incarnate as it were in prophecy, could not fail to attract religious souls, and to rouse or strengthen within them the desire to enter into such divine intercourse. And are we to suppose that this longing, when once aroused, could remain permanently unsatisfied?

You will have observed already that it is only in form that my argument has been *a priori*. What I have thus advanced rests in reality upon historical testimony. The low level of the prophetic guild, as a whole, and the degeneracy of prophecy in some of its representatives, are sufficiently obvious. But in like manner the eminent exceptions of which I have spoken are known to us from history. I have but to name Samuel, Nathan, Elijah and Elisha. That they all came out of the prophetic unions is not certain. Indeed, we know that Elisha did not.[1] The prophets did not form a close caste. The inspiration which was their distinctive mark might appear outside their circle, and if any man experienced it, access to the prophetic unions lay open

---

[1] 1 Kings xix. 19—21.

to him; or he might perhaps come forward as a prophet, without incorporating himself with them at all. Yet, even in the latter case, the form of his activity, the outward aspects of his mission, so to speak, were determined by the prophecy of his time. So, whatever may have been the origin of the men just named, they stand in the relation I have already indicated to the prophetic order as a whole. What is it, then, that exalts them so high above the rest? What distinguishes them from the great mass that they leave so far behind? I repeat the question, because it seems to me no less difficult than important. If I could but give you anything that might claim to be a sketch of the character of Samuel or Elijah, for instance! But you know why no one can do so. The narratives concerning these men are few in number, comparatively late in date, not unfrequently in mutual contradiction, and therefore of doubtful worth. Every conclusion we draw from them is more or less open to suspicion. Of the particulars, even of those which would inspire us with the greatest interest, we know nothing, and can never hope to obtain full knowledge. Yet we could not refrain from asking the question we have emphasized, and we need not leave it altogether unanswered. In the narratives that lie before us, one trait recurs again and again—too naturally to allow of our suspecting deliberate intention on the part of the writers—too regularly to be accidental. The prophets whose names I have mentioned are distinguished by their moral earnestness and courage. Samuel — Saul; Nathan — David; Elijah — Ahab and Ahaziah: I have only to put these names side by side to make my meaning obvious. Is this an accident, or a matter of indifference? I cannot think it. If I am not mistaken, this is the factor which elevates these men above the rest of their order, and at the same time is destined to raise the order itself to higher things. This brings us back to the ethical element in the conception of Yahweh on which we have already fixed our attention.[1] It was in those prophets whom it had most deeply impressed, who were most completely penetrated by the stern and inexorable character of Yahweh's moral demands, and had therefore become the preachers of righteousness, that prophecy reached its full dimensions and bore its ripened fruit.

But let us go further and consult the sequel of the history. The earlier prophets relied for their influence upon the spoken word, to which a section of the people or certain special individuals often gave immediate effect in action. But in the eighth century B.C., the prophets began to extend their activity by writing down the word they had previously spoken. Why first at this period? Times had changed, and prophecy had changed with them. Israelitish literature dates from this century, or at all events from not much earlier. The songs which were originally passed from mouth to

---

[1] Pp. 90 sq.

mouth were now written down, collected and provided with historical notes. From these beginnings historical writing presently developed itself. Experience must have shown that such compositions met with a favourable reception in various quarters, and did not fail of their effect. If the pen had thus shown itself to be a mighty weapon, what was more natural than that the leaders of the people should grasp it? Thus arose, presumably in priestly circles, the earliest collections of laws and moral exhortations,[1] one of which we possess in the Book of the Covenant (Exod. xxi.—xxiii.). Thus, too, the earliest written prophecies, those of Amos and his immediate successors, came into existence. A co-operating cause may have been the changed relations of some of the prophets to the great majority of the people. The wrongs with which they reproached their contemporaries were not of a nature to be righted off-hand in a burst of enthusiasm. Amos and those of kindred spirit with him desired to address themselves to many whom their spoken word could never reach, and it could not fail to further their object if they succeeded in extending to wider circles the opportunity of pondering upon their preaching.

But be this as it may, the prophet's character remained the same after he had become an author. The canonical prophets of the eighth and succeeding centuries are not severed by a sharp line from their pre-

---

[1] Hos. viii. 12. For *ribbó*, Graetz, Gesch. der Juden, II. i. S. 469 f., reads *dibré*, probably correctly.

decessors. Working under the forms of their time and in accordance with its requirements, they are the legitimate successors of Elijah and Elisha. If these are to be regarded as the organs of Israel's national god, then so are those. Or must we say that, although there seems to be no breach of continuity, yet the *contents* of their preaching forbid us to place the canonical prophets in any such relationship to their people and its religion? We must not allow a single essential feature of this preaching to escape us. I hope to lay before you fairly and fully, to the best of my knowledge, all that can serve to illustrate the differences and the conflicts between them and the people. But at the very outset it must be clearly understood that we should be contradicting the prophets themselves were we to begin by loosening the tie that unites them to the Israelite nation. Their own evidence on such a point must at least be heard first, not to say simply accepted as conclusive. We will take this evidence, then, to-day; and thus we shall lay the foundations upon which any further conceptions may rest.

Yahweh Israel's god and Israel Yahweh's people! It surely needs no proof that the canonical prophets endorse this fundamental conception of the popular religion, that not one of them ever thinks of denying it. The whole of their preaching takes this as its starting-point, and leads back to it as its goal. On this latter point I wish to place the utmost emphasis. It is well known that our prophets anticipate evil days for their people. Why they do so we need not at present consider. Enough that they expect Israel's national life to be put to an end, and the Israelites to be carried away into a strange land. But this is not the limit of their anticipations. "The eyes of the Lord Yahweh are upon the sinful kingdom (of Ephraïm), and he will sweep it away from the face of the earth; howbeit he shall not wholly destroy *the house of Jacob.*"[1] The carrying away will be followed sooner or later by the restoration. But this, by its nature, is a new departure, the beginning of a new period. If, then, the relations between Yahweh and Israel in the midst of which the prophets were living had been in their opinion merely temporary, they would certainly have regarded the re-establishment of such relations as destined to be accompanied by a complete change in them. And indeed they did believe that the new era would in many respects be quite different from the old. Israel, humbled by his chastisement, was to return to Yahweh with all his heart and to begin a new life. It is nothing less than a complete transformation. Yahweh makes a new covenant—so Jeremiah puts it—and writes his thorah on his people's hearts, and they all know him, from the least to the greatest.[2] The heart of stone will be taken away and a heart of flesh will be given—so Ezekiel expresses his anticipations.[3] But however great the change may be,

---

[1] Amos ix. 8. [2] Jer. xxxi. 32—34. [3] Ezek. xi. 19, 20.

though the wolf lie down with the lamb and the sucking child play by the adder's hole,[1] nay, though there be new heavens and a new earth,[2] yet the relation between Yahweh and Israel remains the same. The prophecies concerning the heathen (of which more hereafter) do not alter this fact. Consult all the prophets, from the first to the last, and you will find that on this point they are unanimous. The glance of Amos is fixed upon the restoration of the united Israelite nation under the Davidic dynasty, which will be reared again "as in the days of old," that under its lead Israel may "inherit the remnant of Edom and of all the peoples over whom the name of Yahweh has been proclaimed (as the name of their conqueror)." "And," so he concludes, "I, Yahweh, will plant them in their land, and they shall not again be plucked up out of their land that I have given them, saith Yahweh, their god."[3] Hosea finds room for Israel alone in his picture of the future. "I will heal their backsliding and will love them freely, for my wrath is turned away from them. I will be as the dew to Israel. He shall blossom as the lily, and shall spread forth his roots as Lebanon;"[4]—such are the words in which Yahweh describes the close communion there will be between himself and his people. In Isaiah, too, Yahweh stretches out his hand to gather the remnants of his people from

---

[1] Isaiah xi. 6, 8.
[3] Amos ix. 11 sq., 15.
[2] Isaiah lxv. 17; lxvi. 12.
[4] Hos. xiv. 5, 6 (4, 5).

all the places of their captivity, to be his possession. The exiles of Israel and the scattered ones of Judah he draws together. The jealousy of Ephraim and Judah has departed. Together they rush upon the Philistines, plunder the sons of the East, and subdue Edom, Moab and Ammon.[1] A century later, Jeremiah gives utterance to essentially the same thoughts. The new covenant of which we have heard him speak is entered into with "the house of Israel and the house of Judah."[2] Nor is there one of his descriptions of the future in which the same conception is not met with in one form or another.[3] "I will be their god, and they shall be my people," stands as an assurance that in the days to come, whatever else may be changed, the bond between Yahweh and Israel shall not be broken or relaxed. How completely Ezekiel's anticipations are penetrated by the spirit of nationality I need hardly show. Who does not remember his picture of the restored Israel, settled once more in Canaan, ranged round the temple and its servants, or rather round Yahweh who "has established his sanctuary in the midst of them, and whose abode shall overshadow them. He shall be their god and they shall be his people, and the nations shall acknowledge that he, Yahweh, sanctifies Israel (i.e. sets him apart for his service), because his sanctuary is in their midst for ever."[4] The meaning of these utterances is

---

[1] Isaiah xi. 11—14. [2] Jer. xxxi. 31.
[3] Jer. iii. 14 sqq.; xiii. 13—17; xxx. 18—22; xxxi. 1 sqq., &c.
[4] Ezek. xxxvii. 26 b—28.

all the less ambiguous because Ezekiel nowhere brings either Yahweh or Israel into closer relations with the heathen except in a hostile sense. And even the second Isaiah, in so many respects the opposite of Ezekiel, stands with both feet on the ground of nationality. Israel and Yahweh are inseparable from each other. At the very time when the prophet is contemplating the heathen world and representing it as susceptible of the impression of Yahweh's power and majesty, he unites Yahweh most closely with his people, and expresses his expectation that amongst the nations

> "This one shall say: I belong to Yahweh,
> And that one call himself by Jacob's name;
> Another shall unite himself unto Yahweh
> And take Israel's name to add to his own."[1]

But there is no need to multiply quotations. One single remark in conclusion. It is difficult not to be offended by the pictures of Israel's future glory which the second Isaiah so evidently delights in elaborating. "What can this mean?" we are inclined to exclaim, when we hear him prophesy that strangers shall build the walls of Jerusalem and kings shall serve his people.[2] And yet all this can be explained and justified if Israel and Yahweh are one in the prophet's mind. Take away this conception, and you can only be repelled by his boundless national arrogance. We are indeed

---

[1] Isaiah xliv. 5.   [2] Isaiah lx. 10.

doing the prophets ill service if we conceal the fundamental thought of all their preaching. In this respect, "Iliacos intra muros peccatur et extra." Rationalists have branded as "particularism," and supranaturalists have done their best to explain away or evaporate, what is really nothing less than *the very essence of the Israelitish religion*, to which even the greatest prophets could not be untrue without sacrificing that religion itself.

In what, then, does the difference between the prophets and their people consist? Whence the antagonism which after all is as undeniable as the kinship? The answer to these questions I must beg leave to defer till our next meeting.

UNIVERSALISM OF THE PROPHETS.
ESTABLISHMENT OF JUDAISM.

If the canonical prophets stand on the soil of Israelitism and share with it their fundamental idea, whence the divergence between them and their people which sometimes even amounts to hostility and stirs contention? Why are they so loud in their accusations of Israel, and why do the majority of the Israelites refuse to recognize them as their representatives?

The prophets themselves must answer these questions; nor will they refuse to do so when they are laid before them. The antagonism of which we are speaking does not present itself, or at any rate does not force itself into the foreground, everywhere. It is absent or inconspicuous in the prophets who, like Nahum and Obadiah, direct their oracles against a single foe of their people whom they threaten with destruction, or who, like the second Isaiah, come forward, under the deep impression of Israel's national humiliation, as comforters and as preachers of the glad tidings of redemption and restoration. But these are exceptions to the rule. The rule itself is thus formulated by Jeremiah: "The prophets who have been before me, from the first, have prophesied against many lands and great kingdoms, of war, and disaster and pestilence. As for the prophet who preaches peace—when his saying comes to pass, then (but not till then) shall it be seen that Yahweh has indeed sent him."[1] Jeremiah, then, finds the characteristic of the emissary of Yahweh in his being a prophet of evil. And why? Because he is the preacher of repentance, the representative of Yahweh's strict moral demands amongst a people that but too ill conforms to them. These are the demands of which the true prophet is the champion. Here he takes his stand. The god in whose name he speaks is *the Holy One*—if indeed I may use this word in the purely ethical sense which it has for us, but which it had not yet acquired in the usage of the prophets themselves. It is only by going through the prophetic literature itself that one can adequately realize how completely the inviolable and inexorable moral law dominates these men, so to speak, and determines their judgment on all that they observe. Take, for example, the following dirge raised by Amos over his people: "The virgin of Israel is fallen and shall not rise. She lies down deserted in her land, and there is

---

[1] Jer. xxviii. 8, 9.

none to raise her up."[1] The people of her cities shall be decimated by disaster upon disaster;[2] for Yahweh has said to the house of Israel, Seek me, and ye shall live! Go not to Beth-el, to Gilgal or to Beer-shebah, but seek Yahweh, and ye shall live! See to it that he leap not upon the house of Joseph like a fire, an unquenchable fire that consumes Beth-el.[3] As yet the offenders who have given occasion to this denunciation have not been named. But now come the words, "O ye who turn justice to wormwood and fling righteousness to the earth!"[4] Of them, the grandees and judges, the prophet testifies that they hate him who reproves them in the gate, and loathe him who speaks uprightly.[5] "Therefore," he concludes, "inasmuch as ye trample down the needy and take from him a tribute in corn, ye have built houses of hewn stone but ye shall not dwell in them, and planted fair vine-stocks but shall drink no wine from them. For I know your sins that they are many, and your trespasses that they are mighty, for ye accept the money of atonement and give judgment against the poor in the gate."[6] "Woe unto them," cries Micah, "who devise unrighteousness and accomplish evil (in imagination) in their beds, and when morning dawns bring it to pass, because their

---

[1] Amos. v. 1, 2.   [2] v. 3.   [3] vv. 4—6.   [4] v. 7.

[5] Amos v. 10. The two preceding verses disturb the progress of the discourse, and probably are not genuine. Cf. H. Oort, Theol. Tijdschrift, XIV. 118.

[6] vv. 11, 12.

might is their god; who covet fields and take possession of them, houses and seize them; who oppress the owner and his house, the man and his inheritance!"[1] But I need not go on. As it is here, so it is everywhere. In the pictures of the judgment that shall come upon Israel, the sins of the people almost always fill the sombre background; for it is these sins that Yahweh will punish, and indeed *cannot* leave unpunished without renouncing his own moral nature. Isaiah makes the sinners in Zion cry:

> Who amongst us can dwell with a consuming fire?
> Who amongst us can dwell with an ever-glowing furnace?

And the answer declares that they only shall be safe and prosperous who walk in righteousness and speak truth, and whom neither fear nor avarice can force to lay hands on their neighbours' life or possessions.[2]

This profoundly ethical conception of Yahweh's being could not fail to bring the prophets into conflict with the religious convictions of their people. In the consciousness of the latter, Yahweh and Israel were closely and inseparably bound together. It is true that the relations between them were not uniform or incapable of being disturbed. Yahweh never ceases to be the god, i.e. the natural helper, defender and deliverer, of his people, but it does not follow that he is always equally ready to protect their interests. From time to time he hides his face. The misfortunes that fall upon

---

[1] Mic. ii. 1, 2.   [2] Isaiah xxxiii. 15, 16.

Israel proclaim it all too loudly. But this estrangement is only temporary. It leads his worshippers to call with redoubled zeal upon Yahweh, and to offer him more numerous and costly sacrifices than ever. Distress does but multiply vows, to be paid to him when his wrath is appeased or his inaction has come to an end. The bond that unites him to his people, then, is never supposed to be broken. Such strained relations may be compared to misunderstandings between a husband and wife who have never heard of divorce, or at least have never thought of it. The disturbance of their peaceable relations one with the other may be extremely painful, but sooner or later it will be made up. But all this is changed as soon as Yahweh has acquired, as he has in the minds of the canonical prophets, an ethical *character*. I use this expression designedly. Moral *attributes* are ascribed to him by the people also. We have already convinced ourselves of this in dealing with the priestly thorah; and it is well to recall the fact at this point, if only to prevent us from exaggerating the actual distance between prophets and people. But these attributes were only some amongst many. They were not regarded as dominating all else. If not exactly subordinate to Yahweh's connection with Israel, they might at least yield a point in its favour. Only call to mind how in the historical books of the Old Testament—whose authors certainly stood higher in this respect than the great masses—the idea comes into the foreground more than once, that Yahweh had to uphold his own honour, and therefore *could not* neglect to protect and bless his people.[1] Thus, in the conception of the people, Yahweh's might, or, if you prefer to put it so, Yahweh's obligation to display his might, must often have overbalanced both his wrath against Israel's trespasses and the demands of his righteousness. But to the prophets such an idea had become impossible. As soon as an ethical *character* was ascribed to Yahweh, he *must* act in accordance with it. The Holy, the Righteous One, might renounce his people, but he could not renounce himself.

Now consider the necessary effect of this upon the relations between the prophets and the great majority of their contemporaries. If there was a foe to be repelled, or if, in the interest of the people, an attack on a neighbouring tribe was to be made, the national leaders reckoned with certainty upon the help of their god. "Is not Yahweh in our midst? No harm shall overtake us!"[2] Such confidence, they imagined, could only be rebuked by men who questioned Yahweh's power or esteemed that of the enemy's gods more highly. But now they saw opposed to them, in Amos and his successors, men who, far from doubting Yahweh's might, assigned to him greater power and a wider dominion than they themselves had ever done, but who nevertheless denounced their reliance upon his

---

[1] Ex. xxxii. 11, 12; Num. xiv. 13—19; Deut. xxxii. 27; Josh. vii. 9.

[2] Mic. iii. 11.

support as vain and sinful. According to these men, it was no absurd supposition that Yahweh might take the part of Israel's foes against Israel. Nay, they went still further, and declared that Yahweh himself brought upon them, his people, the very thing they most dreaded, the very thing against which they had sought the protection of their god! "I call forth against you, O house of Israel, says Yahweh, the god of hosts, a people that shall afflict you from Hamath to the stream of the plain"—so says Amos.[1] The Assyrians the rod of Yahweh's wrath,[2] and Nebucadrezar Yahweh's servant,[3] are expressions used, the one by Isaiah, and the other a century afterwards by Jeremiah. How can we wonder that such words as these sounded like blasphemy in the ears of the people? Their patriotism rose up in protest, and with it the religious consciousness which as yet coincided with it. But were the prophets really unpatriotic? Were they indifferent to the continued existence and the prosperity of Israel? We have already convinced ourselves of the opposite, and shall presently find further confirmation of it. Yet it is easy to understand that the people and the popular leaders could not see this; for they could only have done so if they themselves had experienced the majesty of the Holy One, even as an Amos had experienced it in its overmastering strength :—" The lion has roared:

---

[1] Amos vi. 14.   [2] Isaiah x. 5.
[3] Jer. xxv. 9; xxvii. 6; xliii. 10.

who should not fear? The Lord Yahweh has spoken: who should not prophesy?"[1]

The loosening of the band between Yahwism and patriotism is a fact of the utmost significance, on which we have much still to say. But before further illustrating it and following up its weighty consequences, we must make ourselves acquainted with the direct influence of the recognition of Yahweh's ethical character on the religious convictions of the prophets themselves.

In the estimation of all who worshipped him, Yahweh was a great and mighty god, mightier than the gods of other nations. There was nothing unusual in such a belief. It was the belief of the Moabite with regard to Camosh, of the Ammonite with regard to Malcám. It is perfectly natural, too, that the recognition of Yahweh's greatness and supremacy should receive stimulus and support from political events. When David waged the wars of Yahweh with a strong hand,[2] and when victory crowned his arms, he made Yahweh himself rise in the people's estimation. Solomon's glory shone upon the deity to whom he had consecrated the temple in his capital. But it lies in the nature of the case that a faith reared upon such foundations was subject to many shocks, and under given circumstances might easily collapse. Born of the sense of national dignity, growing with its growth and strengthening with its strength, it must likewise suffer under the

---

[1] Amos iii. 8.   [2] 1 Sam. xviii. 17; xxv. 28.

blows that fell upon it, must pine and ultimately die when, with the independence of the nation, national self-consciousness disappeared. In any case, Yahweh, if exalted in this way only, remained comparable with all the other gods, of one family with them, if I may so express myself, and of impulses like to theirs. The moral qualities which the people ascribed to him did not affect this fact, for the distinction they established between him and his rivals, however real, was not essential. The case was completely changed when, in the consciousness of the prophets, the central place was taken, not by the might, but by the holiness of Yahweh. Thereby the conception of God was carried up into another and a higher sphere. From that moment it ceased to be a question of "more" or "less" between Yahweh and the other gods, for now he stood not only above them, but in very distinct opposition to them. If Yahweh the Holy One was God, if he was God *as the Holy One, then the others were not.* In a word, the belief that Yahweh was the only God sprang out of the ethical conception of his being. *Monotheism* was the gradual, not the sudden, result of this conception. I assume as established that monotheism does as a fact begin to show itself with unmistakable distinctness in the writings of the prophets of the eighth century, and is taught in explicit terms in the last quarter of the seventh century in Deuteronomy and Jeremiah.[1] But

---

[1] See my essay on "Yahweh and the other gods," Theological Review, 1874, pp. 329—366, and on the present position of the question, Note VII.

I must allow myself—at once in illustration and support of this fact—to call your attention to the contemporaneous movement in the opposite direction which took place in the popular religion.

We can hardly exaggerate the impression produced by the appearance of the Assyrians in Palestine. The last invasion of a powerful foreign foe, that of the Egyptians under Shishak,[1] belonged, in the eighth century, to the distant past. Since then the Israelites and their neighbours had been left to themselves. Their wars against each other had been waged with changing fortunes, but on the whole they had fairly balanced one another. Their horizon was closely bounded. It was, therefore, a very unwonted spectacle that the Assyrian monarchy presented to them, though it did not burst upon them quite without warning. As early as in the ninth century it had already been advancing, and had made its crushing power felt from afar.[2] But it was not till a century later that it appeared in its irresistible might, sweeping all before it, turning the lands into wildernesses, and carrying away their inhabitants captive. It has been truly said that Israel and its neighbours now for the first time came into contact with *the world*. This conception, which had never before risen in the consciousness of these small nationalities, completely shifted their centre of gravity, and made them

---

[1] 1 Kings xiv. 25—28; 2 Chron. xii. 1—12. The incursion of Zerah the Cushite, 2 Chron. xiv. 7—14 (8—15), is too doubtful to be taken into consideration in this connection.

[2] Cf. E. Schrader, die Keilinschriften und das A. T., S. 94 ff.

doubt the power of their gods which they had hitherto tranquilly acknowledged.[1] The religion of Israel, amongst the rest, was thrown into confusion by this disturbing cause. Lack of historical documents prevents our determining with certainty its disorganizing effect in Northern Israel; but in the kingdom of Judah the distinct traces of its influence may still be marked. It is told of Ahaz that he had a new altar placed in the temple at Jerusalem, modelled after one he had seen when visiting the Assyrian king at Damascus.[2] This is a trifle, if you will, but it is not without significance, for it shows that Ahaz was anxious to make the national worship conform to "fashion," always and everywhere an assimilator of foreign ideas, and on that ground very properly called a form of universalism,[3] though unhappily it often brings it to contempt rather than to honour by its exaggerations! More important, however, than this sufficiently innocent innovation is the fact that Ahaz "consecrated his son (to the deity) by fire."[4] If this stood alone, we could not draw any wide inferences from it, and should merely note it in its bearing on the character of Ahaz; but a number of converging details drive us to regard the sacrifice of

---

[1] J. Wellhausen, art. Israel, in the new edition of the Encyclopædia Britannica, Vol. XIII. p. 411 a.

[2] 2 Kings xvi. 10—16.

[3] R. Rothe, Theol. Ethik, 2e Ausg. II. 468 f.

[4] 2 Kings xvi. 3; according to 2 Chron. xxviii. 3, "his sons."

children as the first in a whole series of innovations that found their way into the popular religion of Israel from this time forward. Close by Jerusalem the tophet was built, probably by Ahaz himself,[1] and thus the worship of Molech was encouraged by royal patronage. Manasseh followed the precedent of his grandfather. He, too, "consecrated his son by fire,"[2] and, largely no doubt owing to his example, this practice became far from unusual thenceforth. He also introduced a number of foreign usages, and made the temple at Jerusalem a kind of pantheon.[3] It is from his reign that the worship of "the host of heaven" dates.[4] The origin of all these "reforms," as we may suppose Manasseh would call them, cannot be pointed out with certainty. It is highly probable that not a few of them were adopted directly from the Assyrians, to whom Manasseh, at any rate during the greater part of his reign, was vassal.[5]

---

[1] Cf. Theol. Tijdschrift, II. 562—568, where, besides the well-known places in Jer. and 2 Kings, I have examined Isaiah xxx. 33.

[2] 2 Kings xxi. 6 sq.; 2 Chron. xxxiii. 6.

[3] 2 Kings xxi. 4, 5, 7; cf. xxiii. 12.

[4] 2 Kings xxi. 5; cf. xxiii. 4, 5; Jer. viii. 2; xix. 13; xxxiii. 22; Zeph. i. 5; Deutero-Isaiah xxiv. 21; xxxiv. 4. The evidence of the latest redactor of Kings (2 Kings xvii. 16) is insufficient to prove that the same form of idolatry existed in the kingdom of Ephraim before its fall.

[5] He appears as such in Assyrian inscriptions, in the reign of Ezar-Haddon and of Asur-bani-pal; cf. Schrader, l. c. S. 227 ff., 238 ff.; Fr. Hommel, Abriss der babyl.-assyr. und israel. Geschichte, S. 10.

Egypt also appears to have made sundry contributions.[1] But we need not enter on these questions; for the essential point is simply this, that from the time of Ahaz onwards, i.e. from the time of the first contact with the Assyrians, the popular religion of Israel loses its independence and becomes, so to speak, the sport of the world-power, be it of Assyria herself or be it of Egypt, who for a time disputed the possession of Palestine and Syria with her. And is not this after all a perfectly natural phenomenon? Was it not obvious for the worshipper of the national god, Yahweh, to look about in his perplexity for extraordinary aid? And where should he expect to find it if not in the quarter where the supreme power lay, and whence the very danger he feared threatened his people?

Far different was the aspect worn by these events to the prophets. The victories of Assur had no power over their ethical faith. Their Yahweh could not be dethroned or cast into the shade by Bel or Merodach. On the contrary, strange as it may seem, he became greater in proportion as the world-power made itself felt more mightily. For what was that power, in the view of the prophets, but an instrument in Yahweh's

---

[1] See Ezek. viii. and my Religion of Israel, Vol. II. pp. 77—81. I must add, however, that the inference I still thought myself justified in drawing from Ezek. viii. 7—13, when that note was written, now appears to me to have been rendered questionable by the researches of W. Robertson Smith, in the Journal of Philology, IX. 75—100 (see especially p. 97).

hand to chastise the sins of Israel and its neighbours? Even before the Assyrians appeared in Palestine, Amos, overpowered by his moral indignation, had regarded them in this light and had announced their approach.[1] His successors spoke and thought as he. Who does not remember how high an Isaiah, for example, raises the grandeur of Yahweh, while representing him as the Mighty One whose purposes with regard to his people are served by Assur and by Egypt?[2] And thus the prophets—once more to quote Wellhausen—"absorbed into their religion that conception of the world which was destroying the religions of the nations, even before it had been fully grasped by the secular consciousness. Where others saw only the ruin of everything that is holiest, they saw the triumph of Jehovah over delusion and error."[3] What was thus revealed to the eye of their spirit was no less than the august idea of the *moral government of the world*—crude as yet, and with manifold admixture of error, but pure in principle. The prophets had no conception of the mutual connection of the powers and operations of nature. They never dreamed of the possibility of carrying them back to a single cause or deducing them from it. But what they did see, on the field within their view, was the realization of a single plan,—every-

---

[1] Amos vi. 14 (supra, p. 117), and other passages, in which the Assyrians are not even alluded to, but are none the less presupposed.

[2] Isaiah viii. 9, 10, 12 sqq.; x. &c.

[3] In Encyc. Brit., Vol. XIII. p. 411 a.

thing, not only the tumult of the peoples, but all nature likewise, subservient to the working out of one great purpose. The name "ethical monotheism" describes better than any other the characteristics of their point of view, for it not only expresses the character of the one God whom they worshipped, but also indicates the fountain whence their faith in Him welled up.

This purer and therefore more exalted conception of God could not fail to influence the ideas of the prophets as to the future relation between Yahweh and the peoples not his own. Even as conceived in the popular religion, Yahweh displays his might beyond the limits of Israel, and bends the neighbouring peoples to his will. The greater the national god becomes in the estimation of his worshippers, the more natural it seems to them that his power should be recognized and reverenced in wider circles. A remarkable passage in Amos shows that even in the eighth century the people looked forward with longing to "the day of Yahweh."[1] What conception they had formed of it does not appear; but the humiliation of Israel's foes and their subjection to Israel's god unquestionably formed one feature in it. Now, from an ethico-religious point of view, very little, if any, value can be attached to this popular expectation. What is it but a most ordinary expression of national feeling, the projection into the future of a

---

[1] Amos v. 18.

commonplace patriotism? And in so far as the prophets' anticipations agree with these popular conceptions, it is impossible to assign any higher place to them. Accordingly, many of the descriptions of Israel's restoration and of the rôll which the heathen will take therein have none but literary and æsthetic claims on our admiration. But, as I have said, it lies in the nature of the case that ethical monotheism, even in the period of its genesis, must give a fresh turn to expectations with regard to Yahweh and the peoples. Without deserting the national position—and we know already that the prophets remained true to it[1]—it was possible to think of Yahweh as being to the peoples something else and something more than their conqueror. And, as a fact, even in the earliest prophecies which deal with the future of the peoples, this influence of the purified prophetic conceptions may already be perceived. "In the last days"—so Isaiah[2] and Micah[3] declare, both of them in the words of a predecessor whose name is unknown to us—"in the last days shall the mountain of Yahweh's dwelling-place be established on the top of the mountains and exalted above the hills, and the peoples shall flow unto it. And many nations shall go and say: Come, let us ascend to the mountain of Yahweh and to the house of Jacob's god, that he may teach us of his ways and that we may walk in his paths; for from Zion goes thorah forth, and the word

---

[1] See pp. 105 sqq.   [2] Isaiah ii. 2, 3.   [3] Mic. iv. 1, 2.

of Yahweh from Jerusalem." It is the god of Israel whom the "many nations" reverence, and the central point of the theocracy to which they ascend. But what draws them thither and what they seek there is the thorah of Yahweh, the knowledge of his ways, wherein they desire to walk. Here, then, this unknown prophet adopts the purer, because the truly religious, tone which ever sounds henceforth from the prophetic literature—not unmixed indeed, far from it, but unmistakable none the less. Whether Isaiah himself, in the second half of the nineteenth chapter of his oracles, announces the spread of Yahwism into Egypt, and even the union of Egypt and Assur with Israel in the worship of Yahweh, I should prefer to leave undecided. The authenticity of this passage in his prophecies is too doubtful to warrant us in drawing deductions from it with regard to the pre-exilian period.[1] But the glorious word of Yahweh uttered by Zephaniah is undisputed: "Then will I give the peoples other and clean lips, that they may all call upon the name of Yahweh and serve him with one accord."[2] With him, too, Jeremiah is essentially at one. He, too, speaks of the "flowing of the nations together to Jerusalem, to (the worship or glorifying of) Yahweh's name."[3] He, too, looks for the time when the peoples shall come from the ends of the earth and shall say to Yahweh:

---

[1] Cf. the Commentaries on Isaiah xix. 17—25, and my work, "The Prophets and Prophecy in Israel," p. 248.

[2] Zeph. iii. 9. [3] Jer. iii. 17.

"Nought but untruth have our fathers inherited, nought but emptiness; and amongst them (amongst the supposed gods) is none that brings succour. How should man make gods for himself? They are no-gods!"[1] If elsewhere[2] he shows himself acquainted with the conditions upon which the realization of this prospect depends, and therefore assumes the possibility that, in spite of the dazzling revelation of Yahweh's might and majesty, the heathen may refuse to learn the ways of his people and to swear by his name,—all this, so far from weakening the significance of his prophecy, only serves to bring out its ethical character the more clearly.

As yet I have made no mention of the prophet whose universalism takes the highest flight of all—I mean the second Isaiah. He proclaims the nothingness of the idols, proclaims that Yahweh is absolutely alone, more emphatically than any of his predecessors. Is it surprising, then, that he should expect to see this one God, the first and the last, beside whom there is none other, recognized and adored by even the remotest peoples? "Turn unto me and be saved, all ye ends of the earth, for I and no other am God! By myself have I sworn; righteousness has gone out from my mouth, and a word that shall not be turned aside:

---

[1] Jer. xvi. 19—21. The idea that the worship of other—inferior or imaginary—gods has been destined or allotted to the heathen, is shared by the prophet with Deuteronomy. See Deut. xxxii. 8, 9 (cf. Theological Review, 1876, p. 351); iv. 19, 20; xxix. 25 (26).

[2] Jer. xii. 15—17.

before me shall every knee bend, by me every tongue swear! In Yahweh alone, shall they say, have we health and might; to him shall they come, and all that are inflamed against him shall be put to shame."[1] It is not superfluous, however, to inquire in what sense all this is meant, for in the second portion of Isaiah the heathen are often placed in a servile relation to *Israel.* Is it possible that the same or an analogous idea is expressed here also? In other words, is it as the king and the redeemer of his people that Yahweh is thus honoured, and is it in spite of themselves that the nations recognize his supremacy? To us it is no easy matter to connect or even to harmonize such a political prospect with the expectation of a truly religious relation between Yahweh and the heathen. But to the consciousness of the prophet the two ideas were quite compatible. Undoubtedly his eye is always fixed on the exaltation of his own people and the humbling of the other nations, its foes. But it is equally certain that he expects the prayers of the heathen to ascend to Yahweh. "My house shall be called a house of prayer for all nations."[2] And no wonder, for Yahweh himself comes forward as their teacher: "Hearken to me, ye peoples, and ye nations hear my voice! For thorah goes forth from me, and I will make my ordinance a light for the nations. (The revelation of) my righteousness is at hand; my salvation comes forth, and mine arms

---

[1] Isaiah xlv. 22—24.   [2] Isaiah lvi. 7.

shall judge the people. In me the dwellers by the coast shall hope, and on my arm shall they wait."[1] Nor does the prophet leave completely unanswered the question how all this shall come to pass. It is not to be without Israel's instrumentality. If in the first instance it is the glorifying of "the servant of Yahweh" (i.e. the kernel of the nation set apart by him for his worship) which excites the amazement of the heathen and moves them to submit to Yahweh, this same "servant" is likewise Yahweh's interpreter in the heathen world, and his preaching is the means of converting the peoples to Yahweh. It is but rarely and incidentally that the prophet refers to this aspect of the work of "Yahweh's servant." Perhaps he himself had no clear conception of how he would perform the task. But the scattered utterances in question are, after all, quite unequivocal. "Behold," we read in one passage,[2] "my servant whom I uphold; my chosen in whom my soul delights; I put my spirit upon him: *he shall proclaim right to the peoples.* . . . . He is not maimed nor broken *till he has established right on the earth and they of the coast wait on his thorah.*" Just afterwards, Yahweh addresses him thus: "I have called thee in righteousness, and hold thy hand and keep thee and set thee for a covenant of the people, *for a light of the heathen.*"[3] Elsewhere "the servant" himself is introduced as speaking. "Hearken to me,

---

[1] Isaiah li. 4, 5.   [2] Isaiah xlii. 1, 4.   [3] v. 6.

ye dwellers in the coast, and listen, ye peoples from afar!" And subsequently Yahweh describes the double task that is laid on him thus: "It is not enough that thou shouldst be my servant to raise up the tribes of Jacob and to bring back the redeemed of Israel; wherefore I have set thee as *a light to the heathen*, that my salvation may reach to the end of the earth."[1] All comment seems superfluous. The second Isaiah appreciates the blessing of being called by Yahweh, but also recognizes the duties which that calling involves. It is an exalted place that he assigns to his people, but the responsibility it brings with it is in proportion to its exaltation. Israel is privileged far above the nations, but also destined to share with them the best that it has received from Yahweh.

Was it only as a general expectation that the prophet cherished and proclaimed these thoughts as to the future of Israel's religion? Or did he venture to give them concrete form by applying them to a single individual—though one that was a host in himself—viz. Cyrus? This cannot be a matter of indifference to us if we are to judge his universalism truly, and you will therefore permit me to dwell on it for a moment. I do so the more willingly because very recent discoveries have, in the opinion of competent judges, thrown fresh light on the subject.

The facts, so far as they may be gathered from the

---

[1] Isaiah xlix. 1, 6.

Old Testament, are well known. The second Isaiah speaks with enthusiasm, not only of the task which Cyrus is to perform, but also of Cyrus himself. He calls him "the anointed of Yahweh," "whose right hand he has grasped;"[1] "Yahweh's shepherd," or, according to another reading, which is probably the true one, "Yahweh's companion" or friend, "who shall accomplish all his good pleasure."[2] So far, however, nothing more is implied than that Cyrus is a chosen instrument in Yahweh's hand. But now observe what Yahweh says in another passage:—

"Raised up by me is one come from the North,
Come from the East, who shall call on (or proclaim) my name,
Who shall trample the princes like slime,
As the potter treads down the clay."[3]

The Hebrew idiom admits the alternative translation, "who *calls* on (or proclaims) my name," in the present tense, but the sequel makes it probable that the prophet is thinking of the future. But how can Cyrus even then proclaim the name of Yahweh, whether it be as his suppliant or as his emissary? He has evidently not yet learned to do so at the time when the prophet speaks. In the first prophecy from

---

[1] Isaiah xlv. 1.

[2] Isaiah xliv. 28. For *ro'i*, read *re'i*, both here and in Zech. xiii. 7, where the same emendation is demanded by the parallelism. The metaphor of the shepherd scarcely suits the context.

[3] Isaiah xli. 25. In the third line I have adopted the well-known emendation, *yabús* for *yabó*.

which we have quoted, Yahweh promises him hidden treasures, "so that"—as he says to him—

> "So that thou mayst confess that I, Yahweh, am he,
> Who call (thee) by thy name, the god of Israel.
> For the sake of Jacob, my servant,
> And of Israel, my chosen,
> Have I called to thee by thy name,
> Do I give thee titles of honour, *while thou knowest me not.*
> I am Yahweh, and there is no other;
> Beside me there is no god.
> I gird thee, *while thou knowest me not.*"[1]

As yet, therefore, Cyrus is unconverted, nay, not in any way acquainted with Yahweh. But why may not Deutero-Isaiah have expected the change to come just in consequence of the mighty aid which the god of Israel was about to lend the Persian conqueror? Nay, he explains it all in so many words: Yahweh will clear away all obstacles from before him, and will give him wealth, *in order that he may acknowledge* that Yahweh, the god of Israel, calls him by his name. We see, then, that the prophet makes a genuine advance upon Jeremiah, for instance, who calls Nebucadrezar "the servant of Yahweh."[2] In this case, the Babylonian monarch himself remains passive, whereas Cyrus, the friend and the anointed of Yahweh,

---

[1] Isaiah. xlv. 3 b—5. The interpretation of Cheyne and others, "whilst thou didst not yet know me," i.e. from thy birth onwards (cf. chap. xlix. 1), appears to me inadmissible. The word is *yeda'tani*, not *yada'ta*.

[2] Vid. sup. p. 117, note 3.

is to come forward himself and to call on the name of Yahweh. Now, does this difference find its complete explanation in the glowing idealism of Deutero-Isaiah, and in the very different tasks which Nebucadrezar and Cyrus respectively have to fulfil with reference to Israel? Or did the religion which Cyrus even then professed help to create the expectation that he would ultimately learn to reverence Yahweh? No one can be surprised, I think, that this last question has often been answered in the affirmative.

But before giving our own decision, let us inquire whether there chance to be any other accounts of Cyrus which can give us any light. His decree concerning the return of the Jewish exiles, as given at the beginning of the Book of Ezra,[1] will not help us. It is hard indeed to believe that Cyrus could have thought or spoken as is there represented! And in fact we find that, according to one of our writer's predecessors, whose words he himself adopts,[2] the edict really ran otherwise. On the contrary, we are clearly bound to take cognizance of an inscription in which Cyrus himself boasts of having restored the gods of Babel to their places, declares that he calls daily upon Bel and Nebo, that they may fill up the length of his days and may bless the decree concerning his lot, and further proclaims himself emphatically "the worshipper of Mero-

---

[1] Ezra i. 2—4; cf. 2 Chron. xxxvi. 22, 23.
[2] Ezra vi. 3—5.

dach."[1] The name of Ahura-Mazda does not appear in the whole inscription. Now this, it has been argued, leads us to very unfavourable conclusions either as to the moral character of Cyrus or as to the purity of his religion. Was he a worshipper of Ahura-Mazda, and yet so feeble and indifferent towards him, or so anxious not to offend the Babylonians, that he did not so much as mention the name of his own god, while actually making a merit of his zeal for others? Or did he really know nothing of Ahura-Mazda at all, and does the inscription show him in his true character of an ordinary idolater? The latter alternative has been supposed to find support in the fact that Cyrus calls himself and his forefathers "kings of An-za-an," i.e. Susiana. He himself testifies elsewhere that he is an Achaemenid.[2] This involves his Persian descent, which is therefore beyond dispute. It may, however, be contended that the founder of his dynasty had moved to Susiana, where his posterity had gradually fallen into the religion of the country. But whichever of the above alternatives be adopted, it is contended that in neither case could the person of Cyrus give any grounds for the hope that he would acknowledge and openly confess Yahweh; and that in explaining Deutero-Isaiah's prophecy we

---

[1] The inscription was discovered in 1879, and was first made known by Sir H. Rawlinson. Since then it has frequently been discussed. See Cheyne's Prophecies of Isaiah, I. 301—303; II. 264—270; cf. also Note VIII.

[2] F. Spiegel, die altpersischen Keilinschriften, S. 2.

must therefore leave this personal factor out of consideration.

Is it really so? It seems to me that in this instance there has been too much haste, and that sacrifices too ready and too great have been offered to the one newly discovered document, which is after all only preserved in a fragmentary condition, and is by no means interpreted with certainty. The splitting up of the Achaemenidæ into two branches, one settled in Persia, whence Darius came, and the other in Susiana, from which Cyrus sprang, sounds in itself more like fiction than history; and moreover, when thus presented, it is as inconsistent with the inscriptions of Darius as is the supposed difference of religion between the two branches.[1] I must have better proof than this before I believe that the *whole of antiquity* was mistaken in regarding Cyrus as the founder of the Medo-Persian monarchy. The fact remains, however, that Ahura-Mazda is not mentioned in the newly discovered inscription. But ought this to cause such great amazement? And does it justify such far-reaching conclusions? The inscription is Babylonian, not only in language and in form of writing, but in purport also. The compiler's object is to conciliate the favour of the Babylonians, or, if you will, to reconcile them to their new master. Ought we to forget this fact in estimating the contents of the inscription? Can we regard such a composition as flowing from the pen of Cyrus

---

[1] See, further, Note VIII.

and containing a confession of his personal faith? To do so would be more than hasty. I can see nothing more in it than a political manifesto, and I can only infer from it the belief of the Persian satrap as to what would be acceptable to the inhabitants of Babylonia.

We return to Deutero-Isaiah. He certainly instituted no investigations as to the religious convictions of Cyrus. He simply accepted what common fame reported. But I do not see what hinders us from still supposing that this was enough to enable him to draw a religious distinction between Cyrus and the Babylonian oppressors. This would render it all the easier for him to retain that ideal conception of the person and work of Cyrus which we meet with in his prophecies. The _source_, however, of this conception must not be looked for in the reports concerning Cyrus that had reached the prophet, but *in himself*, in his unconditional monotheism and his unshaken faith. He possesses the courage of his opinions, and therefore sees in the instrument of Yahweh's will the proclaimer also of Yahweh's name.

The Yahwism of the canonical prophets now stands before us in sufficient clearness to enable us to determine its relation to the Israelite nationality. I need hardly remind you again that not one of the prophets ever thinks of severing Yahweh and Israel one from the other. But it lay in the nature of the case that their ethical conception of religion must loosen the bond which united these two—the people and its god—and must give a certain independence to Yahwism. The latter did not cease to be a part of Israel's national life, but it became something else and something more as well. We must not for a moment imagine that this was the result of a preconceived and deliberate plan. The preaching of the prophets had the *tendency* already described, without their having given themselves any clear account of it. Moreover, the tendency itself is not equally marked in them all. In some of them its traces are faint or altogether absent; and in each case in which we observe it, it appears in a special form characteristic of the individual prophet. Let us, however, review the facts themselves, and their significance will at once be apparent.

Is it not highly noteworthy that Amos, our earliest witness, expresses himself so emphatically and unequivocally in this matter? This is no doubt connected with the earnestness and youthful freshness of his Yahwism, which gave a clear outline to the consequences that flowed from it. At the opening of the first of those rebukes which he administers to the kingdom of Ephraim, we find this passage: "Hear the word that Yahweh has spoken concerning you, O sons of Israel, concerning the whole race that I brought up out of Egypt. You alone have I known of all the races of the earth. Therefore I shall visit all your sins upon you."[1] We must not fail to notice how

---

[1] Amos iii. 1, 2.

directly this "therefore" stands opposed to the deduction commonly made by the people, viz., because Yahweh stands in so special a relation to Israel, therefore he will *not* punish, but will overlook and condone, whatever Israel does amiss. At present, however, we are more nearly concerned with this other thought, also expressed in the passage cited: Israel is but one of the many nations of the earth. It is Yahweh who has taken to himself this one nation in distinction from all others. He might have "known" some other nation had it seemed good to him. It is a great, an inestimable privilege which he has as a fact conferred on Israel alone, but which he might have refrained from so conferring. Do not suppose that we are taking Amos too literally at his word in ascribing this conception to him. He returns to it elsewhere in his prophecies more than once. To shake from their slumbers "those who are at ease in Zion," and those "who deem themselves safe on the mount of Samaria," he urges them to go and look upon Calneh, to journey thence to the mighty Hamath, and then descend to the Philistine Gath: "Are ye better than these kingdoms, or is your territory greater than theirs?"[1] Here we are struck by the prophet's silence concerning the guarantee which the Israelites supposed themselves to possess, in the support of Yahweh, against such disasters as

---

[1] Amos vi. 2. The true reading of this verse, which I have adopted in my translation, is pointed out by A. Geiger, Urschrift und Uebersetzungen der Bibel, S. 96 f.

had fallen on these cities. This supposed guarantee Amos entirely ignores. Why should the fate which fell upon these mighty cities spare Judah or Ephraim? Elsewhere, too, he expressly places his people in the same line with other nations. After declaring that the six nations bordering on Israel shall not escape the punishment with which each is threatened "for three transgressions and for four," he hastens to complete the tale of seven by adding Israel, divided into its two kingdoms.[1] Still further to his people's shame, he elsewhere summons the dwellers in the palaces of Ashdod and of Egypt as witnesses of the abominations committed in Samaria.[2] Finally, Yahweh asks, in no doubtful terms, "Are ye not as the sons of the Cushites to me, O ye sons of Israel? Have I not brought Israel out of Egypt, and (that is to say: but likewise) the Philistines from Caphtor, and the Aramæans from Kír?"[3] Thus one of the chief proofs of the inseparable union between Israel and his god is bereft of its force, or rather contemptuously cast aside as worthless. We see Yahweh, as it were, receding from the natural and inherent relation in which he was supposed to stand to Israel. But by this very means Yahwism is exalted into a higher, viz. the ethical, sphere, and at the same time ceases to be exclusively suited and destined for Israel.

---

[1] The six neighbours, in Amos i. 3—ii. 3; Juda and Israel, in ii. 4, 5, and ii. 6—16, respectively.

[2] Amos iii. 9, 10.   [3] Amos ix. 7.

It is certainly no accident that in this same prophet Yahwism begins to assume a broad human character. One might say that it is taking the direction of "natural religion" and of the "*virtutes civiles*," as they have been sometimes called, with grudging sympathy. "Do good!" "Let justice run down like water, and righteousness like an ever-flowing stream!" In these and other such formulae[1] Amos sums up the demands of Yahweh. By this standard he judges and rebukes not only Israel, but Damascus, Gaza, and the rest.[2] The connection between this phenomenon and the prophet's special view of the relation between Yahweh and Israel is not to be mistaken. That Yahwism which, according to the conviction of Amos, might have existed elsewhere than in Israel, cannot be specifically Israelitish. It must commend itself to all in whose bosom beats a human heart. We must beware of attributing to Amos a clear discernment of all that followed from his principle. But we must not overlook the fact that his preaching was big with a revolution on the field of religion which he himself was not to witness, but which he unquestionably prepared.

It has been said of Isaiah, not without justice, that the inviolability of Zion had become a dogma with him. His immovable conviction, however, referred

---

[1] Amos iii. 10; v. 14, 15, 24; vi. 12; cf. Duhm, die Theologie der Propheten, S. 113 ff.

[2] Amos i. 3, 6, 9, 11, 13; ii. 1.

not to the capital of his fatherland, but to the seat of Yahweh, Israel's king. He could therefore unite with this invincible confidence a second expectation, which he expressed in the name of one of his children: Sheár-yashûb.[1] "A remnant repents" is as much a threat as the expression of a hope. Indeed, it is a threat in the first instance. It is the announcement of a fearful judgment which Yahweh will bring upon his people by means of Assur or of Egypt, or of the collision of these two on Judah's territory. The people of Judah that now is must be all but utterly destroyed. Not for it is the glorious future held in store of which Isaiah prophesies. It answers so ill to Yahweh's severe demands, that it must needs be swept away ere Zion can become what it is destined by its divine consecration to be. But "a remnant shall repent." Isaiah could not relinquish this hope, and in so far he was as good an Israelite as any of his political opponents. The actually existing Israel, which in spite of himself he had been forced to renounce, bore in itself "the holy seed"[2] from which the new people, the people after Yahweh's heart, was to spring.

You observe that the severance between people and religion is effected here otherwise than with Amos. The *subject* of Yahwism, the people that is to serve Yahweh in truth, has still to be brought forth. Israel is already there, but not the people of Yahweh.

---

[1] Isaiah vii. 3; x. 20—23; cf. iv. 3, 4.   [2] Isaiah vi. 13.

The future which Isaiah proclaims is foreshadowed in the little circle which he had collected round himself, and into which he retired when his preaching found no acceptance either with the people or with the political leaders. I refer to the "faithful witnesses," Uriah the priest and Zachariah ben Yeberechiah, to whom he communicated his prophecy concerning Damascus and Samaria;[1] and to those "taught of Yahweh," in whose midst he was "to bind up the testimony and seal the thorah."[2] How we long to know more of this little community and its conventicles! But we have to be satisfied with the bare hints to which I have alluded. Yet is not the mere fact that Isaiah thus severed himself, his family and his spiritual kindred, and placed them over against the people, in itself full of significance? I suspect that the circle thus formed exercised an important influence on the further course of Israel's religious evolution. I cannot escape the thought that the priest-prophet to whom we owe the Deuteronomic legislation was of the spiritual progeny of those "disciples of Yahweh" amongst whom was Uriah the priest, and at whose head stood Isaiah the prophet. Be this as it may, Isaiah's separatism—if you will pardon the word—is a remarkable token of the growing independence of Yahwism, a milestone on the way which it must traverse in its course from a national to a universal religion.

---

[1] Isaiah viii. 1—4. [2] Isaiah viii. 16.

Still more clearly speaks the truly tragic figure of Jeremiah. His biography—for we really know enough of him to warrant us in adopting what might otherwise sound a pretentious phrase—need not be repeated here. What gives him his special interest for us at present may be summed up in few words. He stood, as we know, almost alone, with Baruch his faithful servant, against his whole people. It is true that when his life was threatened, there were some of the nobles that took his part. But they defended him more from reverence for the prophet of Yahweh than from sympathy with his conception of Yahwism. At any rate, they made no open confession of any such sympathy. The only man of whom we read that "he spoke according to all Jeremiah's words" was Uriah of Kirjath-jearim, and he was slain with the sword and deemed unworthy of a decent burial.[1] Now Jeremiah's opponents were a very heterogeneous company; but those who set the tone amongst them, and who openly opposed him more than once with a boldness and confidence that we cannot but respect, were fiery zealots for Yahweh. Their specific mark is just that fusion of patriotism and religion with which we are already acquainted. This explains the activity of such a man as Hananiah the Gibeonite, one of the prophets of the patriotic party. The impatience of these patriots under the Babylonian supremacy, their repeated attempts to

---

[1] Jer. xxvi. 20—23.

deliver their fatherland, the anticipations with which they cheered and inflamed each other, the stubborn heroism with which they resisted the overpowering force of the enemy,—all this is inseparably connected with their faith in Yahweh, the god of Israel. Had Jeremiah no feeling for these things? Was the humbling of his people nothing to him? Nay! for he was an Israelite heart and soul. Yet not a word of sympathy with the friends of freedom ever escaped his lips. Firmly, but not without a fierce inward struggle, he repressed every impulse of that patriotism with which all the rest were glowing, that he might bear exclusive witness to what in his eyes was the only true worship of Yahweh, the worship which Israel could not renounce without sacrificing all his privileges. His line of action struck his contemporaries as anti-national, and he himself was cast into prison as a foe, nay as a traitor, to his fatherland, and escaped death only by a lucky chance. We know him better, and shall beware of subscribing to this hostile judgment. The man whose toil and zeal for the true good of his people never flagged throughout his life, and who at last esteemed a share in his people's reproach more highly than the treasures of Nebucadrezar and the luxury of the Chaldæan court,—this man was not wanting in love for his people. But it remains true that in him religion and patriotic feeling for a time stood over against each other, and their reconciliation, impossible in the present, could only be looked for in

L

the future. Hence his complete isolation. "The true Israel was narrowed to himself."[1] Yet this individualism is but the form under which the nascent universalism reveals itself. Jeremiah himself regarded it in no other light. We have already seen[2] that he never relinquished the hope that Yahweh would again be the god of Israel, and Israel again the people of Yahweh. But it was to be a new covenant then entered into: the thorah of Yahweh laid in the inmost parts of his servants and written on their hearts; no mediators any more between him and his own, for "they shall all know him, from the least to the greatest." Doubtless it is with "the house of Israel and the house of Judah" that this covenant must be struck; but it remains in reality independent of the relation in which Yahweh has stood to his people from the exodus out of Egypt downwards;—it is a *new* covenant, and as such no longer confined to a single nation, but fitted and destined for "many peoples."

At the end of the line we have thus far followed stands the second Isaiah, the spiritual son of Jeremiah and the heir of his thoughts as to the future of Yahwism. From the point of view we now occupy, we can easily recognize in his conceptions and anticipations the independent reproduction and elaboration of the hints we have noted in Jeremiah. The distinction

---

[1] Wellhausen, in Encyc. Brit. Vol. XIII. p. 417 a.
[2] Supra, p. 128.

between the fleshly and the spiritual Israel has found its classic expression in the Deutero-Isaiah's "servant of Yahweh." Where, as in the celebrated fifty-third chapter, this spiritual Israel or "servant of Yahweh" is described as an individual, some scholars have thought—mistakenly, indeed, but not without occasion—that they could trace a description of Jeremiah's own lot. We have seen that the task of "the servant" includes not only the restoration of Israel, but also the proclamation to the heathen of the true religion, the ordinance and the thorah of Yahweh. Let us admit that this idea is merely indicated and not in the least developed. But even in its embryonic form it is a striking result, worthy of the remarkable movement that emanated from the prophets of Israel and was continued by the most eminent amongst them throughout wellnigh three centuries. No preconcerted plan underlay it, and we may now add that no system issued from it. But unity and connection are not wanting. Now that the whole or at least the most prominent portions of it lie before us, we can easily perceive that the final outcome was already contained in germ in the initiative of the shepherd of Thekoa. Yahweh, the Holy One of Israel, was predestined to become the God of all peoples.

The second Isaiah was very likely in his grave before the year 500 B.C. To think of this is to remind ourselves that Israel's preaching to the heathen remained for centuries no more than a pious wish. How is this?

How comes it that the Israelitish religion, so far from spreading abroad, adopts a rigidly exclusive character, and becomes a wall of partition between the Jews and the nations?

If we may start from the assumption that fact is the expression of thought, and that we understand the reality the better the more clearly we perceive its reasonableness, then we must answer: "Because the extension of Israel's religion, though already proclaimed, was not yet ripe for execution; because Israel had yet to be prepared for the task; because nothing can make itself felt externally until reduced to internal order and vigour." In a word, before the servant of Yahweh can be "a light to the heathen," there must be a servant of Yahweh duly trained for his task.

The prophets had not succeeded in making their conception of Yahwism the possession of the people. This is not meant as a reproach. Neither the wish to reform the nation in its entirety, nor zeal and perseverance in the attempt, had been wanting. But the demands of the prophets were too lofty to be at once allowed and complied with by the masses. This does not prove, however, that their labours bore no immediate fruit. Their inspired word cannot have returned to them empty; and who shall say how many felt its influence and retained it to their lives' end? But this was not what they purposed, or at least was but a small part of it. They intended their Yahwism to sink into the consciousness of the nation and to take shape in its life. No less than a complete transformation was involved, a breach with the deeply-rooted heathen practices and the rearing up of a fresh national existence. Did it not really lie in the nature of the case that the fragmentary and unregulated activity of the prophets must fail in bringing such a reformation to pass?

The prophets themselves could not long be blind to their comparative powerlessness, nor could they refrain from asking what fresh means to their end remained for them to adopt. Of their deliberations on this point we know nothing. Only as a rare exception does history allow us a glance into the laboratory in which a reformation is being prepared. But we know the result. Are we to suppose that Hezekiah's measures for purifying the worship[1] were the result of mutual consultations, and were recommended to the king by the prophets, perhaps by Isaiah? We suspect as much. But our information as to the scope and bearing of these measures themselves is too scanty to enable us to speak with certainty.[2] Our ignorance in this par-

---

[1] 2 Kings xviii. 4 sq., 22 (Isaiah xxxv. 7).

[2] The more elaborate narrative of the Chronicler (2 Chron. xxix.—xxxi.) is subject to very grave suspicion (cf. K. H. Graf, die historischen Bücher des A. Testaments, S. 168—173), and therefore cannot be used to supplement 2 Kings xviii. 4. In the last-named passage we must distinguish between the *one specific fact*, the breaking of the brazen serpent, the historical character of which is supported by Isaiah's polemic against the images of the other gods and of Yahweh (chap. ii. 8, 19 sq.; xxx. 22; xxxi. 7), and the

ticular case, however, is of less consequence than might well be supposed. Hezekiah's reformation did not last. Manasseh, the next king, hastened to restore the former state of things. The changes Hezekiah had introduced vanished without a trace, and their true significance cannot have been seen and appreciated until long afterwards, when they turned out to have been the prelude to the great events of the eighteenth year of Josiah's reign.

It was in this year that "Hilkiah's book of law" was brought to the knowledge of the king, and, when confirmed by Huldah's prophetic authority, put into practice by him.[1] Now here the prophetic aspirations of the time had found complete expression. A great part of the book, or—to give it the name under which we all know it—of the Deuteronomic thorah, consists in prophetic exhortation to fidelity to Yahweh, prophetic warning against service of "the other gods." By the side of these stand legal ordinances derived from usage or from older law-books, and a whole series of moral precepts which likewise breathe the spirit of

---

general formulæ under which the final redactor of Kings describes Hezekiah's reformation, and which remind us at once of 2 Kings xxii. sq. The destruction of the images, then, is far better guaranteed than the suppression of the "bamôth." For the rest, Jer. xxvi. 18, 19, confirms the fact that Hezekiah did in some way play the part of a reformer; for the humbling of Hezekiah and his people, there mentioned, must have translated itself into action, or the memory of it would not have been so long preserved.

[1] 2 Kings xxii. 1—xxiii. 25.

prophecy. But beyond all this, the Deuteronomist enters upon a field on which his predecessors had not stepped—that of the cultus. In the character of the sacrifices and feasts in honour of Yahweh he makes no change. But, penetrated as he is by the conviction that the mingling of Yahwism with the adoration of other gods must be brought to an end, and that this cannot be, so long as the "bamôth," the true centres of the syncretism in question, exist, he confines the worship of Yahweh to "the place which he shall choose," to the temple at Jerusalem.[1] This centralization is the means by which he proposes to extinguish idolatry and to give undisputed supremacy to the Yahwism that stands before him as his ideal.

The attempt to carry out this programme was made under what seemed at first very favourable auspices. The king was completely won over to it. No doubt it was in conflict with the convictions and customs of the masses,—so much so, indeed, that it would never have been accepted if not imposed by the strong arm of authority. It was even necessary in sundry cases to appeal to force, where primeval sanctuaries, beloved by the people of the neighbourhood, were swept away. But, on the other hand, the attitude of the people towards Josiah's reformatory measures was not one of unmingled hostility, and they would not, therefore, offer an unconditional opposition to them. Before

---

[1] Deut. xii. 5, 11, 14, 18, 21—26; xiv. 23—25, &c.

proceeding to action, the king summoned the representatives of the nation to the temple at Jerusalem, and made them swear to obey Hilkiah's book of law.[1] We are not to suppose that there was a regular and free discussion at this gathering, followed by a decision according to the majority of votes. The final result testifies to the power of the royal initiative rather than to the existence of a strong and unanimous conviction on the part of the people. But it is equally clear that Josiah would not have ventured to ask the consent of his subjects, and would still less have been able to carry away "the priests and the prophets" by his impetuous enthusiasm, if there had not been many points of contact between the Deuteronomic law and the popular feeling. Though the populace had not followed the prophets of Isaiah's school on the path they had laid down, yet they could not remain unmoved by the commands now laid upon them in the name of Yahweh, the god of Israel. Least of all could they be indifferent to the moral precepts which the king read out to them; for they had long known that Yahweh maintained the right and rewarded mercy. Neither can Josiah's hearers have met by a simple rejection the command to serve Yahweh alone, and him in that sanctuary only which he himself had chosen. The prestige of the temple had steadily risen during its existence of almost four centuries, and the delivery of Jerusalem

---

[1] 2 Kings xxiii. 1—3.

from the Assyrians, with Isaiah's commentary on that great event, had contributed in no small degree to raise the reverence for it into an article of the popular faith. Thus we may explain the sanction given to Josiah's plans in a moment of excitement and enthusiasm by the great majority of the assemblage. The Deuteronomic thorah gained what its champions desired—the opportunity of revealing itself in its might and exerting its influence uncontrolled. . . . .

Yet none the less it failed. Justice compels us to admit that the circumstances, at first so favourable, soon turned against it. Josiah's death on the battle-field of Megiddo[1] was a terrible blow to the reformers. It is their conviction which is reflected by the author of Kings in the well-known words: "Like unto him was there no king before him, that turned to Yahweh with all his heart, and with all his soul, and with all his might, according to all the thorah of Moses; neither after him arose there his like."[2] The last statement is only too true. Not one of Josiah's successors was completely devoted to his principles, and Jehoiakim was even hostile to them. Nor must we forget that the kingdom of Judah only continued to exist for twenty years after Josiah's death, and that during that period it was exposed to all manner of disturbances and disasters. At any rate the fact remains that very little of what the Deuteronomist contemplated,

---

[1] 2 Kings xxiii. 29, 30; cf. 2 Chron. xxxv. 20—25.
[2] 2 Kings xxiii. 25.

even if it ever came about, survived the defeat at Megiddo. If we may believe Jeremiah, the moral condition of the people underwent no improvement. This in itself would be enough to explain the bitter disenchantment that followed his early joy in Josiah's reformation.[1] But, besides this, the adoration of other gods by Yahweh's side did not cease; nay, after a short time it was practised more zealously than ever.[2] What did it signify, against this, that devotion to the temple of Jerusalem was strengthened in many hearts? To the Deuteronomist, the single sanctuary was no more than a means—highly valued indeed, and therefore warmly advocated—to secure the introduction and maintenance of the true Yahwism. To the great masses the temple was a fetish. Instead of being the seat of a pure monotheism, it had become once more, though perhaps in less degree than formerly, the scene of all manner of idolatrous practices. Accordingly, Jeremiah, as we saw but now,[3] despaired of a gradual reformation of the existing state of things. To accomplish any true good, Yahweh must begin again from the beginning, and make *a new covenant* with the house of Israel and the house of Judah. A glorious expectation and a striking proof of Jeremiah's invincible faith! But at the same time a judgment on his own contemporaries, and on the working of that scheme by

---

[1] Cf. Jer. xi.   [2] Cf. Religion of Israel, Vol. II. pp. 56—59.
[3] Vid. sup. pp. 128, 146.

which Josiah and those that felt with him had hoped to bring and to keep the people to the way of Yahweh. Is there any appeal from this sentence? Must we not grant that the prophet is right, and that, judged with reference to its immediate purpose, the Deuteronomic thorah was another failure?

We rest in this judgment all the more confidently when we find that a renewed attempt in the same direction likewise fell short of satisfactory results. The Jews who returned from the captivity in the year 536 B.C., and who settled at Jerusalem or in its neighbourhood, had quite outgrown idolatry. In so far they stood above their ancestors. Jeremiah's prophecies of evil had not been fulfilled in vain. But in other respects we cannot aver that Yahwism asserted itself with any vigour amongst them. Want of enthusiasm, of energy and of inspiration, is the special characteristic of the period that extends from Zerubbabel to Ezra. Towards the end of this time the danger was far from imaginary that, in consequence of the numerous mixed marriages, the Jews might be gradually merged amongst their neighbours, and in consequence might lose their national characteristics, including their religion. Now during this period they were once more living under the Deuteronomic thorah, and, as far as we can see, it once more failed to secure to itself the hearts of the people. Deep and stirring was its exhortation, "Thou, O Israel, shalt love Yahweh, thy god, with all thy heart, and with all thy soul, and with all thy might;"¹ but however loud the echo might be in certain hearts, yet "a people of the heritage, consecrated to Yahweh,"² was not formed.

Meanwhile, the train was completely laid for a great change. In Judæa itself the priests had enjoyed great and increasing influence since 536 B.C. In Babylonia, if I may so express myself, the theory that corresponded to the practice had been elaborated. Even in the first half of the captivity, Ezekiel sketched the plan of a new Jewish state, with the temple for its central point. His successors maintained and further developed his idea. Finally, in the year 458 B.C., the conception seemed to be ripe for realization, and in Judæa the ground seemed ready for the new edifice to rise upon it. Thither went Ezra, with the king's authority, at the head of a second band of returning exiles, and armed with "the law of his God."³ Some years later, when Nehemiah, on whose sympathy he could entirely rely, was governor, he saw that the moment had come for realizing his plans. The priestly law was read aloud, and the whole people solemnly accepted and swore to observe it.⁴ *Judaism was established.*

What the prophetic preaching had failed to effect, what Deuteronomy, the prophetic thorah, had only

---

[1] Deut. vi. 5.   [2] Deut. xiv. 2.   [3] Ezra vii.—x.
[4] Neh. viii.—x.; cf. my Religion of Israel, Vol. II. chaps. vii. and viii., and, on the most recent objections to this view of Ezra's person and work, Note IX.

which Josiah and those that felt with him had hoped to bring and to keep the people to the way of Yahweh. Is there any appeal from this sentence? Must we not grant that the prophet is right, and that, judged with reference to its immediate purpose, the Deuteronomic thorah was another failure?

We rest in this judgment all the more confidently when we find that a renewed attempt in the same direction likewise fell short of satisfactory results. The Jews who returned from the captivity in the year 536 B.C., and who settled at Jerusalem or in its neighbourhood, had quite outgrown idolatry. In so far they stood above their ancestors. Jeremiah's prophecies of evil had not been fulfilled in vain. But in other respects we cannot aver that Yahwism asserted itself with any vigour amongst them. Want of enthusiasm, of energy and of inspiration, is the special characteristic of the period that extends from Zerubbabel to Ezra. Towards the end of this time the danger was far from imaginary that, in consequence of the numerous mixed marriages, the Jews might be gradually merged amongst their neighbours, and in consequence might lose their national characteristics, including their religion. Now during this period they were once more living under the Deuteronomic thorah, and, as far as we can see, it once more failed to secure to itself the hearts of the people. Deep and stirring was its exhortation, "Thou, O Israel, shalt love Yahweh, thy god, with all thy heart, and with all thy soul, and with all thy might;"[1] but however loud the echo might be in certain hearts, yet "a people of the heritage, consecrated to Yahweh,"[2] was not formed.

Meanwhile, the train was completely laid for a great change. In Judæa itself the priests had enjoyed great and increasing influence since 536 B.C. In Babylonia, if I may so express myself, the theory that corresponded to the practice had been elaborated. Even in the first half of the captivity, Ezekiel sketched the plan of a new Jewish state, with the temple for its central point. His successors maintained and further developed his idea. Finally, in the year 458 B.C., the conception seemed to be ripe for realization, and in Judæa the ground seemed ready for the new edifice to rise upon it. Thither went Ezra, with the king's authority, at the head of a second band of returning exiles, and armed with "the law of his God."[3] Some years later, when Nehemiah, on whose sympathy he could entirely rely, was governor, he saw that the moment had come for realizing his plans. The priestly law was read aloud, and the whole people solemnly accepted and swore to observe it.[4] *Judaism was established.*

What the prophetic preaching had failed to effect, what Deuteronomy, the prophetic thorah, had only

---

[1] Deut. vi. 5.   [2] Deut. xiv. 2.   [3] Ezra vii.—x.

[4] Neh. viii.—x.; cf. my Religion of Israel, Vol. II. chaps. vii. and viii., and, on the most recent objections to this view of Ezra's person and work, Note IX.

half accomplished, that was brought to pass by Judaism. In this form Yahwism became *the religion of the Jewish people*, and that people henceforth identified itself more and more fully with it, till the identification was complete. In other words, the priests of Yahweh, from Ezekiel to Ezra, saw their attempt crowned with complete success. We need hardly remind ourselves that this proves nothing as to its value from a religious point of view. Indeed, we might rather incline to regard the very success of these men as itself throwing suspicion on the merits of their cause. May not the authors of the priestly legislation have consulted the needs and capacities of the people throughout, and deliberately brought down their requirements to the requisite level? But no; we are not justified in taking any such view of their work. I will not deny that sometimes they consciously descended to the position of the masses. Still less will I deny that their followers, the Scribes, made important concessions to the popular usage. But it is impossible to explain all their work and the fruits which they gathered in from it upon this principle. The system to which their legislation gives shape is the natural outcome of their special views, and its practicability can only have been a secondary recommendation in their eyes. Let us then examine the system more closely. For its own sake it is well worthy of our attention; and we have just now a special additional reason for studying it. If we have felt any interest in tracing the development of the prophetic ideas, we must now desire further to know what became of them when the priestly thorah was introduced. Are we really to suppose that Ezra and his fellow-workers renounced them, and set them aside to make room for their own new creation?

It will be seen presently that I am far from rating the distinction between the prophetic and the priestly conception of Yahwism low. But before everything we must do justice to their points of mutual connection and agreement. Ezra himself recognized the prophets as the servants of Yahweh who had proclaimed his commandments.[1] He never dreamed that he was breaking down what they had built up. Is it likely that he was mistaken?

The conception of God that underlies the priestly legislation is that of the prophets—or perhaps we should rather say is its development in one special direction. Yahweh is to the authors of this legislation, with Ezekiel at their head, the Only One, the exalted and unapproachable God, stern in his demands and inexorably strict in maintaining them.[2] The parallels, or at least the germs of all this, may be traced in the pre-exilian or exilian prophets.[3] But what these pro-

---

[1] Ezra ix. 10—12.

[2] See, e.g., Ezekiel i. x., and on Yahweh's justice, xiv. 12—23; xviii.; xxxiii. 10—20; cf. R. Smend, der Prophet Ezekiel erklärt, S. xvi. ff.

[3] Cf. the sketch of the ideas of the prophets of the eighth century B.C., in my Religion of Israel, Vol. I. pp. 40 sqq.

phets put side by side with it, Yahweh's goodness and mercy, falls into the background with the priestly legislators, Ezekiel again sounding the key-note. The distance between Yahweh and the "son of man" has become greater. It is no longer as in the days of Amos, when "the Lord Yahweh did nothing without revealing his counsel to his servants the prophets."[1] This relation of confidence has been superseded by one of deep awe, not to say fear and trembling. In a single word, the balance that oscillates—shall we say inevitably?—between the immanent and the transcendental conception of God, now inclines to the last-named.

The priestly conception of religion awakes our interest even more than the priestly idea of God. We have found the prophetic view of religion to be ethical to the very core. Can we say the same of the priestly view? The main contents of Ezra's legislation might well seem to sanction an opposite conclusion, and to stand in contrast with Hosea's word, "mercy and not sacrifice."[2] But any such judgment would really be unfair. The priestly legislators do not aim at completeness. What was already adequately regulated in the Deuteronomic thorah, they do not manipulate afresh. Its moral injunctions were not slighted, much less annulled by them, but simply assumed. Moreover, the moral law is not wholly unrepresented in

---

[1] Amos iii. 7.   [2] Hos. vi. 6 a.

their own contributions. Let us not forget that the nineteenth chapter of Leviticus, an elaboration, as it were, of the law of the ten commandments, flowed from the pen of a priest, to whom accordingly we owe that royal word, "Thou shalt not avenge nor bear any grudge against the children of thy people, but thou shalt love thy neighbour as thyself: I am Yahweh;" and that other which is like unto it: "The stranger that dwelleth with you shall be unto you as one born among you, and thou shalt love him as thyself; for ye were strangers in the land of Egypt: I, Yahweh, am your god!"[1] Elsewhere, too, the moral precepts shine through the ritual, so to speak.[2] The religion of the priestly lawgiver, then, is itself ethical—but not as the religion of the prophets is. Let us try to give ourselves an account of the difference. I think it may be reduced to two main points.

"Be holy, for I, Yahweh, am holy!" In these words the priestly thorah itself sums up its conception of religion.[3] It is with this demand that it comes to the whole people and to every several Israelite. What does this include? "Holy" signifies a relationship. It is applied to the person or thing which is consecrated to the deity, which belongs to him and is set aside for his service. What does it mean, then, to be consecrated to

---

[1] Lev. xix. 34.

[2] Lev. xxiv. 10—23; xxv. 17, &c.; Num. xv. 39, &c.

[3] Lev. xix. 2; xx. 7, 26, cf. 24; xxi. 8, 15, 23; xxii. 9, 16, 32; xi. 44, 45; Num. xv. 40, 41.

Yahweh? In virtue of what can this consecration be testified of any man, and how is he distinguished from the unconsecrated? The answer to these questions—which reveals the character of the priestly conception of Yahweh's demands—cannot remain doubtful for a moment. Holiness is *purity*. This, in the estimate of the priests, is the chief of all excellences, the first mark of the Israelite. The prophets could never have adopted the priestly motto, simply because they looked at the matter otherwise. "What does Yahweh require of you, but to do justly and to love mercy and to walk humbly with thy God?" Thus spoke Micah;[1] and in the other prophets likewise the human virtues, justice and mutual love, stand in the foreground. The priest will likewise insist upon all this, and sometimes very finely, as we have just been reminded. But his epitome runs otherwise: "Be holy, for I, Yahweh, am holy!" The centre of gravity for him lies elsewhere than for the prophet; it lies in man's attitude, not towards his fellow-man but towards God, not in his social but in his personal life. I must leave it to you to work out this contrast. You remember how purity is further defined in the priestly laws, how it is made to include chastity, for instance, in the widest acceptation of the term.[2] The passages on contracting uncleanness and on the means of removing it are also in your minds; so that you can hardly wonder at the charge of materializing

---

[1] Mic. vi. 8.   [2] Lev. xviii. xx.

the ethical conception which has been brought against the priestly legislator. But we will abstain from passing judgment. Our present object is simply to give a faithful outline of the priestly ideal.

A second mark of this ideal may be found in the assumption of worship amongst the duties of the people consecrated to Yahweh, and of every Israelite in particular. The minute detail with which the temple service is regulated stands off in sharp contrast from the silence of the prophets, which does not indeed evince absolute repugnance on their part, but certainly proves indifference. Yet it is not, as it might easily seem, one and the same thing which is here left to take care of itself, as already only too deeply engaging the interest of the Israelites, and is there laid upon them, in the name of Yahweh, as a sacred duty. To begin with, what may be called in a single word the *heathen* elements of the popular Yahweh-worship were of course rejected and excluded by the priestly legislator, as they had been by the Deuteronomist before him. And, yet more, the worship acquires under his regulations a character wholly different from that which it had borne before the Babylonian captivity. The change is so great as to constitute an actual breach with the past. The priestly thorah regards the service of Yahweh as existing for its own sake, as an institution that has its own significance and value independently of the participation and the dispositions of those in whose name it is offered to Yahweh.

Accordingly it leaves as little as possible to the initiative of the worshipper. Day by day, on the sabbath, on the feast days, the fixed and accurately defined sacrifices must be laid on the altar. The cost must be met by the community, but in other respects all goes on without its intervention. It is true that free-will offerings are recognized, but they are only considered as secondary. The same is true of vows, which are in some cases rather restrained than encouraged by the law.[1] Connected likewise with this statutory character of the cultus is the priestly estimate of the different kinds of sacrifice. In Deuteronomy, as in the popular usage, the thank-offering still occupies the largest space. Yahweh is as it were the host, "before whose face" the children whom he has blessed "make themselves glad."[2] In the priestly thorah, on the contrary, the burnt offerings and propitiatory sacrifices[3] stand in the foreground. What else, indeed, could we expect after the preceding survey? The pre-exilian practice was out of harmony both with the character of Yahweh, as conceived, for example, by Ezekiel, and with the sense

---

[1] Cf. Religion of Israel, Vol. II. pp. 283—285.

[2] A Deuteronomic formula which occurs in chaps. xii. 7, 12, 18; xiv. 26; xvi. 11, 14; xxvi. 11; xxvii. 7, and is repeated in Lev. xxiii. 40; cf. Isaiah ix. 2 (3); Amos v. 23.

[3] The propitiatory sacrifices are but very seldom mentioned in the pre-exilian literature. 1 Sam. iii. 14; 2 Kings xii. 17 (16), where the reference is to fines in money received by the priests; Deut. xxi. 1—9 (quite different in ritual from the later ordinances). On Hos. iv. 8, which does not come under this category, vid. sup. p. 89.

of sin, aroused and strengthened by the deep humiliation of the people; and it must therefore submit to a drastic change. Moreover, the regulations about cleanness, or rather the inevitable transgressions of them, necessarily involved the multiplication of sin-offerings. Severe punishment of these trespasses, for the most part involuntary, could not be thought of; but the disturbed relation to Yahweh must be restored by sin and guilt offerings, and once a year by the day of atonement.

Is it a higher position that the priestly legislator takes in these ordinances? Or does he estrange himself from "nature and truth" in them? It is enough for me to ask the question and so direct your attention to it. Our present task is not so much to estimate the facts as to state them; but a part of that very statement must be that, together with the priestly thorah as a whole, the Jewish people heartily accepted the worship, as regulated in accordance with its precepts. The fact deserves express mention, because it is not, like the attachment of the old Israel to its offerings and feasts, a thing that completely explains itself. The masses were naturally influenced by the outward splendour of the temple and its servants, and by the solemnity of the devotional ceremonies. But the more highly cultivated likewise came under the spell. To be present at the temple was in the eyes of the pious an inestimable privilege. We may differ in opinion as to what it was that they sought and found there. It has recently been said, not without reason, that "the emotion with which the worshipper approaches the second temple, as recorded in the Psalter, has little to do with sacrifice, but rests rather on the fact that the whole wondrous history of Jehovah's grace to Israel is vividly and personally realized as he stands amidst the festal crowd at the ancient seat of God's throne, and adds his voice to the swelling song of praise."[1] But even if we suppose this applicable only to a comparatively small number, the fact is in any case undeniable that the Levitical cultus was dear to the pious Jew, and that in the temple he felt that he was near to God. The Psalms bear eloquent testimony to this fact. "One thing have I desired of Yahweh; that do I seek after: to dwell in the house of Yahweh all the days of my life, to behold the beauty of Yahweh and to gaze upon his palace."[2] "O Yahweh, dear to me is the abode of thy dwelling, and the place where thy glory abideth."[3] "How lovely are thy dwelling-places, O Yahweh of hosts! My soul has longed and thirsted for Yahweh's courts. My heart and my flesh cry out to the living God!"[4] Why should I cite more passages? The eighty-fourth Psalm, the first verses of which I have just quoted, the forty-second and forty-third Psalms, and many more, have been familiar to us from our childhood. It was the

---

[1] W. Robertson Smith, The Old Testament in the Jewish Church. Twelve Lectures on Biblical Criticism, p. 380, cf. 238 sq.

[2] Psalm xxvii. 4.   [3] Psalm xxvi. 8.

[4] Psalm lxxxiv. 2, 3 (1, 2).

temple of Zerubbabel and Joshua which drew from the poets these tones of fervent longing; it was the priestly ritual for which their hearts so thirsted.

Truly it was no light or insignificant task that the priests of Yahweh had thus accomplished. The conflict between the two conceptions of Yahwism has disappeared. If in the days of Jeremiah they still stood off one from the other so sharply that they might be called, with no great exaggeration, two religions, they are now reconciled. And it is the conception of the small minority that has triumphed. It is true that it has not issued unscathed from the conflict. Something of its idealism is lost, and it has been forced to clothe its spiritual ideas in a material form. The victory has been dearly purchased, but who shall assure us it could have been won on any other terms? We may rest content with the actual result. And yet in one respect we feel that we can hardly do so. Was not the religion of the prophets on the very point of spreading its wings to pass beyond the boundaries of Israelite nationality? In Judaism we have so far found no trace of that ideal or of the attempt to realize it. Nay, even in the preliminary preparations for its establishment, Judaism rudely rejected the foreign elements.[1] It was "they who had severed themselves from the people of the land"[2] who entered, under the guidance of Ezra and Nehemiah, into an

---

[1] Ezra ix. x.   [2] Neh. x. 29 (28).

engagement to live after God's law; and the first point to which they pledged themselves was not to give their daughters to the sons of the land, nor themselves to take the daughters of the land to wife.[1] "Separation," then, was the watchword under which the priestly thorah was introduced. The Jewish people fenced itself round, so to speak, with a host of regulations and customs; and when once it had set foot upon this path, it continued, under the guidance of the Scribes, to advance ever further and further upon it.

Is not this a melancholy repudiation of a glorious past, or at least the frustrating of the promise contained in it? Must the prophetic Yahwism, that had already so far loosened itself from the ties of nationality, now be rivetted once more to a single people,—and that people, after the ten tribes had been severed from it and merged amongst the heathen, too insignificant to be numbered among the nations?

The spectacle of the establishment of Judaism could not fail to produce such an impression. Had we witnessed it, we could have seen nothing in the religion which Ezra and Nehemiah raised to supremacy amongst their people but a *national* institution, in the strictest sense of the term. And nevertheless this view is incomplete and therefore wholly unjust. With the light of succeeding centuries cast back upon these events, we may easily convince ourselves that the international and universal elements were by no means wanting. They do not lie on the surface; but they are there, and we cannot even say that they slumber. It is on this inward aspect of Judaism that our attention must be fixed when next we meet.

IV.

JUDAISM AND CHRISTIANITY.

If we judge Judaism by its first establishment, we must attribute a rigidly national and exclusive character to it. Though not denying this, I have nevertheless asserted that it was not without the internal leaven of universalism. And if it really had appropriated this treasure bequeathed by the prophets, you may reasonably ask where it had concealed it!

To begin with, let us note that the Jewish religion was only in appearance a sub-section of the Jewish national life. In reality, it had an independent existence. Judaism was inaugurated by the public reading of the Law, and continued to bear the character of legalism stamped ever more and more deeply upon it. *The Thorah*—at first the written letter only, afterwards the oral tradition also—passed as the complete revelation of Yahweh's will, and its authority was therefore recognized and reverenced as supreme. From the first this was no mere theory; and it gradually became a more and more palpable fact. For, from Ezra downwards, the Law had its own special representatives amongst the Jews in the persons of *the Scribes;* and thus it ceased to be dependent on the assent of individuals and on their possibly divergent explanations. Not, indeed, that the Scribes were themselves the magistrates and could ensure the carrying out of their decisions, for the fact was the reverse. But this only left them all the more free, and enabled them all the better to consecrate their undivided attention to their task, which accordingly absorbed them so completely that the Thorah soon became their only love. It was to the Thorah, not to the greatness or the freedom of the fatherland, that their hearts were given. They took part in the revolt against Antiochus Epiphanes, but only because he forbade the free exercise of religion, and only as long as the Law was in jeopardy—not a moment longer. When Alcimus, a creature of the Syrians, but a descendant of Aaron, assumed the high-priestly office, they were ready at once to pay him reverence.[1] It was not by them, but by the Hasmonæans, that the war of Jewish freedom was fought out. In harmony with their attitude at this crisis was their conduct under Alexander Jannæus, and during the struggle between Aristobulus and Hyrcanus II.[2] If any one should urge that by such exaggerated indifference to politics they became faithless to the religion

---

[1] 1 Mac. vii. 12—15.

[2] Flavius Josephus, Antiq. xiii. 13, § 5; xiv. 3, § 2.

they upheld, and thus overshot their own mark, I answer that the Jewish people itself judged otherwise. It did not always go with the Scribes, but it never ceased to reverence them as the true representatives of its religion. In such matters as this public opinion is not deceived; and on its authority we may safely assume that, in the centuries immediately preceding the Christian era, it was not impossible to be a deeply religious man and at the same time a lukewarm patriot, or, in other words, that in Judaism religion and nationality were no longer inseparably united.

The Jews, in the dispersion, furnish a striking proof of the fact. We cannot treat this interesting subject in all its bearings here; but we shall presently have to return to it, and must now content ourselves with a few special remarks. The very fact that so many Jews, though far from the soil of the fatherland, remained Jews nevertheless, in itself fully deserves our attention. The phenomenon seems natural enough as long as the abode in a foreign land can be regarded as provisional and temporary—that is to say, during the Babylonian captivity. But when it survives this period, it gives a striking proof of the extent to which religion had already been emancipated from dependence on the conditions of national existence. At what a distance do we stand from the antique idea which finds expression, for instance, in David's well-known appeal to Saul, "If men have stirred thee up against me, they are cursed, for they have driven me out this day from dwelling in Yahweh's heritage, saying to me, 'Go, serve other gods'"![1] But we need not ascend so far for illustrations. In the eighth century B.C., in the kingdom of Ephraim, the Yahwism of the people had still so little independence that it could not survive the shock of transportation to a foreign land. In Palestine, amongst the Assyrian colonists, Yahweh was served;[2] but the exiles of the ten tribes vanish without a trace, together with the religion which alone could have saved them from absorption among the heathen. To the Jews of the diaspora, on the other hand, their Judaism was like a protecting sheath that secured their continued existence.

And, conversely, religion itself must have felt the influence of life in a foreign land, far from the temple and therefore from all the ritual of worship. Whatever could mitigate the loss, was sought out, retained and developed. To this *the synagogue*, more especially, owes its origin. It appears to have been in Babylonia, whether before the end of the captivity or amongst those who remained behind afterwards, that the custom rose of assembling on the Sabbath-day for mutual edification by reading aloud, by exhortation and by prayer. Its influence cannot well be overrated. Whilst in other respects the recognition of but one sanctuary seemed to place Judaism in complete dependence upon the place where that sanctuary stood, the synagogue,

---

[1] 1 Sam. xxvi. 19. [2] Vid. sup. pp. 80 sq.

which could easily be reared anywhere, securing to the Jews of every region the privileges of religious communion, made them attach all the higher value to those spiritual blessings that they could carry with them everywhere. In this way it contributed most powerfully to the independence of religion.

One more aspect of the dispersion of the Jews beyond their fatherland must receive our attention here. Wherever they established themselves, they were brought into continuous and lively intercourse with the people of the land, which must necessarily result, under favourable circumstances, in an interchange of ideas. This could not possibly fail to exercise some influence on the religious ideas of the Jewish colonists. Judaism becomes one thing in the Greek world, at Alexandria for instance, another in Babylonia, and yet another at Rome. Whether all these shades of the one Judaism were possessed of true vitality may reasonably be questioned; but the very fact of their coming into existence at all is a remarkable phenomenon, for it reveals, and cannot fail in its turn to develope, a power of self-adaptation already considerable. What an intensely interesting fact, for instance, is the translation of the Law into the Greek language, as an evidence of what Judaism had already become, even more than as an instrument of future influence upon the heathen world! The whole of Jewish Hellenism, so full of movement and variety, is a striking proof of the capacity for development, and therefore of the independent vitality, of Judaism.

But for all that, it remains confined to the one people of the Jews. It shows, indeed, that even beyond the limits of Judæa it can exercise the same power which it wields within them; but what has come of the universalism that the prophetic conception manifested? We are now to see that there was far more of it left than would be supposed from a superficial examination.

Let us remember, in the first place, that the prophetic ideas had not fallen into oblivion amongst the Jews. As for the Scribes, we know that they devoted their best powers to the Law, to its redaction, and to the application of its precepts to life. Yet even by them the other religious writings of Israel, and specifically the prophetic books, were by no means slighted. It was they who preserved these precious remains from destruction and who multiplied the copies of them. Would it be rash to assume that the pious community still valued the inspired word of Yahweh's emissaries fully as much as the often dry details of the Thorah? In any case, they were made acquainted with the one no less than the other; and for them, too, the hints as to the destiny of Israel's religion were preserved from forgetfulness. When we note how such a man as Jesus ben Sirach (about the year 200 B.C.) reverences the prophets—singling out Isaiah's inspiration to glorify especially [1]—we need not hesitate to ascribe to his people in general, together with a know-

---

[1] Ecclesiasticus xlviii. 24, 25.

ledge of the prophetic writings, the retention of one of the most flattering of the prophetic expectations.

But we are not left to mere probable surmises. Positive proofs are at hand that the prophetic conceptions lived on. Such proofs lie before us in the Psalter. When the poet of the twenty-second Psalm has described the deliverance of the righteous man from his deep humiliation, he adds: "All the ends of the earth shall observe it, and turn unto Yahweh; and before thee shall bow down all the kindreds of the heathen, for to Yahweh belongs dominion, and he rules amongst the peoples."[1] Another psalmist concludes his song of triumph with these words:

> "Yahweh is king over all the peoples,
> Yahweh sits on his holy throne.
> The princes of the nations are gathered together to the god of Abraham,
> For to Yahweh belong the shields of the earth: greatly exalted is he!"[2]

"Thee do the peoples praise, O Yahweh! thee do the peoples, all of them, praise"—so runs the refrain of the sixty-seventh Psalm,[3] which is throughout sung to the glory of Yahweh, the ruler of all the earth, and which utters the hope that "all the ends of the earth" will

---

[1] Psalm xxii. 28, 29 (27, 28).

[2] Psalm xlvii. 9, 10 (8, 9). For "Elohim" I have three times substituted Yahweh, as the poet himself undoubtedly wrote. In v. 10 a (9 a) the pointing of the LXX. is followed.

[3] vv. 4, 6 (3, 5).

fear him, because of the benefits he has conferred upon Israel.[1] The review of Israel's guidance by Yahweh, in the sixty-eighth Psalm, closes with the prayer that kings may bring him treasures to Jerusalem, that nobles may come up from Egypt, and that the Ethiopians may stretch out their hands to him.[2] "Jerusalem, the religious centre of the world," is the theme of the eighty-seventh Psalm. But enough. The Book of Psalms, as a whole, has been called the answer of the community to God's revelation; and amongst its claims to this title we must note the fact that it catches up the promise of the spread of God's dominion, and repeats it as a joyful expectation.

The Book of Daniel, though itself very unlike the writings of the prophets, bears emphatic testimony to the influence which they still continued to exercise. The prediction that within half a week of years the temple which Antiochus Epiphanes had desecrated should be restored to its true purposes, and that "the people of the saints of the Most High" should then assume dominion over the world,[3] is the fruit, as the writer himself tells us,[4] of his study in "the books," and especially Jeremiah's prophecies. Circumstances conspired to draw him more especially to the political aspects of the Messianic predictions; and who shall

---

[1] v. 8 (7).

[2] Psalm lxviii. 30, 32 (29, 31), partly imitated from Isaiah xviii. 7.

[3] Dan. ix. 24—27; vii. 25—27, &c.   [4] Dan ix. 2.

blame him for thinking in the first instance of the frustration of the heathens' attack upon Yahweh, or for regarding the humbling of their pride as the most urgent need of the moment? But even he looks to the acknowledgment of Yahweh's supremacy by the peoples as the result of their approaching chastisement. His Nebucadrezar cannot escape this supremacy, and therefore himself gives his subjects an account of the punishment which had fallen on his self-exaltation, and which had only been removed when he humbled himself;[1] while Darius the Mede issues a decree "that men should bow down and tremble, throughout his whole kingdom, before the God of Daniel, for he is the living God, who abides to eternity, whose kingdom passes not away, and whose dominion endures to the end."[2]

But why call in more witnesses, and prove the influence of prophetic ideas on the later apocalypses likewise? We can already see, clearly enough, that there was small danger of the Jews being content to take rank simply as one out of the many nations of the earth, and to claim no more for their religion on the part of the heathen than mere toleration. However distinctly their Thorah may have seemed to be designed, and however clearly it gradually showed itself to be calculated to sever them from other nations and as it were shut them in, yet in so far as they

---

[1] Dan. iv.   [2] Dan. vi. 27 (26).

listened to the voice of their prophets they could not possibly regard this isolation as the complete realization of their destiny.

But is it quite correct, after all, to regard the Thorah as exclusively directed to the formation of a single people, consecrated to Yahweh? This much at least is certain, that it is placed in a framework that promises far more than this. I refer especially to the historical introduction to the priestly laws, which, even in its present fusion with the Yahwistic narratives, dominates the whole, gives it its colour and character, and determines the impression which it leaves on the reader. The conception of this introduction is indeed sublime.[1] It is that of a progressive revelation of God, with the Sinaitic legislation as its key-stone. *Elohim* creates the heaven and the earth in six days, and hallows the seventh day, on which he rests from his labour. The blessing which he pronounces on the first human pair he subsequently repeats after the rescue of Noah and his family from the flood; whilst at the same time he lays his commandments upon the new race of men, and establishes the rainbow as the sign of the covenant he has made. To Abraham he reveals himself as *El Shaddai*, God Almighty; and enters into a closer relationship with him and his posterity, the seal of which is circumcision. Mindful of this, he takes pity on Jacob's posterity in

---

[1] Compare with what follows, Religion of Israel, Vol. II. pp. 158—173.

Egypt, reveals himself to Moses as *Yahweh*, redeems the people, by the hand of Moses and Aaron, from slavery, leads them to Sinai, where he declares how he desires to be served, and finally, when a dwelling has been built for him, establishes himself in the midst of Israel. "There"—at the altar before the tent of meeting—"will I draw near to the sons of Israel, and it (the altar) shall be hallowed by my glory. And I will hallow the tent of meeting and the altar, and Aaron and his sons will I hallow to serve me as priests. And I will dwell in the midst of the sons of Israel and be to them for a god. And they shall know that I, Yahweh, am their god, who have brought them up out of Egypt, to dwell in their midst. I, Yahweh, am their god!"[1]

To our feeling there is a want of congruity in this progression, which begins with the creation of the world and at first embraces all mankind, and yet culminates in minute precepts about the sanctuary, the priests and their vestments, the sacrifices and ceremonial cleanness—precepts which, by their very nature, can only be put into practice within the narrow limits of one small people. Even when we substitute for the ritualistic code the purpose it was meant to serve, viz. the formation of a community consecrated to Yahweh, the disproportion still remains. It may be partly explained by the course which the development of reli-

---

[1] Exod. xxix. 43—46.

gious ideas had taken in Israel. The god of that one people gradually became, in the conception of his worshippers, the Only One, and therefore in reality too exalted for the limited relations within which he was still confined. In the prophets, whom we have learned to recognize as the authors of this transformation, the result, for a variety of reasons, appears far less repellent. In them we see it, as it were, ripening before our very eyes. Their conception of the service of Yahweh is spiritual and ethical, and the majority of them at any rate do not fail to contemplate the spread of Yahwism in wider circles. In the priestly thorah, on the other hand, the contrast between the point of departure and the point arrived at is most palpable. The system erected on the broad basis of a theory that embraces heaven and earth is very carefully finished, —but of very minute proportions!

The real question, however, is not whether *we* are struck by a want of consistency in this, but whether the authors of the priestly thorah and the Scribes who followed them were themselves conscious of the discordancy. In my opinion, we can hardly doubt that they were. In the days of Ezra and Nehemia, Malachi appears as a prophet. Yahweh, so he declares, will not accept the lean and blemished sacrificial beasts which the priests are not ashamed to offer him; "for," says he, "from the rising of the sun to its setting, my name is great amongst the heathen, and in all places is incense offered to my name and a pure sacrifice, for my name is great among the heathen."[1] And immediately afterwards: "For I am a great king, and my name is feared amongst the heathen."[2] These words have been incorrectly referred to the Jews in the dispersion, but—to say nothing of the fact that by the middle of the fifth century B.C. they had not yet spread through the heathen world, "from the rising of the sun to its setting"—the Jews could not be said to offer incense and sacrifice to Yahweh " in all places," for they were only permitted by the Law to do so at the temple of Jerusalem. Neither can Malachi's utterance be taken as a prediction. The original will bear no such interpretation; and besides, the prophet cannot have recognized any place of sacrifice except Jerusalem even in the future. No! the reference is distinctly to the adoration already offered to Yahweh by the peoples, whenever they serve their own gods with true reverence and honest zeal. Even in Deuteronomy the adoration of these other gods by the nations is represented as a dispensation of Yahweh.[3] Malachi goes a step further, and accepts their worship as a tribute which in reality falls to Yahweh,—to Him, the Only True. Thus the opposition between Yahweh and the other gods, and afterwards between the one true God and the imaginary gods, makes room here for the still higher conception that the adoration of Yahweh is the essence and the truth of all religion.

Why have we dwelt so long, in this connection, upon a single prophetic utterance? Because the man who spoke it stood by the cradle of Judaism. His contemporaries, the authors of the priestly thorah, in all probability did not share his ideal conception of heathendom; but their monotheism and that of their followers was as pure and as absolute as his. Now, if this be so, is it not almost monstrous to suppose that they expected the true religion to be *ultimately* confined to the single Jewish people? Or if we shrink from making any decisive assertions about them individually, are we to believe that all who accepted the Thorah, with its broad historical premises, were reconciled to its permanent destination for the Jews alone? Here was an antinomy which may not have been generally recognized, but of which some at least could not fail to be conscious, even if unable as yet to perceive how it could be resolved.

At one point we see the universalistic principles breaking through the shell, as it were. I refer to the regulations of the priestly thorah concerning *the gérim*, the strangers settled in Israel, who must be distinguished alike from the aliens and from the foreign labourers who merely passed through the land. "One law shall there be for the stranger and for the home-born." Such is the rule which the lawgiver lays down[1] and applies to special cases. Even in the seventeenth chapter of

---

[1] Exod. xii. 49; Levit. xxiv. 22; Num. ix. 14; xv. 29.

Genesis the "gêrîm" are included in the ordinance of circumcision;[1] and in the Sinaitic legislation they come under the precepts of the ritual,[2] under the regulations as to cleanness,[3] and under the general criminal law.[4] They likewise share the privilege of admission to the feast of the passover.[5] Now these ordinances unquestionably characterize the spirit of the priestly lawgivers. With respect to one of them, we may demonstrate this very clearly by comparing it with the more ancient precepts from which it diverges. "Ye shall be holy men unto me, and flesh that has been torn in the field by beasts ye shall not eat. Ye shall cast it to the dogs." So runs the ordinance in the Book of the Covenant.[6] The Deuteronomist doubtless had it in view when he wrote: "Thou shalt not eat anything that dieth of itself. To the stranger that is within thy gates shalt thou give it, that he may eat it; or thou shalt sell it to the alien, for thou art a people hallowed unto Yahweh, thy god."[7] Here, then, is a contrast resting on a religious distinction. What is forbidden to the Israelite is allowed to the "gér" in the gates, because he does not belong to the people chosen by Yahweh. Now let us listen to the priestly thorah:

---

[1] Gen. xvii. 12, 13, 23, 27; cf. Exod. xii. 44.
[2] Levit. xvii. 8; Num. ix. 14; xv. 29.
[3] Levit. xvi. 29; xvii. 10, 13, 15, 16.
[4] Levit. xxiv. 16, 22.
[5] Exod. xii. 48, cf. 19; Num. ix. 14.
[6] Exod. xxii. 30 (31).   [7] Deut. xiv. 21 a.

"Every one who eats what has died of itself or has been torn of beasts, *be he home-born or stranger*, shall wash his clothes and bathe himself in water and be unclean till the evening. And if he wash not (his clothes) and bathe not his body, he shall bear his sin," i.e. he shall suffer punishment.[1] Here no distinction is made any longer. The prohibition has become intrinsically binding. The practice against which it is directed is not to be allowed at all, either in a stranger or an Israelite. It is true that the precept is at the same time weakened by the indication of a means of escaping the penalty. Any one who will take the trouble to purify himself may now break the commandment with impunity. But in the form in which he still upholds it, the priestly legislator applies it to every one that belongs to the *community*. This conception of the "community" has now become local instead of genealogical. Is there progress here? In one sense there is not. The underlying religious idea which is expressed in its purity in the Book of the Covenant, and is still preserved by the Deuteronomist, is almost obliterated in the priestly thorah. But against this we must weigh the fact that the latter oversteps the boundary-line between Israel and the peoples, and does so in full consciousness of what it is doing.

Might we not assume that experience had led the

---

[1] Levit. xvii. 15, 16.

authors to this momentous step? Even during the Babylonian captivity, or at any rate in the period immediately following the return, it seems not to have been unusual for strangers to unite themselves with the Israelitish community. To the author of "the oracle concerning Babel," incorporated in the prophecies of Isaiah, this extension of the circle of Yahweh's worshippers was still a thing of the future, though on the point of being realized. For he proclaims in the same breath that "Yahweh will have pity on Jacob, and will choose Israel once more, and will plant them in their land," and "that the strangers will join on to them and cleave to the house of Jacob."[1] To the second Isaiah—or more probably a still later prophet—this joining on is an accomplished fact, and his heart impels him to utter the words of cheer: "Let not the alien who has joined himself to Yahweh say: Surely Yahweh will sever me from his people!"[2] There is no ground, says the prophet, for any such fear; for "the aliens who join themselves to Yahweh to serve him and to love the name of Yahweh and be his servants, all who take heed not to desecrate the sabbath and who keep my covenant, I will bring to my holy mountain and will make glad in my house of prayer.

---

[1] Isaiah xiv. 1. The word here and subsequently translated "join themselves on" is the Niph'al of the Hebrew "lawah." Cf. S. Maybaum, die Entwickelung des altisraelitischen Priesterthums, S. iv. ff.

[2] Isaiah lvi. 3.

Their burnt-offerings and thank-offerings shall be acceptable to me, for my house shall be called a house of prayer for all the peoples."[1] In the face of the facts to which this utterance bears witness, the lawgiver was compelled to take up a definite position. Was he in full agreement with the prophet just quoted? It may well be doubted.[2] He was very likely more in accord with Ezra, who began his work in Judæa with such stern measures against the strangers. Yet in one point at least he tempers his exclusiveness. The "gêrim" are received into grace, and incorporated, not into Israel, but into the community. We might have wished and perhaps expected more, but this must not prevent our recognizing the great significance of even this first step. Judaism is extending its borders. Proselytism has begun. The very word by which this phenomenon is designated is the Greek translation of the Hebrew "gér," which was gradually applied to those who had attached themselves to Israel rather than to those who had no portion in it. We will not "despise the day of small things"[3]—mindful of the stone which was quarried by no human hand and became a great mountain and filled the whole earth.[4] Before the collection of Psalms was closed, "they that feared Yahweh," i.e. the proselytes, had already taken their place after "Israel" and "the

---

[1] Isaiah lvi. 6, 7.   [2] On Levit. xxii. 25, see Note X.
[3] Zech. iv. 10 a.   [4] Dan. ii. 34, 35.

house of Aaron," and had heard the exhortation of the temple-choir addressed to them also: "Praise Yahweh, for he is good, for his mercy endureth for ever."[1]

We see, then, that from the first Judaism was something more than it seemed, something more than one of the many forms of religion exclusively destined and adapted to one single people. It now becomes my task to point out how this promise of something broader and more exalted was fulfilled, or, in other words, how there grew up out of Judaism a world-religion—Christianity.

The general outlines of the history of Judaism and the fates of the Jewish people down to the fall of Jerusalem will be assumed as familiar. We shall only dwell upon such portions of them as are needed to enable us to see and understand this one noteworthy transition from national to universal religion. On the other hand, I shall not attempt to shut out the light that shines back from Christianity itself upon the earlier centuries. Rather shall I seek to trace the antecedents of Christianity in Judaism as expressly as the advance and internal development of Judaism in the direction of a religion of the world. We must freely acknowledge that the phenomena which we now describe in this way as an advance and development, would have appeared far less striking and far less

---

[1] Ps. cxv. 9—11; cxviii. 2—4; cxxxv. 19, 20.

important had we not known in what they really issued. Why, then, should we affect to look at the facts as they were seen by contemporaries, rather than under the aspects which later generations only could perceive and estimate?

But while preparing for the task thus defined and limited, I am met by an objection which, whatever else we may think of it, has at least the merit of going to the root of the matter. "The 'development' of which you are speaking"—so I am told—"is simply a fiction. Judaism did no doubt develope—into Talmudism. Christianity rose on the soil of Judaism, but to derive or explain it from it is a hopeless task. It is a new creation, and we can no more understand it without the person of its founder than we can regard that founder himself as the product of his time and his people. Would you explain Jesus away? If not, re-cast your question. By formulating it as you have done, you secure in advance the impossibility of a solution."

My answer may be short and simple. Before all things let me declare that I have no thought of ignoring the person of Jesus or lowering its high significance. To me, too, the rise of Christianity would be an insoluble riddle were I to set aside him who for eighteen centuries has taken rank as its founder. Whence he sprang —from Israel or from God, as it is sometimes, but I think very incorrectly, put—we need not now decide. Our opinions on this subject may possibly diverge widely. But I may rely on the assent of all in declaring that what Jesus founded can only be called a new *creation* in a very improper sense of the word. "If there be such a thing as creation out of nothing, then it is the incommunicable prerogative of the Deity, and must be left out of consideration in reviewing any human development."[1] In the course of the history of our race, nothing comes into existence that does not link itself on to what exists already, that does not—however new and unheard-of it may be—presuppose the existing state of things, and become impossible, even in imagination, when detached from it. As far as our knowledge reaches, the spiritual life of man, especially including religion, is likewise subject to this law. Are we to admit an exception in the case of the rise of Christianity? Unquestionably we must, if adequate grounds can be shown for doing so. But this is far from being the case. Nay, Ernest Renan could say from this very chair, "Christianity at its origin is no other than Judaism;"[2] and even those who are far from giving him their assent must admit that the points of contact and agreement are innumerable. In Holland, not long ago, a Jewish scholar summed up in the following thesis the result of a comparison with the Talmud carried through the first

---

[1] S. Hoekstra Bz., de ontwikkeling van de zedelijke idee in de geschiedenis, bl. 114.

[2] On the Influence of the Institutions, Thought and Culture of Rome on Christianity (The Hibbert Lectures, 1880), pp. 16 sq.

chapter of the Sermon on the Mount. "The ethics of the gospel are no other than appear in the Talmud, are the same that were handled in the schools of the Sopherim and the Tannaïtes, the same that are held as law to this day by the Talmud-Jews."[1] You think this is far too strongly expressed, and I am the first to acknowledge that it cannot be accepted till fenced with many reservations.[2] But the agreement exists, and it is simply impossible to deny it. If so, how can we set Christianity and Talmudic Judaism diametrically opposite to each other, and deny the connection of the one, while asserting that of the other, with the Judaism of an earlier time? Such a method would be utterly unhistorical, and our duty clearly lies in another direction. We must be equally on our guard against hasty identification and against explaining away a connection which the facts themselves proclaim. When Christianity was founded, it is clear that materials borrowed from Judaism were employed. What were they? Such is the question we are now seeking to answer. And even in asking it we have marked off the character of our investigation more accurately than was possible before. It is not the founding of Christianity itself that I am attempting to describe to you; nor is it the person and the work of its founder. Let that remain for one of my successors in this place. I shall deem

---

[1] T. Tal. Een Blik in Talmoed en Evangelie, bl. 126.

[2] Cf. H. Oort, Evangelie en Talmud, uit het oogpunt der zedelijkheid vergeleken, bl. 37 vv., 97 vv., and elsewhere.

that I have done enough if I can show you in the Judaism of the commencement of our era the indispensable antecedents of the work of Jesus, and if I can enable you to see in what he established the fulfilment of the promise which, as we know already, lay in the Yahwism of the prophets.

But no sooner have we disposed of this first objection than we are faced by another equally fundamental. If the former disputed the possibility of discovering the origins of Christianity at all, the latter challenges our selection of the field on which to seek them. For have we not assumed that it is *in Judaism* that we shall find the antecedents of Christianity? We can certainly appeal to tradition in confirmation of this view; but what if this tradition be nothing more than a venerable prejudice? "The origin of Christianity from Roman Griechenthum"—so runs the untranslatable second title of Bruno Bauer's "Christ and the Caesars."[1] Do not suppose that I am about to attempt, by way of an episode, a refutation of this singular book! When I tell you that Seneca and Philo of Alexandria appear in its pages as the founders of Christianity, probably but few of you will wish to hear anything more of it. And yet the eccentricities of this veteran writer deserved mention. A traditional opinion can only be safely

---

[1] Christus und die Cäsaren. Der Ursprung des Christenthums aus dem römischen Griechenthum, von B. Bauer (2e [Titel-] Aufl. 1879). Cf. the further illustration of some of the details in Das Urevangelium und die Gegner der Schrift: "Christus und die Cäsaren" (1880).

followed when it has borne the test of a searching criticism. Now Bruno Bauer's book has demonstrated once for all that in order to make the denial of the Jewish origin of Christianity look, I will not say like the truth, but like a theory capable of discussion, we must set aside the whole of the New Testament, the well-known testimonies of Tacitus, Suetonius, Pliny the Younger and—one might almost say everything else! Here we must deny and reverse all things, there we must ascribe conclusive evidential force to accidental or trivial details, before we can gain even the semblance of a right to come forward with such a denial. The Apocalypse alone, regarded as the work of Galba's contemporary, or even as written under Domitian, is enough to demolish Bauer's reconstruction of history. Any one of the Pauline Epistles annihilates it. Not only the Founder of Christianity, but Paul and Peter with him, must be banished to the realm of fiction. In a word, we must give full swing —no longer to criticism, but to pure caprice. Truly a tradition that can only be attacked across such ruins as these is for the present safe enough. Roman "Griechenthum" must remain content with the secondary but by no means unimportant part which has long been assigned it in the spread and development of that Christianity which sprang up quite outside it.[1]

---

[1] Cf. further, Note XI., where the relation of Bauer's thesis to that of E. Davet in " Le Christianisme et ses Origines" (Tom. I. II. l'Hellénisme; Tom. III. Le Judaisme) is also dealt with.

P. 192, n. 1, for "Davet," read "Havet."

With confidence, then, we approach our task; but at the very outset we find once more that the ways part. The Judaism in which we are to seek the materials for the edifice of Christianity is a complex phenomenon. Where are we to make our search? In Hellenism, in Palestinian Judaism, or in both? It will be no small simplification of our work if we can make sure of this at the outset. Nor does it seem impossible to do so. Let us begin by defining the point at issue. It would be a mistake to imagine that the foreign or at any rate the Greek-speaking Jews, the so-called Hellenists, all without distinction followed one line of development, diverging from that of the Palestinian leaders. Very many of these Greek Jews, even in Alexandria, and still more elsewhere, placed themselves under the guidance of the mother community, and reflected, in their own way of course, the varied shades of opinion which might there be observed. More than one of the Greek Apocrypha of the Old Testament might have been written in Palestine, as far as the ideas it expresses go. The author of the Second Book of the Maccabees, for instance, is a Pharisee of the Pharisees. It must be understood, therefore, that when we contrast Hellenism with Palestinian Judaism, we mean by the former that peculiar fusion of Judaism and Greek philosophy which took place more especially at Alexandria, which has left in the apocryphal Book of Wisdom a sample of what it produced, but which finds its true representative and spokesman in Philo.

The real question, therefore, is whether, not indeed Philo himself, but the movement which culminated in him, must be reckoned amongst the factors of the nascent Christendom, or perhaps regarded as the most important of them all. The temptation to answer this question in the affirmative is great. Indeed, if it were but a little modified, the affirmative answer would be the true one. In very early years Hellenism began to exercise an influence on the conception and presentation of Christian truth. In the Christian religion which spread amongst the heathen, a Hellenistic element was already incorporated. Paul had felt its power; it continued to work amongst his followers; and the Logos doctrine of the fourth Gospel is essentially that of Philo. The earliest development of Christianity, then, assuredly did not take place outside the influence of Hellenism. But in granting this, we are at the same time laying down the limits within which that influence worked. Hellenism did not contribute to the *rise* or the foundation of Christianity. In the first three Gospels we find no trace of it. Yet it is here that the teaching of the Founder of Christianity is presented to us in its most original form; and if the atmosphere which he and his first disciples breathed had really been impregnated with Hellenistic ideas, we could hardly have failed to detect them here.

And might we not have anticipated that this would be the outcome of a comparative study of the documents of Christianity? At any rate, when the result is obtained, it is easy to see how completely it corresponds to the first impression which Hellenism and the earliest Christianity make upon us when compared together. We shall not challenge the place of honour taken by Philo and the Hellenistic school in general, in the history of the development of religious and ethical ideas. Their idealism, the broad and humane spirit of their moral exhortations, deserve, together with their universalism, no stinted praise. But yet there is something in their writings that is always coming between us and them to disturb our sympathy; something that ever represses our rising assent when we are just on the point of being carried away. It is, in a word, their want of naturalness, their artificiality and affectation, that produce this feeling of constraint. We may conceive, though not without difficulty, how Philo contrived to combine dependence upon Greek philosophy with reverence for the divine authority of the Law. We may persuade ourselves, though this too needs an effort, that he really believed in his own method, and considered that his allegorical interpretation of Scripture was justified. But what semblance of enthusiasm can possibly rise in us as we follow his intricate argumentation? It is not the lordly flight of the eagle, but the astounding feats of the acrobat, that we witness. We are struck with admiration indeed, but still more with astonishment. And now I would ask, Where in all this is the power that can produce a new religion? Christian *theology* might gain much from Hellenism, and accordingly made ample—perhaps too ample—use of it. But the Christian *religion* cannot have sprung from this fountain. It remains undeniable that Philo and the gospel touch each other at diverse points, often reflect identical religious dispositions, and have many maxims of morality in common; but in essence and in character they are severed. However far you produce the line on which Hellenism is moving, it will not bring you to Christianity.

Before closing this preliminary review, I will once more state in unequivocal terms the position from which I have started. The international religion which we call Christianity was founded, not by the Apostle Paul, but by Jesus of Nazareth—that Jesus whose person and whose teaching are sketched in the Synoptic Gospels with the closest approximation to truth. The celebrated Edward von Hartmann has done us the service of formulating the opposite opinion with his customary clearness and incisiveness. In his History of the Development of the Religious Consciousness of Man,[1] Jesus appears as the founder of "das Judenchristenthum," a Jewish sect or heresy, or rather a mere phase or shade of Judaism, yielding to none of the schools that then existed in rigid orthodoxy and national exclusiveness, and only departing from the ruling official idea in this,—that it turned to the poor and despised, and, by preaching the near approach of

---

[1] Das religiöse Bewusstsein der Menscheit im Stufengang seiner Entwickelung (1882).

the kingdom of God, endeavoured to convert them and to raise them up to perfect righteousness after the Law.[1] Out of this Jewish Christianity, which had no enduring worth and no future, Paul made a religion of the world by interpreting the atoning death and the resurrection of the Messiah as the condemnation of the legal point of view, and so removing the barrier between Jews and heathens, and making Jewish monotheism accessible to all the world.[2] I spoke of the *service* rendered by von Hartmann in respect to the historical problem on which we are now engaged, and you may perhaps be inclined to ask wherein the service consists. I find it in the fact that the identification of religion and dogmatics, which pervades almost the whole of his book, is here driven to such a point, and the onesidedness of the view brought out so clearly, that one would say the author had expressly set himself to cure us of it for ever. There is indeed but little to urge against his thesis if we begin by regarding the formula of universalism as the all-important matter, for this formula appears far more clearly and explicitly in the teaching

---

[1] Ibid. S. 514—532. See especially S. 529 : "diese judenchristliche Richtung, die man nicht einmal eine Sekte innerhalb des Judenthums nennen konnte ;" S. 530 : "das Judenchristenthum war das für die Armen und Elenden in Judäa mundgerechtgemachte Judenthum ;" S. 525 : "das Judenchristenthum nichts anderes als nationaljüdische Gesetzesreligion mit verstärkter messianischen Erwartung und mit bestimmter Beziehung dieser messianischen Erwartung auf die Persönlichkeit eines bei Lebzeiten verkannten und getödteten Propheten."

[2] Ibid. S. 546 ff.

of the Apostle to the Gentiles than in the earliest accounts of Jesus. And yet the former preached, not himself, but "Jesus Christ, and him crucified."[1] Are we to suppose that he did not know what he was doing? That it was only a blunder or a certain irony of fate that made him tack on his preaching of "there is no difference"[2] to the person of a well-meaning, upright, amiable, but singularly legalistic and narrow-minded Jew?[3] Let him believe it who can! Those who, like myself, reject it as little better than absurd, will also allow that the religion of the world already existed in principle when Paul began to spread it amongst the heathen. We may therefore advance fearlessly on the path that lies before us. There, in the Judaism of Palestine, we may perhaps discover something more than the antecedents of von Hartmann's "Judenchristenthum," and may thus find our method, in the merits of which we are already confident, justified at last by the result also.

---

[1] 1 Cor. i. 23; ii. 2.

[2] Rom. iii. 22; x. 12; cf. Gal. iii. 28.

[3] Cf. von Hartmann, l.c. S. 551 sq. All that is there granted is: "Andrerseits konnte er (Paulus) nicht daran zweifeln, dass Jesus, wenn derselbe das paulinische Evangelium zu lehren für opportun gehalten hätte, es hätte lehren *können*, da er sonst sein Wissen von demselben nicht auf eine Offenbarung Jesu Christi hätte beziehen können." No research was necessary, however, since the cancelling of the law was already (logically) established. On the question itself, see A. H. Blom, Paulinische Studiën, ii. and vii., in Theol. Tijdschrift, 1879, bl. 344 vv.; 1881, bl. 53 vv.

Upon Palestinian Judaism, then, our attention must be fixed from this point onwards. But it must be Palestinian Judaism as a whole, and not simply some *one* of the religious schools into which it was divided at the time of which we are speaking. An express declaration on this subject is needed; for there is one of these schools or parties which certain writers are never weary of attempting to bring into close and even immediate connection with Christianity. It is *Essenism*. The secret of this persistency is not hard to discover. It is revealed as soon as we notice the form under which the theory in question is generally presented to us. It is that of the romance. Almost all the accounts of Jesus which attempt the so-called "natural" explanation of his life—including the most recent, published not long ago in this country[1]—make him an Essene, or at any rate give him Essenic antecedents. This hypothesis is indeed the only one that feeds the fancy. Philo and Flavius Josephus have given us a graphic picture of the life of the Essenes,[2] the charm of which we cannot deny, and which needs little embellishment to serve as the background of a romantic history of Jesus. There is another reason, of a more serious nature, which prompts the ever-repeated attempt

---

[1] Rabbi Jeshua. An Eastern Story (London, 1881).

[2] Philo, Quod Omnis Probus Liber, § 12, and Apol. pro Judæis fragm. apud Euseb. in Præp. Evang. viii. 11; Josephus, Antiqq. xiii. 5, § 9; xv. 10, §§ 4, 5; Bell. Jud. II. 8, §§ 2—14.

to seize upon Essenism in explanation of the origin of Christianity. Essenism itself has been represented—I might almost say obstinately—as resulting from the action of foreign influences upon Palestinian Judaism. Josephus himself gave the lead in a certain way, and he has his followers even yet. The Hellenism thus supposed to be the immediate parent of the Essenes next affords the opportunity of bringing them into indirect connection with various systems of Greek philosophy, with Zarathustra, and even with Buddhism. And so, finally, if the Essenes in their turn contributed to the rise of Christianity, then a means has been found of bringing the latter into connection with the West or with the Eastern religions, and the enigma of its origin is supposed to be brought at any rate a step nearer to its solution.

But the question why the hypothesis of a close connection between Christianity and Essenism is attractive to many minds, and is therefore readily accepted by them, must of course yield to the inquiry whether there is really any adequate reason to suppose that such a connection existed. Now, unless I am much mistaken, the negative answer to this latter question, which always had probability on its side, has recently been supported so conclusively that ere long every one must accept it. In the first place, it is now established that Essenism is a *Jewish* phenomenon, and specifically a product of *Palestinian* Judaism. When it was noticed that Essenism rose towards the middle of the second century B.C., immediately after the attempt of Antiochus Epiphanes to hellenize the Jewish people, its Palestinian origin could not but be regarded as highly probable *a priori*. When it had been shown[1] that almost every trait of the life and thought of the Essenes finds its parallel in Talmudic Judaism, the probability rose almost to certainty. But yet the hypothesis of a foreign origin still had a safe retreat in *the Therapeutæ*, that enigmatical colony of ascetics, on the Mareotid lake in Egypt, upon whom Philo pronounced so glowing a panegyric in his treatise, "De Vita Contemplativa." In spite of all differences, there was still so much similarity between these Therapeutæ and the Essenes that it was impossible not to bring them into connection with each other; and since, for many reasons, the Therapeutæ could not be derived from the Essenes, what remained but to represent the latter as having come from the former? And this again opened a channel, albeit a circuitous one, by which heathen, and especially Neo-Pythagorean, influences might be supposed to have flowed into Palestine. I do not say that this view was open to no objection, but it was one for which something might be said, and which actually had defenders of no mean rank.[2] But what has now happened? It was no new matter for the

---

[1] Cf. H. Graetz, Gesch. der Juden, III. 657 ff. (3te Ausg.), and the essays of Frankel there quoted; also J. Derenbourg, Hist. de la Palestine d'après les Talmuds, &c., p. 166 svv.

[2] E.g. Zeller. See note 2 on next page.

Philonic treatise "De Vita Contemplativa" to excite the suspicion of attentive readers, and provoke surmises of spuriousness and a later origin.¹ But until lately it was impossible to say that criticism had completed its task with regard to this book, and the hypotheses concerning its antiquity and its purpose continued to be widely divergent. The blank has now been filled. A young Strassburg scholar has succeeded in obtaining a satisfactory answer to the riddle. The treatise was composed in the third century, or quite at the beginning of the fourth, in defence and commendation of the asceticism then practised by many Christians. It was, therefore, written by a Christian, but in the name of Philo, from whom, in accordance with his assumed character, the author borrowed many thoughts, and to whose genuine writings he tacked on his essay.² This demonstration has been accepted by the most competent judges, including those who had previously espoused a different opinion.³ And herewith falls the last prop of the foreign origin of Essenism, the purely Jewish character of which is now finally established.

We come next to the connection of Essenism itself

---

[1] Cf. Religion of Israel, Vol. III. pp. 217—223, & the writers mentioned there.

[2] P. E. Lucius, die Therapeuten und ihre Stellung in der Gesch. der Askese. Eine kritische Untersuchung der Schrift *de vita contemplativa* (Strassburg, 1880).

[3] Amongst others, by E. Schürer, in Theol. Literaturzeitung, 1880, Sp. 111—118, and A. Hilgenfeld, in Zeitschr. f. wissensch. Theol. XXIII. (1880), S. 423 ff.

with Christianity. The hypothesis of this connection has been supported by proofs which cannot bear the test of serious inquiry even for a moment. When Graetz, for instance, draws a parallel between the Essenic doctrine of the Messiah and the kingdom of heaven and the corresponding Christian conception,[1] we ask in amazement what sources he commands whence he can derive any knowledge of this Essenic doctrine? There are other arguments which, though not fictitious like this one, are nevertheless counterbalanced by others no less weighty than themselves, and are therefore inconclusive. The agreement of Essenism and primitive Christianity in certain moral precepts, their common rejection of the oath, and their similarity in fostering the spirit of brotherhood, are insisted upon on the one side; but on the other we note the difference of their views as to personal ceremonial cleanness and the observance of the sabbath, points in which the Essenes were as strict as the first Christians were lax or indifferent. In my opinion, this weighing of the *pro* and *contra* must by itself result in a declaration of the independence of Christianity. The agreement is in details of secondary importance, the difference is one of principle. Essenic separatism, the formation of a small and strictly closed society to realize the ideal of ceremonial purity, has nothing Christian in it; and conversely the Christian propaganda for the rescuing of sinners is in

---

[1] l.c. S. 292, with a reference to Note 10, iii., that is, to S. 662, where, however, no resemblance of a proof is offered.

no way Essenic. The truth of the matter is, that to enable us to uphold the identity of the two, we must first create an Essenism of our own invention. And yet I must admit that this line of argument does not silence all opposition. Accentuate your review of Essenism differently, regard the severance from society, for example, not as a part of the ideal, but simply as a means dictated by necessity, and you will at once reach a different conclusion with regard to the point at issue. Now, if I am not mistaken, a hypothesis put forward by the same scholar whom I have mentioned already, offers us the prospect of bringing this apparently endless controversy to a satisfactory conclusion. It was shown but now that we had already found very firm ground beneath our feet in deriving Essenism from Palestinian Judaism. We were already practically certain that the Essenes sprang from the "hasidím" or "devout" who appear more than once in the accounts of the revolt against Antiochus Epiphanes.[1] But we had not yet found any answer to the question what it was precisely that drove the Essenes out of Jewish society, and was thus the immediate occasion of the rise of the Essenic *order*. This immediate cause of severance has now been discovered in the opposition to the high-priests Jason, Menelaus and Alcimus, afterwards persevered in against the Hasmonæan successors

---

[1] 1 Macc. ii. 42, vii. 12 sqq.—irreconcilable with 2 Macc. xiv. 6, as has been shown, most recently, by Lucius in the treatise referred to below, S. 91 ff.

of these tyrants,—men of a very different spirit, indeed, but whose appointment did not, any more than theirs, come up to the strict requirements of legalism. The erection of the temple of Onias at Leontopolis in Egypt, and its continuance down to the year 70 A.D., as well as the attitude assumed by the Scribes towards the Hasmonæan high-priests, are, on this hypothesis, parallel phenomena, which bring out the significance of the Essenic secession all the more clearly.[1] Now, we may question whether Lucius is right in deriving almost all the usages of the Essenes from their special attitude towards the *personnel* of the temple staff; whether, for instance, their common meals should be regarded as an imitation of the sacrificial feasts, from which they found themselves excluded; or whether the presents they sent to the sanctuary at Jerusalem, at which they never appeared themselves, are to be looked upon as an ever renewed protest against the servants of the temple: but in any case, if the breach with Jewish society had the cause which is now suggested, it is perfectly natural that avoidance of the national sanctuary should be the distinguishing mark of the Essenes. By relaxing this point they would, in their own estimation, have lost their *raison d'être*. The application of all this to our subject is obvious. A connection between Essenism and Christianity can no longer be thought of. Scruples against participation in the temple ser-

---

[1] P. E. Lucius, der Essenismus in seinem Verhältniss zum Judenthum (Strassburg, 1881), especially S. 75 ff.

vice, or doubts as to the legitimacy of the officiating high-priest, are things which it has never yet entered any man's head to attribute to the Founder of Christianity or to the earliest Christians. If any reliance whatever is to be placed on the accounts we possess, then such ideas were entirely foreign to them, and their attitude towards the sanctuary was that of the nation at large. But in that case they were not Essenes, either in the narrower sense (so much we had long known) or in the broader; for it was just this personal participation in the common worship that placed the other Jews outside the boundary-line which circumscribed the Essenic order.

Does it follow that we must leave the Essenes altogether out of view in the research upon which we are engaged? Not at all. They are of great service to us in our diagnosis of Palestinian Judaism. At a given moment the order severed itself from the parent stem and went on its own way. But the very things which it henceforth displays within narrow compass, and therefore all the more distinctly, must have come with it in germ and principle as the legacy of its earlier and still dependent life, and must therefore have lived and worked in the Jewish people also. If the birth of Essenism is in itself a witness to the power of religion in those days, so likewise the form which it assumed at its establishment, or which it subsequently developed, is a record of the elements of which that religion was composed. There they lie before us, in all their motley diversity, in the descriptions of the life of the Essenes. Anxiety as to ceremonial purity comes strongly into the foreground. Every pollution is avoided, or if unavoidable is removed, with the utmost scrupulosity. Other external ordinances are accepted in the same narrow spirit and observed with the same petty strictness. Yet what deep reverence for the moral ideal was there! We know from Flavius Josephus[1] the form of oath which the Essene must take when received into the order. It was the only oath ever permitted him. To what, then, did he pledge himself when on this single occasion he invoked the holy name of God to attest his word? He pledged himself, it is true, to observe the laws of the order and not to divulge its secrets; but firstly and chiefly he pledged himself to uprightness, faithfulness and submissiveness, to humility, simplicity and truthfulness. The man who formulated this oath must have sat at the feet of Israel's prophets and psalmists. "Who shall abide in Yahweh's tabernacle, and dwell upon Yahweh's holy mountain?" This question, it has been truly said,[2] the Essene must have asked and answered with the poet of the fifteenth Psalm. Let us bear this well in mind! Serious objections may be urged against the Essenic life, not from any arbitrarily selected point of view, but from that of Israelitism itself. Not without justice has its separatism been condemned as a

---

[1] Bell. Jud. II. 8, § 7. [2] Lucius, l. c. S. 106 ff.

relinquishment of the ideal of Law and Prophets alike.[1] So much the more noteworthy, then, is the fact that in this outgrowth of Judaism the prophetic conception of the life well-pleasing to God asserted itself so powerfully! We must not lose sight of this in our further study of the Palestinian Judaism from which Essenism had indeed withdrawn, but out of which it had sprung and of which it therefore testifies.

In reviewing a composite phenomenon we are sometimes at a loss how best to group its component parts. No such perplexity awaits us here. Palestinian Judaism, regarded from a religious point of view, finds its obvious and natural centre in *Pharisaism*. In the Jewish *state* the high-priest takes the highest place, while the distinguished families of priests and laymen who together with him make up the Sadducees, range themselves around him. We should have to begin with him if our object were to sketch the political history of the Jews. But in religion the Sadducees represent no special principle. Here it is the Scribes who lead and rule, supported by their pupils, the Pharisees, who put their theory into practice. If the Scribes consecrated themselves wholly to the study of the Law and its application to life, or more truly to the subjection

---

[1] "Der Essenismus ist nicht "die Blüte des Judenthums," sondern das bewuszte Aufgeben der Realisirung derjenigen Idee des Gottesvolks, welche Gesetz und Propheten fordern und verheizen" (Demmler, in Theol. Studien aus Württemberg, I. (1880), S. 53).

of the life of the people in all its branches to the precepts of the Law, the Pharisees are absorbed in its observance and in the realization of righteousness, regarded as conformity to its ordinances.

It is no longer needful to indite an apology for the Pharisees. The polemic against their shortcomings in the New Testament, especially in the Synoptic Gospels,[1] is not meant as a complete description of their purposes and efforts, and ought never to have been taken as such. Most assuredly there were false brethren amongst them—of what religious circles may not the same be said?—but to regard them all as hypocrites or mere formalists is the height of injustice, and is inconsistent with the New Testament itself,[2] no less than with the evidence of Flavius Josephus and the Talmud. No; Pharisaism was an attempt—so thoroughly earnest as to claim our profound respect—to realize the principle of Judaism itself, viz., complete obedience to the will of God expressed in the Thorah. The Pharisees, to speak with Wellhausen,[3] are *the virtuosi of religion*.

The fact that amongst the post-exilian Jews such men arose, that they drew together, and formed recog-

---

[1] e.g. Luke xii. 1; Matt. xxiii. 13 sqq.; v. 20.

[2] Acts xxvi. 5; Phil. iii. 5.

[3] Die Pharisäer und die Sadduciäer. Eine Untersuchung zur inneren jüdischen Geschichte (Greifswald, 1874), S. 20. I may also refer to his admirable description of Pharisaism altogether (S. 8—26, 26—43).

nized unions or corporations, is of decisive significance. In the first place, it demonstrates afresh how the Scribes had gradually succeeded in making religion an affair of the people, and what a power that religion had become. But even this is not enough to say. Pharisaism was not only an indication of the place religion now occupied, but was in its turn the guarantee that it should never again be thrust from it, that it had taken it once for all. In the Scribes, Judaism had its official representatives, who lent it powerful support in their capacity as such. But these men, to whom the preaching of religion had become a calling, must yield the palm of influence and power to the volunteers who had given themselves up to their guidance. The unofficial character of the latter did but heighten their moral authority. Nothing is more natural, therefore, than to find that the people cherished the utmost reverence for them, and, when occasion rose, were always ready to follow and support them. The sense of the masses is seldom misled in such things, nor was it at fault in this special case. On our side we can but subscribe to the judgment. We have, as will soon appear, very serious objections to urge against the principle of legalism supported by the Pharisees, and its inevitable consequences. But we cannot withhold the tribute of honour due to the uprightness of their intentions and their perseverance in their task. Pharisaism reveals an energy fraught with the promise of great things. It may have been wrongly directed, but if so, was it not capable of being turned into the right channel and made to serve the true advancement and development of religion?

These are no questions with which, from the vantage ground of centuries, we descend upon Pharisaism to disturb its self-complacency. No! its own most flourishing period proclaims loudly and unmistakably enough its own insufficiency. Within, and still more around it, in the life of the Jewish people, all manner of phenomena might be noted which, to any one capable of observing and fathoming them, could admit of no other interpretation than this.

Let us first look within Pharisaism itself, or, which comes to the same thing, within the schools of the Scribes, whence issued the rule observed by the Pharisees. In these schools some of the great teachers, though not all of them, manifested a very decided disposition to regard righteousness in some other light than as the observance of the countless precepts of the Law. They sought to simplify religion and strike some deeper ground of principle. We all know the answer given by Hillel, Herod's contemporary, to the heathen who begged him to describe the religion of the Jews in a few words: "*What thou wouldst not have done to thee, do not that to others.* This is the whole law; all the rest is but the interpretation. Go, then, and learn what this means!"[1] In the tract of the Mishnah called the Pirké

---

[1] Talmud babli, Sabbath, fol. 31 a.

Abôth, we find at any rate some sayings, ascribed to various periods, which rise above the point of view of legalism and are akin to Hillel's utterance. Antigonus of Sochoh used to say: "Be not as slaves that minister to the lord with a view to receive recompence; but be as slaves that minister to the lord without a view to receive recompence; and let the fear of Heaven (i. e. the fear of God) be upon you!"[1] The following saying is handed down from Gamaliel, the son of Rabbi Judah the holy: "Do his (God's) will as if it were thy will, that he may do thy will as if it were his will. Annul thy will before his will, that he may annul the will of others before thy will."[2] One of the disciples of Johanan ben Zaccai, Eleazar ben Arak by name, answered his master's question as to which was the good way that a man must cleave to by saying, "A good heart;" and Johanan approved his answer above those of all the other disciples.[3] In the haggadic portions of the Gemara, and in the numerous midrashîm which have come down to us, the like purely religious and ethical utterances, together with stories and parables of similar import, are very frequent. In the form in which we possess them, they date from a later period; but it is practically certain that the Scribes gave similar lessons from the first. When they preached in the

---

[1] Pirké Abôth, I. 3 (p. 27 in the edition of Ch. Taylor, Cambridge, 1877).

[2] Ibid. II. 4 (p. 43 in Taylor's edition).

[3] Ibid. II. 12 (p. 49 in Taylor's edition).

synagogues, we may suppose they usually adopted this form of teaching, generally linking it on to the sections of the Law and Prophets which were read aloud to the congregation, but sometimes quite freely in accordance with the promptings of their own hearts or the requirements of the moment.[1] There is really nothing surprising in this. For amongst the Scribes there were men not only earnest and conscientious, but likewise gifted with deep piety of heart and with warm emotions; men, too, of imagination and talent; in a word, successors of the prophets, an echo of whose preaching, we can hardly doubt, sounded sometimes in the ears of their hearers. Now the reason why I mention this aspect of the work of the Sopherîm, natural as it seems, as something special, is, that it offers such a contrast, or at least such a conspicuous want of agreement, with the rigid legalism which was the essence and the enduring characteristic of their work. Whenever they extol the inward disposition as the highest, or even as the one thing needful, whenever they condemn mercenary piety or seek an ally in the conscience of their hearers, they remind us of a captive bird pecking at the wires of its cage, or, if you will, raising its song as though it were soaring freely in its own element. The spontaneity, the spirit of

---

[1] Cf. J. Derenbourg, l.c. p. 159 sv., 202 svv.; J. Freudenthal, die Fl. Josephus beigelegte schrift Ueber die Herrschaft der Vernunft (iv. Makk.), eine Predigt aus dem ersten nachchristl. Jahrhundert (Breslau, 1869). especially S. 4 ff.

devotion, the initiative energy which they thus reveal, do not go together with the scrupulous care to observe the six hundred and thirteen commandments of the written, and the far more numerous precepts of the oral, Thorah. But, you will say, in the Scribes they did go together. And in the face of such a fact, what is the meaning of declaring them incompatible? This: that the spiritual and emotional elements in the teaching of the Scribes were little more than its helpless protest against its own essential character. Just because it could not relinquish its legalism without renouncing itself, it was powerless to do justice to anything that lay outside it. All this must remain for ever a dash at an inaccessible goal, a promise without fulfilment. The words of Hillel sound beautiful enough, and were doubtless uttered in sincerity: "Be of the disciples of Aaron (the peaceful); loving peace and pursuing peace; loving the creatures and bringing them nigh to the Thorah."[1] But how when the theory has to be put into practice, and it appears that this Thorah, with its "hedge"[2] raised by the Sopherîm and made yet stronger and higher in accordance with the seven rules drawn up by Hillel himself,[3] is inaccessible to "the creatures" who are to be brought to it? In

---

[1] Pirké Abôth, I. 13 (p. 34 sq. in Taylor's edition).

[2] Ibid. I. 1 (p. 25 in Taylor's edition); cf. Taylor's note on the passage.

[3] See my Religion of Israel, Vol. III. pp. 213 sq.

truth, it is but too clear that the teaching of the Scribes and the Pharisaism inseparable from it are smitten with internal contradiction. There is no real correlation between the dispositions and emotions which they rouse and on which they desire to rest, and the practical goal to which they direct their efforts. Such discords are not felt by every one in whose life-system they exist,—what is called a happy inconsistency has never been rare in the world, and was no less frequent then than it is now,—but they eat into the spiritual life in which they have established themselves. Sooner or later they come to consciousness—and then? How is it possible—by advancing on the path once chosen, I mean—to find the reconciliation?

"Love men and bring them nigh to the Thorah." This saying of Hillel's leads us of itself to the second group of phenomena which seems to me to reveal the insufficiency of Pharisaism. Amongst "the men," or, as the expression really stands, "the creatures," of whom Hillel speaks, the Jews settled in Palestine surely take the first place; yet who could dare to say that these "children of the kingdom" enjoyed the knowledge of the Thorah or the blessing of a life in accordance with its precepts? We have no right whatever to accuse the Scribes of neglecting their duties towards their people. They did what they could. Nor can we say that there was any section of the nation for whom they had laboured wholly in vain. Their exertions had made a portion, and truly no despicable portion, of Judaism the universal possession of the Jews. Monotheism, about the beginning of our era, and even earlier, had sunk into the popular consciousness. The privilege which Israel enjoyed above the heathen was generally acknowledged; the resultant obligation to live after God's commandments was denied by no one. But if we go on to ask whether the Judaism of the Scribes had realized its ideal of a people consecrated to the Holy One, or, if this is too much to require, whether it was at any rate on the way to its realization, then we must face a very sad result. A considerable portion of Palestine's Jewish population utterly failed to comply with the demands which the Sopherîm made, and from their point of view could not help making, upon it; and it was therefore unclean, nay abominable, in their eyes. To this class belonged, in the first instance, those whom the New Testament calls "the lost sheep of Israel,"[1] the sinners and the publicans, whom the Talmud styles "ammé ha-árez," which is equivalent to "(Jewish) heathens." But besides these, the large numbers whom the earliest Christian literature includes under the name of "the multitudes," though not standing so low as the others, were far from irreproachable in the estimation of the Scribes. Many, though perhaps not all, fell under the sentence put upon the lips of "the chief priests and Pharisees" in the fourth Gospel: "This multitude that know not the law are

---

[1] Matt. x. 6; xv. 24; cf. Matt. ix. 36; Mark vi. 34.

accursed."[1] This has been denied, and the Jewish *bourgeoisie*, the middle class proper, has been described as completely answering to the demands of the Sopherîm.[2] It seems hard to decide in such a case. We are moving in a sphere which is hardly amenable to statistics even under the most favourable circumstances, and in this special case the difficulty is enhanced in proportion to the meagreness and incompleteness of our sources of information. And yet there is one fact which the optimistic view does not take into account, and with which it seems to me irreconcilable. That fact is Pharisaism itself. It loses its very meaning if it cannot be regarded as a protest against the unsatisfactory condition of the people in general, from the point of view of legalism. The Pharisee takes upon himself no single duty which every Jew is not equally bound to observe. Pharisaism is simply Judaism itself, and nothing more; and yet it is the practice, not of the whole nation, but of a sect—of some few thousand men to whom the people look up with profound respect, but who are seen by that very fact to be essentially different from the people itself. Geiger, who in other respects has done much to give us a true insight into the nature and

---

[1] John vii. 49.

[2] Graetz, l.c. S. 305, "Der judäische Mittelstand, die Bewohner kleinerer und gröszerer Städte, war grösztentheils derart von Gottergebenheit, Frömmigkeit und leidlicher (!) Sittlichkeit durchdrungen, dasz die Aufforderung die Sünden zu bereuen und fahren zu lassen für sie gar keinen Sinn hatte."

mutual relations of the Jewish parties, was mistaken in identifying the Pharisees with the Jewish *bourgeoisie*.[1] But even the errors of a master are often instructive. As Geiger imagines it was, so it really *ought to have been*. Theoretically speaking, there was not the least reason why the whole of the people—the utterly untutored and the castaways alone excepted—should not have complied with all that the Pharisees observed. But practically it was not, and could not be so. The burden of the commandments was too heavy, obedience too complicated, for the whole nation to take up and bear. The feat was possible only to a comparatively small number who made it the business of their lives. But if what these few did was the duty of all, then we must avow that Pharisaism condemns, while it reveals, the form of religion of which it was no arbitrary outgrowth, but the historically necessary development.

What happens when the consistent application of a principle which is only half true leads to a dead-lock such as that to which Judaism was brought about the beginning of our era? Subterfuges are sought—and found. If the ideal has proved inaccessible, something short of the ideal is accepted instead. But this is at best a melancholy alternative, in which the conscience cannot rest. The unrealized ideal never ceases to dis-

---

[1] Urschrift und Uebersetzungen der Bibel, S. 100 ff. (e.g. S. 150, "Die Pharisäer bestanden aus dem national und religiös gesinnten Bürgerthume"); Das Judenthum und seine Geschichte, I. (1865). S. 86 ff. (e.g. S. 89 : "die Abgesonderten, das Bürgerthum").

turb us, and goads us from time to time into renewed efforts, which (on the hypothesis from which we have started) can only result in renewed disappointment. A restless striving and longing remains. How the heart of many a Jew must have beaten, as he thought of the countless trespasses from which he shrank, but which he could not escape! How often must he have been oppressed by the violation of God's commandments which his conscience bound him to observe, but which he could scarcely hope even to know, how much less to fulfil! It is true that a man ends by banishing such painful thoughts and acquiescing in the inevitable. But is this a solution of the difficulty? No! Such quietness of soul is bought at too great a price.

Fortunately there was another way of escape, and we are free to believe that some at least did not fail to find it. There was, as we have just seen, an internal contradiction in the system of the Scribes, a prophetic element that did not harmonize with its main principle of rigid legalism. With this most attractive side of the work of the Sopherîm the believing Jew first came into contact in the synagogue; and afterwards, too, when he had become acquainted with the "halacha" (the Thorah in its manifold application), it continued to fascinate him. Here a note was sounded that waked an echo in his heart. Then why not give heed to it? If the Scribes appealed to his conscience and sought in his religious aspirations a point of attachment for their preaching, what did they more than the pious men of ancient time had done? Was it not the spirit of the Prophets and Psalmists that worked in them and sounded from their lips? To its guidance he might safely trust himself. Nurtured in reverence for the prophetic word, and with his attention constantly fixed on it by the Scribes themselves, he might thus rise to a different view of the religious and moral life from that which the Scribes, in virtue of their principle, systematically fostered. Need I describe this other view more narrowly? You remember how the prophets had pictured the dispositions pleasing to God, what affections they had fostered, and how, setting the ritual completely on one side, they had extolled the most purely human virtues as manifesting the truest piety. There can be no manner of doubt that under the dominion of Judaism this conception still had its upholders.[1] And yet I ought not really to speak of the formation of *another theory* subsequently erected in opposition to the official one. For it was by the preaching of the synagogue and the reading of the Holy Scriptures that the seeds were scattered of *a religion* which could not find its consum-

---

[1] From this point of view, the remarks of Flavius Josephus, Contr. Ap. II. 16, deserve attention. Note the words, for instance: "He (Moses) did not make piety a part of virtue, but he recognized and established the virtues as parts of piety; I mean righteousness, endurance, temperance, mutual harmony between the citizens in all things. For with us, all actions and occupations and words are derived from the pious disposition towards God; for of all these things he (Moses) left none without regulation." Cf. also II. 19, on the reception of these ideas into the life of the people.

mation in the observance of the covenant made with God and the expectation of the reward he had attached thereto. These seeds were not dropped in vain. Sometimes they fell upon good ground. Essenism has already taught us how strong the purely moral elements in Judaism were, and how successfully they vindicated their place by the side of the others. The same fact must have been abundantly evident in the unobtrusive lives of many who still retained their places in Jewish society. They had not risen above the principle of legalism. The Pharisee had not ceased to be their ideal of piety and righteousness. Hence in some cases, no doubt, a certain want of self-reliance. Were they really on the right way? *Ought* they to experience the peace they enjoyed? Their religion was, in a certain sense, illegitimately acquired, a stolen possession, which might therefore be taken away again. But as a matter of fact they had, were it only provisionally, risen to a higher standpoint than that of Pharisaism—a standpoint which ere long was to be possessed and defended in right as well as in fact.

Our review of Palestinian Judaism must now take a wider sweep. The life it led may have appeared, so far, to have been one of isolation, so to speak, having little or no contact with other religions and their confessors. But this was not so at all. In Palestine, Judaism was shut in and pressed on every side by the overmastering power of the heathen world, and outside Palestine it had its branches everywhere. This could not remain without influence on the thoughts and feelings of its confessors, on their expectations, on what they did and what they left undone. In truth, this influence was most penetrating. What we have to say on the subject falls under two heads—*Messianism* and *Proselytism*.

As to "the Messianic idea," if we are not to be overwhelmed or at least carried out of our course by the wealth of the subject, we must be content to relinquish the consideration of all details and all matters under dispute, and confine ourselves to the main point, as to which there is fortunately no difference of opinion. I assume it as proved, therefore, that the Messianic expectations had not expired in post-exilian Israel; that they survived especially, not in the ranks of the ruling aristocracy, but amongst the Scribes, the Pharisees, and the people who were led by them; that the pressure of Herod's rule no less than that of the Romans had revived and strengthened them. About the beginning of our era, these expectations had not yet taken any definite shape, and Judaism possessed no rounded system of Messianic dogma. But there was a conviction, dominant everywhere, that the subjection of God's people to the heathen was an anomaly that could not last. As surely as Israel had been chosen out of all the nations of the earth by the Almighty, and belonged to him as a "kingdom of priests and a holy people,"[1]

---

[1] Exod. xix. 6 a.

so surely must Israel win freedom and dominion. In mutual agreement so far, the Jews part at this point into two companies. In the one, the Messianism has produced _Zelotism_. Wider and wider spreads the thought that the dawn of the better time must not be passively expected, but must be hastened by heroic deeds. Josephus, almost the only witness we can consult, is forced to reveal the constant growth of Zelotism, gladly as he would conceal it, sweeping the whole people with it at last in the year 66 A.D. But this result came about in spite of the spiritual leaders, the Scribes and their faithful disciples the Pharisees. From the first they consistently maintained their expectant attitude, and as long as they commanded the hearts of the people, they taught them to hope indeed, but also to endure. It is remarkable how often the thought of suffering and dying for the Law finds expression in the pages of the Jewish historian, as he tries to place his people and its religion in the true light against the attacks of Apion. "It is implanted in every Jew," he says,[1] "from his very birth, to regard them (the words of the Law) as God's commands, to abide in them, and, if need be, gladly to die for them." Elsewhere he extols the courage of his fellow-believers in facing death for the sake of the Law—not, he adds, "that easiest form of death which a man meets on the battle-field, but that which is

---

[1] Contr. Ap. I. 8.

accompanied by bodily torture and is deemed the most terrible of all."[1] They firmly believed, he had just informed us, that they who had observed the laws and, if needful, cheerfully died for them, would live again in a far better existence. "I should hesitate to set this down," he adds, "had not the facts made it manifest to all that many of my countrymen have on many occasions nobly preferred to suffer any extremity rather than utter a single word contrary to the Law."[2] In whatever other respects Josephus may have been false to the traditions of his people, here at least it is the true Pharisee that speaks.

Let it not be thought that this passive aspect of devotion to the Messianic idea may be disregarded in judging the Palestinian Judaism because it manifested itself in no external movement. On the contrary, it seems to me to have far higher religious significance than the zeal of a Judas the Gaulonite,[3] which evaporated in the very deeds of violence it inspired. It means something to live in a world that is the very opposite of what it ought to be, and to stand against it with a protest, unuttered indeed, but all the more earnest and deep on that very account, in the name of the Only True, whom the world knows not, but must some time, whether it will or no, learn both to know and reverence. We cannot say with certainty in what

---

[1] Contr. Ap. II. 32.   [2] Contr. Ap. II. 30.

[3] Josephus, Antiqq. XVIII. 1, § 1; Bell. Jud. II. 8, § 1; cf. my Religion of Israel, Vol. III. pp. 256 sq.

mood this position will be held. It may be in hatred, concentrated hatred, of the godless masters of the world. Or it may be with an inward estrangement from the ungodly world itself and all its glory, with a falling back upon those spiritual blessings which the world cannot give, but cannot take away, —in a word, renunciation of the world or fleeing from it, a kind of spiritual Essenism, of which we have more than one actual example preserved to us in the accounts of the great Scribes. In what proportion these and perhaps other emotions were stirred in the Jewish hearts by the Messianic idea must remain a mystery; for who has power to fathom the inner life of bygone generations? But this at least is certain, that as a whole the religious life of the Jews was modified in character and changed in colour by the future on which they dwelt. In other respects there was nothing in their mode of life to irritate or provoke their neighbours. It is true they declined to fall in with other people's ideas and usages. The Jew was independent, and made a point of remaining so. But this might be regarded simply as a harmless eccentricity or a fit subject of ridicule. It was widely different, however, when he, the scion of an insignificant tribe, came forward, or rather went quietly on his way, cherishing in his heart this protest against the whole existing disposition of earthly things, this hope of a total revolution, these claims to universal dominion. Although such thoughts and anticipations were not preached from the house-tops, yet they could not remain concealed, and they had, as a matter of fact, become known amongst the Romans, and still more amongst the neighbours of the Jews.[1] Need we wonder if many an one, dissatisfied with the social conditions under which he lived, and having outgrown the traditional religion, cast an inquiring look to that quarter of the mysterious East whence perhaps the light might break?

But let me not speak as if nothing more came of it than this attitude of uncertain inquiry. Great numbers, in almost every quarter of the then known world, had actually joined the Jews already. *Proselytism* had gradually assumed amazing dimensions. Here, too, I must refrain from entering upon details; and after all it is only the main fact itself, as to which there is no difference of opinion, that has special interest for us in this connection. Flavius Josephus certainly deserves our confidence when he makes an assertion concerning his own times which any one of his readers could bring to the test of the facts; and he does not hesitate to declare that "many of them (the Greeks) have agreed to submit themselves to our laws; some having persevered, whilst others, lacking the patience to endure, have fallen away again."[2] And once more, later on: "For a long time back, great zeal for our religion has

---

[1] Suetonius, Vesp. 4; Tacitus, Hist. v. 13.
[2] Contr. Ap. II. 10.

laid hold upon multitudes; nor is there any city of the Greeks, or indeed any city at all, even though barbarian, nor is there any nation, where the observance of the seventh day, on which we rest from toil, has not made its way, and where the fasts and lamp-lightings and many of our prohibitions as to food are not observed. And they try to imitate our mutual harmony, and our industry in handicrafts, and our patient endurance under persecutions for the Law's sake. .... As God penetrates the whole world, so the Law has made its way amongst all men. Let each one look for himself at his own land and his own home, and he will not withhold belief from what I say."[1] It was the Jews of the diaspora more especially that attracted the proselytes.[2] But in Palestine, too, and from Palestine as a centre, Judaism spread amongst the heathens, whether as a natural result of their intercourse with the Jews, or in consequence of the activity of missionaries sent out to convert them. It is far from improbable that in the first century of the Christian era such direct attempts were not unfrequent.[3] In a word, Judaism was by no means without consciousness of its own broader destiny, and was already engaged in extending its borders in many directions.

The most striking proof of the importance of this movement is the fact that the question of the conditions

---

[1] Contr. Ap. II. 39.

[2] See the authorities in my Religion of Israel, Vol. III. p. 274.

[3] Cf. Matt. xxiii. 15, and Note XII.

under which heathens should be admitted into Judaism had already been asked and variously answered. There is a celebrated account given by Flavius Josephus of the conversion of the royal house of Adiabene to the Jewish religion;[1] and still more interesting, for our present purpose, than the fact itself, is the doubt of Izates as to whether he must submit to circumcision, and the contradictory opinions on the subject given by Hananiah and Eleazar. The former would be satisfied with the observance of the main points of the Law; the latter maintained that reverence for that Law must show itself at the very outset by submission to *all* its ordinances, including circumcision. When I say that what Josephus tells us on this subject forms a kind of commentary on the Epistle of Paul to the Galatians, it is as much as to declare that the question between national and universal religion had already been, I will not say answered, but at least asked, out there on the banks of the Tigris! From the point of view of the Law, Eleazar—determined to maintain every jot and tittle—is unquestionably right. But if his rule is to be followed, then Judaism must remain what it is, the religion of one single people; and the handful of converts it may make will but serve to bring out its national character all the more clearly. In that case, what is to become of the far wider destiny which we have seen shadowed forth in so many phenomena? What comes, to begin with, of the prophetic univer-

---

[1] Antiqq. XX. 2—4; cf. the Talmudic accounts, Derenbourg,

salism? What comes, again, of that plastic power of adaptation which Judaism has already displayed in foreign countries? What comes, above all, of the treasures of piety and morality which lie stored within it, and for which so many hands are already held out in longing? Are all these promises of a glorious future to be sacrificed to rigid legalism—in a word, to Pharisaism? And that, too, although this consistent carrying out of the legal principle "is condemned already;" although in Palestine itself it has failed in its most immediate task; although by its side, partly in Essenism, but far more in the lives of some of the people, another and a better conception of religion has appeared,—as yet hardly venturing to show its head, but impressing us as having risen to the task which is reserved for Judaism!

The limit fixed for this portion of our investigation is now reached. When we have included Buddhism within the circle of our observations, I shall return once more to Judaism and the relation in which Christianity stands to it. But we have already traced through its course the ascent of Judaism towards an international religion, the birth of which now stands before our eyes as a historical necessity. Yet always, let me say it again, with one most important reservation. I think I have shown that the conditions of this transition are present, that the material is as it were collected for the new edifice; or, to express it differently, that the problem has been set, and that too in such definite terms as to bring the solution as close as possible. One thing only is wanting, and that is *the solution itself.* The elements lie mingled one with another, and the "Let there be light" must still be spoken. But is not this equivalent to the avowal that our whole undertaking has failed? No doubt it would be so if I had promised to explain the origin of Christianity independently of the person of its Founder. But you will remember that at the outset I declared that I could do nothing of the kind. What I did undertake to show was, that Jesus ought not to be regarded as the "deus ex machina" who suddenly appears to bring order out of the confusion and misery wrought by men, and that he might be strictly demonstrated not to have stood in opposition to the whole Jewish people in every phase and shade of its religion. Have I not satisfied these promises? "Christianity," I read not long ago, "the person of Jesus Christ, is not the last shoot of the Israelitish nationality, but the completion of the revelation of God which underlies its history."[1] I say nothing of the contrast, for it would bring us upon a field we are not now treading. But for us the denial here made has fallen away. Christianity not the last shoot (or rather the fruit) of the Israelitish nationality? But have we not seen how more than one of the components of Judaism pointed forward towards

---

[1] "Das Christentum, die Person Jesu Christi, ist nicht der letzte Ausläufer des israelitischen Volkstums, sondern die Erfüllung der ihm zu Grunde liegenden Gottesoffenbarung" (H. J. Bestmann, Gesch. der christlichen Sitte, I. 318).

the things that should be, and as it were forced the development of that germ which the Israelitish religion had for centuries, nay from the very beginning, borne within itself? Have we not witnessed "the birth-pains"—not the imaginary but the real ones—"of the Messiah"?[1]

And now we may take one more step forward. Up to the moment when the facts themselves gave the answer, it remained a secret what the solution would be. But we may safely say that its *form* could hardly be doubtful to one who comprehended the course of Israel's religious history. We have recognized prophecy as the moving power of its development. Priests, and subsequently Scribes, zealously co-operated, and thereby did priceless service to their people and so to humanity. But at the turning-points of this age-long process of evolution the prophet stands. Every direct approach to the final goal is his work. The Judaism of the "time of fulfilment" owes to his influence those thoughts, those aptitudes and dispositions, which immediately proclaim the new era that is to be. It seems then to lie in the nature of the case that in the transition from the national to the universal the chief part is reserved for the prophet. What Amos, Isaiah, Jeremiah and "the great Unknown" had begun, it was reserved for Him to finish.

So it seemed that it must be, and so it was.

---

[1] Compare J. Drummond, The Jewish Messiah (London, 1877), Bk. ii. chap. v., especially p. 221.

V.

BUDDHISM.

RETROSPECT AND CONCLUSION.

"SIMPLICITY the seal of truth!" Were this life-motto of my great countryman universally valid, then the view I have upheld of the origin of Christianity from Palestinian Judaism would need no further recommendation. But we have so often found the ways of history circuitous, that we are almost more inclined to doubt whether the straight path can be the true one than to assume that it must be so! In any case, it is no superfluous question to ask whether other factors than those of which we traced the influence when last we met may not have contributed to the formation of Christianity. May not the process really have been more complex than we have supposed it?

There is definite occasion for asking these questions. When Christianity was born in Palestine, there was a world-religion in existence already. Have we any right to leave it out of consideration? It is an established fact that contact with strangers was not without its influence upon the religion of Israel after the exile; that Persian ideas, for example, gained access, not simply to individual minds, but to the nation as a whole. Now, at the beginning of our era, *Buddhism* had already overstepped the boundaries of its fatherland more than two centuries ago. Difference of nationality had proved no barrier to its spread. Is it not therefore extremely natural that repeated attempts should have been made to raise this, the first in the series of universal religions, to the position of parent of the other two, or at any rate to give it a side influence in the production of Christianity, and thereby, indirectly, of Islam also?

We cannot altogether ignore these attempts, though they need not detain us long. A single glance is enough to teach us that inventive fancy plays the chief part in them.

What is the nature of the proofs alleged by those who maintain that Buddhistic influences were at work in the production of Christianity? Positive evidence that Buddhistic ideas had penetrated to Western Asia is not forthcoming till a far later time. The Indian "Gymnosophists" whom Philo mentions once or twice[1] are not Buddhists at all, and, moreover, he only knows

---

[1] Quod Omnis Probus Liber, § 11 (II. 456 Mang.); de Abrahamo, § 33 (II. 26 Mang.).

them by vague report. Clement of Alexandria is the first who mentions the Buddha; and he speaks of him as the human founder of a religion, whom his followers, "because he was so surpassingly venerable," reverenced as a god.[1] What he has to tell us leaves the impression that even in those days, about the beginning of the third century of our era, Buddhism was still a remote phenomenon. If it had made its influence felt in Egypt or in Palestine centuries before, Clement at least had not the faintest suspicion of the fact. If there is no evidence of the reality of this influence, then, are we to deny its possibility? I for one dare not go so far. The way which Buddhism would have to travel in order to reach either Palestine or Egypt was long, but it was neither unknown nor impassable; and if we think of the Babylonian Jews as the medium of communication, the distance is notably curtailed. But the total absence of historical witnesses should make us very cautious in assuming such an "actio in distans," and renders it at least our imperative duty to submit the quality of the proofs which are usually urged in support of the theory of Buddhistic influences to a very close examination. The well-known volume on "the Angel-Messiah of the Buddhists, Essenes and Christians,"[2] no doubt teems with parallels of every

---

[1] Strom. I. 15, § 71 (p. 359 Pott.).

[2] The Angel-Messiah of Buddhists, Essenes and Christians, by Ernest de Bunsen (London, 1880).

description; but, alas! it is one unbroken commentary on Scaliger's thesis that errors in theology—or, as he really puts it, "disputes in religion"—all rise from neglect of philology.[1] A writer who can allow himself to bring the name of "Pharisee" into connection with Persia,[2] has once for all forfeited his right to a voice in the matter. But the very title of the book ought really to have preserved us from any illusion as to its contents. "The Angel-Messiah" of the Buddhists, who know nothing either of angels or a Messiah, and of the Essenes, who were certainly much occupied with the angels and their names, but of whose Messianic expectations we know nothing, absolutely nothing![3] By such comparisons between unknown or imaginary quantities, instituted without any kind of accuracy, we could prove literally anything. Unquestionably there are points of agreement between the Gospel narratives, especially in Luke and John, and the legend of the

---

[1] Non alunde dissidia in religione dependent quam ab ignoratione Grammaticæ (Scaligerana, ed. Tan. Fabri, p. 86).

[2] L.c. p. 86, where as yet we only read, "the Sadducees and the Pharisees, the name of the latter having *possibly* been derived from Pharis (Faris), the Arabian (!) name for the Persians." But on p. 92 the ancestral tradition of the Pharisees is brought "with increasing certainty" into connection with "Persia, the Pharis of the Arabians(!), and from which name that of the Pharisees may have been derived." In the note on p. 86 we are further invited to compare "Phares and Pharesites or Pherisites (Perizzites)." That *pherûshî*, *Pharets* and *Pherizzi*, have nothing to do either with each other or with *Pharás* (the Hebrew name of Persia), needs no proof.

[3] Vid. sup. p. 203.

Buddha; and also between the preaching of Jesus and that of his great predecessor. To make a complete collection of these parallels, and to illustrate both them and the no less noteworthy points of difference, I hold to be far from a superfluous task; and it is satisfactory to know that it has actually been undertaken by a competent hand, with results that have quite recently been given to the world.[1] It would be premature as yet to pronounce a final judgment on the outcome of the running comparison thus instituted; but meanwhile I think I may safely affirm that we must abstain from assigning to Buddhism the smallest direct influence on the *origin* of Christianity. The utmost that can be maintained is, that a few features in the evangelical tradition may have been borrowed from it; and even this must remain very doubtful, inasmuch as the resemblances upon which the hypothesis is built present themselves, remarkably enough, in some of the stories which are dependent on the Old Testament, and in which, of course, the coincidence with certain traits in the life of Çâkya-Muni *cannot* by any possibility be more than accidental.[2] In a word, however attractive the hypothesis that brings Jesus into connection with the Buddhists may possibly appear, and however readily

---

[1] Prof. Dr. Rudolf Seydel, das Evangelium von Jesu in seinen Verhältnissen zu Buddha-saga und Buddha-lehre, mit fortlaufender Rücksicht auf andere Religionskreise (Leipzig, 1882).

[2] Cf. Note XIII.

it may lend itself to romantic treatment,[1] yet sober and strict historical research gives it no support, and indeed condemns it.[2]

But, what we do not require to explain the origin of Christianity is nevertheless of intense interest to us for its own sake. The study of Buddhism—with a view, as before, to the relation in which it stands to the national religion of India—is not the least important part of our task. But this only serves to increase the fear and trembling with which I approach it. Believe me, it is no mock-modesty that dictates these words. If a burning desire to fathom any subject could qualify a man to deal with it, then indeed I should have every right to be heard; for I confess that there are few questions which inspire me with deeper interest than those which refer to the character of the primitive Buddhism and the manner in which it rose. But something more than this is needed, viz. study of the sources, and yet again study of the sources. And for

---

[1] Such as it receives at the hands of G. Birnie, De invloed van de Hindoe-beschaving, ook met betrekking op Java (Deventer, 1881), bl. 97, where it is not thought improbable that Jesus visited Alexandria and there made acquaintance with Buddhism. A little before this (bl. 94 v.), the treatise "De Vita Contemplativa" has been treated as Philo's, and—which is quite equally hazardous—as evidence of the spread of Buddhistic asceticism in Egypt.

[2] Cf. with the foregoing, Prof. J. Estlin Carpenter, The Obligations of the New Testament to Buddhism (The Nineteenth Century, Dec. 1880, pp. 971—994); and Rhys Davids, Lectures, &c., pp. 151 sq.

this task I have not even qualified myself by the necessary preparation. Now such a defect might be made bearable, though never wholly compensated, if the pioneers on the field were unanimous in the results they announce. But every one knows how far they remain at variance, in spite of the advances recently made, or rather in part because of them. If, notwithstanding, I venture, not only thankfully to make use of the facts which are established to every one's satisfaction, but also to express an opinion on questions still waiting their solution, I do so in the hope that the doubts, perhaps the errors, of one who stands outside may give the special students of the subject some idea of what we look to them to give us, and may move them to bring forth out of their treasure-house yet more than we have received already. I am far indeed from any intention of "singing the siege of Troy after Homer." I know too well that, in Buddhistic phrase, my place is not in "the community," but amongst the "adherents." I will only allow myself, as an interested spectator of the researches of recent years, to record my impressions, to express a wish, or at the very most to hazard an occasional conjecture. Even in this I shall often allow the specialists themselves to speak for me, and as soon as possible I shall take my place once more at their feet, mindful of the lesson of the Dhammapada: "If you see an intelligent man who tells you where true treasures are to be found, who shows what is to be avoided, and administers reproofs, follow that wise man; it will be better, not worse, for those who follow him."[1]

The close connection between Brahmanism and Buddhism is denied by no one. But there was a time when this connection was represented as consisting in unqualified opposition. Buddhism was supposed to have been the denial and rejection of Brahmanism, and to have sprung from it as the French revolution, for instance, sprang from the "ancien régime." And even now the echo of this thought still falls upon our ear from more quarters than one. Not many years ago (1868), the celebrated Indian scholar Weber reprinted an essay in which he described Buddhism as being "in its origin one of the sublimest and most radical of all reactions in favour of the common human rights of individuals against the grinding tyranny of the so-called divine rights of birth and rank." "It was the work of a single man," he adds, "who rebelled against the Brahmanic priests in the beginning of the sixth century B.C., and by the simplicity and moral power of his teaching brought the Indian people to a complete breach with its own past."[2] Max Duncker

---

[1] v. 76, according to F. Max Müller's translation, Sacred Books of the East, Vol. X. Part i. p. 23. A. Weber's translation runs: "Wen man sieht als gleichsam Schätze verkündend, als Mängel erschau'nd, Als tadeln lehrend, einsichtig—solchem Weisen man an sich schliess'. Wer einem solchen sich anschliesst, besser wird's dem, nicht schlimmer, gehn" (Indische Streifen, I. 130 f.).

[2] Indische Streifen, I. 104. The sequel runs: "Mitten unter die trostlosen Verrenkungen aller menschlichen Gefühle, wie sie das

expresses himself with no less emphasis: "In the doctrine of Buddha the philosophy of the Indians .... had broken with the results of the history of the Arians on the Indus and the Ganges, with the development of a thousand years. .... And this doctrine, which annihilated the entire ancient religion and the basis of existing society .... rested solely on the dicta of a man who declared that he had discovered truth by his own power, and maintained that every man could find it. That such a doctrine found adherence and ever increasing adherence is a fact without a parallel in history."[1] In like manner, Prof. Monier Williams describes the Buddha as "the deliverer of a priest-ridden, caste-ridden nation,—the courageous reformer and innovator who dared to attempt what doubtless others had long felt was necessary, namely, the breaking down of an intolerable ecclesiastical monopoly by proclaiming absolute free trade in religious opinions and the abolition of all caste privileges."[2]

---

brahmanische Kastenwesen und Staatsthum mit sich führte, unter die lebendige Sehnsucht nach einer Erlösung aus dem irdischen, individuellen Dasein, welches sich für die grossen Massen des Volkes nur in so qualvollen, eingeschnürten Formen zeigte, und aus dem ewig wechselnden Kreislauf der Wiedergeburten .... trat jener Mann mit seinem Evangelium von der gleichen Berechtigung aller menschen ohne Unterschied der Geburt, des Standes oder Ranges, ja des Geschlechtes sogar, und von der durch die richtige Erkenntniss und den richtigen Wandel allein, aber auch von Jedem, früher oder später zu erreichenden Auflösung des individuellen Daseins."

[1] History of Antiquity, Vol. IV. pp. 455 sq.
[2] Indian Wisdom, p. 55.

There is something imposing and therefore attractive in this representation; and we cannot wonder at its having come into existence, or at its still remaining in favour with certain scholars. This Çâkya-Muni forces us to yield him our sympathy and reverence. Marvellous his mission may be, but inexplicable it is not—always supposing that the state of things which he attacked has been correctly described:—" aux grands maux les grands remèdes." But this is precisely what is now so often denied. The "priest-ridden, caste-ridden nation" of which the Buddha is said to be the redeemer, is the creature, we are told, of the Western imagination. In the legend of the Buddha, at any rate, we find no traces of it. And even this is only one out of many facts which have gradually led to a notable change in the conception of the relations between Brahmanism and Buddhism. Let me mention the most important of these facts, not in the order in which they came to light or have had their weight allowed in the judgment formed on Buddhism, but as they stand before me now, absolutely compelling us, when taken in their mutual connection, to tone down the traditional opposition.

The edicts of king Açoka still supply the firmest foundations for our knowledge of the earlier Buddhism. Immediately on the discovery of these monuments, the spirit of appreciative tolerance which breathes through them was observed as a striking characteristic. Açoka declares that he desires above all things "that the good name and sterling worth of all the sects may increase." "He who extols his own party, doubtless does so out of love of his sect, in order to glorify it; but none the less will he greatly injure his own sect by so doing. Wherefore unity is best, so that each may learn to know and to praise the other's religion. For this is the wish of the king, that the members of every party be well instructed and cleave to a doctrine of goodwill."[1] In complete accordance with these sentiments, he elsewhere couples "Brahmans and (Buddhistic) monks" together, and exhorts his subjects to genuine charity towards both.[2] He himself practises the lesson, for, as we learn from another inscription, "The king, ten years after his coronation, came to true insight. Wherefore he entered on a course of righteousness, consisting herein: that he sees Brahmans and monks about him and bestows gifts upon them, sees old men about him and honours them with gold, receives his subjects from city and country, exhorts to righteousness and seeks righteousness."[3] "Want of respect for Brahmans and monks" is one of the evils which he laments as on the increase.[4] Here you will observe that the representatives of the two hostile religions

---

[1] Girnar xii. The translation follows that of Kern, in his treatise Over de jaartelling der Zuidelijke Buddhisten en de gedenkstukken van Açoka den Buddhist (Amst. 1873), p. 70. Compare T. W. Rhys Davids, Lectures, &c., App. II. pp. 230 sq.

[2] Girnar ix. xi. (Kern, bl. 85, 78).

[3] Girnar viii. (Kern, bl. 59). [4] Girnar iv. (Kern, bl. 52).

stand peaceably side by side, while one protecting hand is stretched over both alike. But does this really warrant any inferences as to their mutual relations? Is it not "the humane king," as his title of honour runs, rather than the disciple of the Buddha, that is here speaking? In other cases, remote and recent, the civil authority, in the interests of peace, has imposed silence on the contending parties, and has taken them all alike under its protection. Now I certainly dare not vouch for Açoka's untarnished orthodoxy, and can give no answer to the doubts with which it has been assailed.[1] But it is very generally allowed that in these addresses to his people, as elsewhere, he speaks as a pronounced Buddhist.[2] Nor does he by any means compromise this character by mentioning the Brahmans with respect and predilection; for the very same thing is done by the Buddha himself—that is to say, by the sacred literature that introduces him as speaking.

Of the many passages that might be cited in support of this assertion, I will content myself with one or two. A verse of the Dhammapada runs thus: "He who, though dressed in fine apparel, exercises tranquillity, is quiet, subdued, restrained, chaste, and has ceased to find fault with all other beings, he indeed is a Brâhma*n*a, an ascetic (*s*rama*n*a), a friar (bhikshu)."[3]

---

[1] See Kern, l.c. bl. 81 v., 107.

[2] Inscription of Babhra (Kern, bl. 37).

[3] v. 142 (Max Müller, p. 39). According to Weber (l.c. S. 110), Selbst reich geschmückt, wenn wer Besänft'gung übet, Ruhig, be-

The last word is the ordinary designation of the members of the Buddhistic order, and the parallel between them and the Brahmans is no less noteworthy than it is unequivocal. Equally clear is the teaching of the entire twenty-sixth chapter of this same work, with its refrain, "him I call indeed a Brâhma*n*a"—him, for example, "who has cut all fetters, who never trembles, is independent and unshackled," or him "who in this world, leaving all desires, travels about without a home, and in whom all concupiscence is extinct."[1] Here "Brahman" is unquestionably a title of honour, to which the writer assigns the highest value. But it may be asked whether this is not peculiar to himself, and an exception to the general rule. Far from it. Oldenberg says it is "worth mentioning that *in the Buddhistic texts* the word 'Brahman' by no means carries with it the idea of an enemy to the cause of Buddha. It affords no parallel to the 'Pharisees and Scribes' of the New Testament, for instance, who appear throughout as the opponents of Jesus."[2] It is of course undeniable that Buddhism makes high demands of the Brahmans, and denies that they who fail to comply with them have any right to bear this name of honour. The Dhammapada declares: "I do not

---

zähmt, an sich halt und keusch lebet, Keinem Wesen irgendje Zücht'-gung zufügt, Der "Brâhmana" ist, der "Asket," der "bhikkhu."

[1] *vv.* 383—423 (Max Müller, pp. 89—95), especially *vv.* 397, 415 (pp. 91, 93).

[2] Buddha. Sein Leben, seine Lehre, seine Gemeinde (Berlin, 1881), S. 174, n. 2.

call a man a Brâhma*n*a because of his origin or of his mother. He is indeed arrogant, and he is wealthy: but the poor, who is free from all attachments, him I call indeed a Brâhma*n*a."[1] We may say generally that nothing is commoner than sharp castigation of the devotion to externalities, the conceit and the pride of the Brahmans.[2] But in this respect they themselves are quite abreast of the Buddhists. Dr. Muir has collected a whole string of passages that prove this, and the purport of them all may be summed up in the one maxim:

> "Nor study, sacred lore, nor birth,
> The Brahman makes; 'tis only worth."[3]

Nothing is further from the minds of the men who use such words than the abrogation of the Brahman caste and its privileges. One might say with more justice that they were its most zealous defenders. He who calls the nobility to its duties strengthens the foundation on which it rests. The man who contrasted the Jew who was a Jew outwardly, and the circumcision of the flesh, with the Jew who was a Jew inwardly, and the circumcision of the heart, is the same who answered the question, what advantage the Jew really had over the heathen, with a hearty, "Much, every way!"[4]

---

[1] *v.* 396 (Max Müller, p. 91).

[2] Oldenberg, l.c. S. 195.

[3] Metrical Translations from Sanskrit Writers (Trübner's Oriental Series, VII.), No. lxxxvii. (p. 70), and in general Nos. lxxviii. sqq. (pp. 65 sqq.).

[4] Rom. ii. 28 sq.; iii. 1 sq.

One more consideration, which appears to me to silence all opposition. If the abrogation of caste had lain within the purpose of the Buddha, then, when his disciples came into power, they would have proceeded to effect or at any rate to attempt it. Nothing of the kind seems to have taken place. In Ceylon, under Buddhist supremacy, there are the castes! Nay, it is even a question whether the Buddhists did not introduce them there.[1] If we are to suppose, on the other hand, that there, as elsewhere, the existing facts were too strong for them, how are we to explain that even in their dogmatics room is found for the distinction between higher and lower castes? Here at least they moved freely. It is a fact, however, that according to the orthodox doctrine the successive Buddhas are always born either as Brahmans or as Khshatriyas.[2]

Permit me to express the conclusion in the words of Dr. Oldenberg: "We can understand," he says, "how in our times Buddha should have had the roll assigned to him of a social reformer who broke the oppressive chains of caste and won a place for the poor and humble in the spiritual kingdom which he founded. But if any one would really sketch the work of Buddha, he must, for truth's sake, distinctly deny that the glory of any such deed, under whatever form it may be conceived,

---

[1] The Religions of India, by A. Barth. Authorized Translation, by Rev. J. Wood (Trübner's Oriental Series), p. 125.

[2] Oldenberg, l.c. S. 334.

really belongs to him. If we permit ourselves to speak of the democratic element in Buddhism, we must at any rate keep the full prominence of this fact before our eyes: that the idea of reforming the life of the state, in any direction whatsoever .... was absolutely foreign to the circles in which Buddhism arose."[1]

We have heard enough already to break the point of the contrast which I began by recalling to your minds; but there are other facts which compel us further to modify, if not wholly to relinquish it. Continued researches bring out ever more and more clearly the close internal relationship between Brahmanism and Buddhism, or—to express it at once in a more definite form—the great extent to which Buddhism was indebted to Brahmanism for its doctrine and its organization.

Religion and metaphysics owe their origin to one and the same effort of the human spirit. However strained the relations in which they but too often stand to each other, in their deepest foundations they are one. It is true that, even while admitting this, we must nevertheless be on our guard, as a general principle, against selecting for the special gauge of comparison between any two religions the metaphysical systems which are united to them; for it often happens that this union is of later origin, and that the philosophical system grew up without any connection with

---

[1] L. c. S. 155 f.

the religion which now seems inseparable from it. But in the case of Buddhism it was not so. Here the metaphysic is no foreign element brought in from elsewhere, but is the veritable foundation upon which the whole edifice is raised. Now this foundation was laid by Brahmanism. Before the rise of Buddhism, speculation had already been landed in the antithesis between the one infinite and unalterable Being and the multiplicity of finite beings which only seem to exist, between the blessed repose of the Brahma and the suffering of the world. Moreover, it had already indicated the path by which redemption from that suffering must be won, viz. the removal of the ignorance which takes the show for the reality, and the quenching of the desire for continuance of individual existence.[1] Now what are these but the deepest root-thoughts of Buddhism itself? It may have formed a differing conception of the "Being," it may have denied the "Universal Soul" and the human soul alike, and may possibly have represented the final practical goal otherwise; but it is one and the same conviction, and one way of salvation.

In their ethical systems, likewise, the intimate relationship of the two religions comes clearly into the light. But instead of expatiating on this point, I will at once call your attention to the far more significant fact that the mode of life of the Buddhistic monks is

---

[1] Cf., e.g., Oldenberg, l. c. S. 33—55.

copied, even down to minute details, from that of the Brahmanic ascetics. But why not rather say that the latter is a copy of the former? The question is natural enough, and, considering the absolute want of the historical sense which characterizes the Indians, it might well seem easier to ask than to answer it. And yet I should suppose that in this special case the originality of Brahmanism rests on very firm foundations. In "the sacred laws of the Aryas,"[1] of Âpastamba and Gautama, which are supposed to precede Manu's book of law chronologically, we find the order of the ascetics recognized, together with those of the disciples, the householders and the hermits. Their mode of life is carefully regulated. In Gautama's "Institutes" they are usually called "samnyâsin," but now and then "bhikshus," like the Buddhist mendicants.[2] Nor is the name all that they have in common. One is rather tempted to inquire in what they differ. The ascetic has no provisions, leads a life of chastity, does not change his abode during the rainy season, never enters a village except to beg, and then only once a day, after the inhabitants have finished their meal; he banishes covetousness, controls his tongue, his eyes, his deeds; he wears a garment to cover his nakedness, made, according to some, of an old rag

---

[1] Translated by G. Bühler. Part I. Apastamba and Gautama. In Sacred Books of the East, Vol. II.

[2] L.c. Gautama's Institutes, chap. iii. 2, 11 (Bühler, pp. 190, 191).

which he has first washed.¹ .... But why go on? We have already seen more than enough to prove the close conformity of the Buddhists to the Brahmanic practice, and the points of difference, which are not wanting, do not invalidate the proof. In order, however, to show that Gautama is not alone in laying down these rules, permit me further to cite the shorter redaction of Âpastamba: "He [the samnayâsin or ascetic] shall live without a fire, without a house, without pleasures, without protection. Remaining silent and uttering speech only on the occasion of the daily recitation of the Veda, begging so much food only in the village as will sustain his life, he shall wander about neither caring for this world nor for heaven. It is ordained that he shall wear clothes thrown away (by others as useless). Some declare that he shall go naked. Abandoning truth and falsehood, pleasure and pain, the Vedas, this world and the next, he shall seek the universal soul. (Some say that) he obtains salvation if he knows (the universal soul). (But) that (opinion) is opposed to the Sâstras. (For) if salvation were obtained by the knowledge of the universal soul alone, then he ought not to feel any pain even in this (world). Thereby that which follows has been declared."² The meaning of this last line is, that the necessity of what follows has been demonstrated by the previous argu-

---

[1] L. c. chap. iii. 11—19 (pp. 191 sq.).
[2] Chap. ii. 9, 21, vv. 10—17 (Bühler, l.c. pp. 152 sq.).

ment; and, as the editor informs us, it is *the Yogas* that follow, that is to say, the elaborated system of bodily and spiritual exercises that was also adopted by the Buddhists.[1]

To avoid all misconception, I must add at once that asceticism occupies quite a different place in Brahmanism from that which it takes in Buddhism. On this point the two witnesses we may consult, though differing in details, are essentially at one. Âpastamba is acquainted with the opinion that a life of privation and chastity stands higher and bears nobler fruits than any other, but he expressly combats it, and declares that to have posterity is a great blessing. And "even though some (ascetic) may gain heaven through a portion of (the merit acquired by his former) works or through austerities, whilst he is still in the body, and though he may accomplish (his objects) by his mere wish, still this is no reason to place one order before the other."[2] Gautama goes a step further. He concludes his summary of the rules for ascetics and hermits with these words: "The [i.e. my] venerable teacher (prescribes) one order only, because the order of householders is explicitly prescribed (in the Vedas)." His commentator agrees with this view and further elaborates it. "The duties of a householder .... are

---

[1] See the proof of this in Kern, Geschiedenis van het Buddhisme in Indië, Deel I. 334, 349, 366 sqq.

[2] Chap. ii. 9, 23, v. 3—ii. 9, 24, v. 15 (Bühler, pp. 156—159).

frequently prescribed and praised in all Vedas" and law-books. Wherefore "this alone is the order (obligatory on all men). But the other orders are prescribed only for those unfit for the (duties of a householder). That is the opinion of many teachers."[1] This has anything but a Buddhistic ring. We are all the more certain, therefore, that we are really listening to exponents of Brahmanism, and must consequently attach the more significance to one special trait in Âpasamba's description: the ascetic relinquishes everything, *including the Vedas*. There is no question of this.[2] Indeed, strictly speaking, it is already involved in his withdrawal from society, which prevents the possibility of his performing the prescribed sacrifices or being present at their performance. But, besides this, the attempt to gain "knowledge of the Universal Soul," as conceived by Brahmanism, is in principle incompatible with submission to the authority of the Vedas. Of course this does not mean that every ascetic who had dedicated himself to the effort in question had already broken with the authority of the Vedas, or must gradually relinquish it. But it does mean that their rejection is allied to asceticism, and must of necessity appear in connection with it. We are therefore quite ready to believe Dr. Oldenberg

---

[1] Chap. iii. 36, with the comment (Bühler, pp. 193 sq.).

[2] Cf., e.g., F. Max Müller, Lectures on the Origin and Growth of Religion, as illustrated by the Religions of India (The Hibbert Lectures, 1878), pp. 340 sq., 349 sqq.; Barth, l.c. p. 81.

when he assures us—though confessing at the same time that he cannot prove it—that even before the rise of the Buddha " many, if not most, of the ascetic fraternities had escaped from the authority of the Vedas."[1]

I have spoken of the ascetic fraternities; for it is a fact that they too are pre-Buddhistic. It was far from infrequent for a saint, fleeing from the world, to gather about him a circle of disciples; and in so far as Çâkya-Muni did the same, there was nothing novel or strange in his mission.[2] It is even a question whether we must not go further, and suppose that in his time an ascetic fraternity, to which his own bore a most striking resemblance, had been formed just before it. I refer to that of the Jainas. Investigations into this interesting question are at this very moment being eagerly pursued, and as yet the discussions concerning it are by no means closed.[3] You will remember that in the legend of the Buddha no unimportant place is taken by his contest with the six false teachers.[4] Now one of them, the second in the rank, is Jnâtiputra, the Nirgrantha. But this is a surname of Wardhamâna, who is also called Mahâvîra, " the great hero," and is reverenced by the Jainas as their master, the

---

[1] L. c. S. 64.

[2] Rhys Davids, Lectures, &c., pp. 153 sqq.

[3] The literature is given and the question itself further illustrated in Note XIV.

[4] See, e.g., Kern, l.c. bl. 143—152, cf. 111 v.

founder of their order. The extreme significance of this identification strikes us at once. If we accept it as substantiated, then light is thrown on the hitherto mysterious origin of Jainism, its true relation to Buddhism is defined, and the historical character of the Buddha-legend is supported at any rate at this special point—a result which we shall be better able to appreciate hereafter. But all these prospects—so fair as almost to rouse our suspicion—can only be realized if we have before us a really undesigned confluence of two streams originally independent of each other. In other words, we must be satisfied that Jnâtiputra was not placed amongst Buddha's converts *because* he was the founder of Jainism, and, on the other hand, that the Jainas did not borrow their supposed prototype from the legend of the Buddhists itself. It must be confessed that neither of the suppositions hinted at seems very probable. If the Buddhists had wished to humble Çâkya-Muni's rival, they would have pointed to him emphatically as the founder of Jainism, and this is not done. And, on the other hand, if the Jainas had been at a loss for a name for their "Mahâvîra," they would hardly have gone in search of one amongst the teachers who were defeated and put to shame by the Buddha. But, while admitting all this, we must decline, or at least we must hesitate, to build upon this identification. The written documents we have at our command are separated by too wide an interval from the facts. The two streams of Buddhistic tradition do indeed run parallel here, and we may therefore feel confident that the contest with the false teachers was early taken up in the tradition. But if we are told[1] that these teachers belong to the mythical element in the legend, and were originally neither more nor less than the planets, and if the inference is drawn that the historical names which some of them bear must be referred to misconception or to intentional alteration of the tradition, are we in a position to refute the statement? If matters stand thus with regard to the Buddhistic evidence, we are still less able to rely upon that of the Jainas. Authorities seem to agree that their sacred books do not date from earlier than the fifth or sixth century of our era.[2] This means that they are separated by about a thousand years from the times of the Founder! The scarcity of trustworthy data for the history of India is so great that there is a very natural and proper desire to cherish with the utmost care the few records that give or promise any light, and an extreme reluctance to reject a single item as altogether useless. Nothing, then, is more legitimate than to keep in view the coincidence between the accounts of the Buddhists and the Jainas, and to pursue the line of investigation it suggests. But for the present it would seem rash to infer from the facts laid before us that the founder of Buddhism had only to take over,

---

[1] See Kern, l.c.

[2] Cf. Barth, l.c. pp. 147 sq., and the writers there referred to.

in a more or less modified form, what another had already conceived before him.

In this summary of the points of contact between Brahmanism and Buddhism, I have not aimed at completeness, and do not in any way profess to have attained it. I am satisfied if I have been able to justify the impression produced on my own mind by the researches of the recent ten years, viz. that the sharp contrast which was at first supposed to exist between the two religions has made way, on nearer inspection, for close and manifold relationship. It can hardly surprise us that Indian scholars are now vieing with each other in the recognition of this connection, or, in other words, in asserting the dependence of Buddhism upon Brahmanism. One declares that the Buddhists are in "many points merely Brahmanists in disguise;"[1] another calls Buddhism, "in the natural, genetic classification, a variety of Hinduism,"[2] and even denies it all originality; a third expressly protests against the prevalent misconception "that Gautama was an enemy to Hinduism, and that his chief claim on the gratitude of his countrymen lies in his having destroyed a system of iniquity and oppression and fraud. This is not the case. Gautama was born, and brought up, and lived, and died a Hindu."[3] But instead of filling in, as I might

---

[1] F. Max Müller, Lectures on the Origin and Growth of Religion, &c., p. 137.

[2] Kern, l.c. I. 281 and passim.

[3] T. W. Rhys Davids, Buddhism, being a sketch of the Life and Teachings of Gautama, the Buddha, p. 83.

easily do,[1] this "catalogus testium veritatis," I will call attention to one more fact, which would be almost conclusive even if it stood alone. I refer to the place occupied by the Jâtakas in the Buddhistic literature. The name signifies, according to the traditional interpretation, "birth-histories" or "birth-stories." You will remember to what this name refers. Whenever the Buddha has told one of the stories in question, we find it added at the close that he himself, in one of his previous existences, had taken a part in the action. Thus the whole becomes the description, in a long series of pictures, of all that the Buddha, in his infinite variety of forms, from all eternity, has experienced and accomplished. Now nothing is more obvious, or more universally allowed, than that the stories themselves had originally nothing to do with Buddha and his previous existences, and were simply taken down from the mouth of the people. The application is sometimes very forced, and is evidently a new patch on an old garment. In so far, at least, there is nothing whatever to conflict with the opinion lately expressed by Kern, that "jâtaka" really means no more than "story," and was only brought into connection with "birth" as an after-thought.[2] This brings out yet more clearly what we may well call the unmistakable

---

[1] See, e.g., Rhys Davids, in the "Birth-Stories," which are cited below, I. xxvii. sq.; E. von Hartmann, l.c. S. 318, and elsewhere; Barth, l.c. pp. 115 sqq.

[2] L.c. I. 256 vv.; cf. 303, n. 2.

fact, that the Buddhists appropriated a large measure of the popular wit and wisdom of the Indians, carrying it with them and spreading it everywhere, so that after many wanderings it was even enabled to reach our own quarter of the globe.[1] This is a clear proof that, as the Founder "lived and died a Hindu," so too the religion was in its origin intimately connected with the national life of India, and bears, especially in the most popular and cherished portion of its religious literature, the ineffaceable stamp of the Indian character.

It is only across the ruins of error that we can approach the truth. It is no unreasonable hope, therefore, that in convincing ourselves of the incorrectness of a formerly prevalent opinion, we may have approached nearer to the answer of the real question before us, viz., how Buddhism grew out of Brahmanism, the universal out of the national religion. And, if I am not mistaken, we have indeed discovered at least the direction in which we must look. It is not in the popular belief, nor in any social needs and aspirations, but in philosophical speculation and asceticism, that Buddhism finds its immediate antecedents. You will naturally expect, however, that I should enter into fuller explanations.

But here a colossal difficulty blocks, I will not say

---

[1] On this point cf. T. W. Rhys Davids, Buddhist Birth Stories, or Jātaka Tales: Translation, Vol. I. pp. xxix sqq.

my way, but ours. To avoid the necessity of either anticipations or cumbrous circumlocutions, I have hitherto allowed myself to follow the common usage, and have more than once spoken of "the Founder of Buddhism." You will hardly have blamed me for this, and may even expect that this Founder will occupy the chief place in the review to which we must now proceed. And yet you are aware of the considerations which imperatively forbid me to go on as I have begun. The legend of the Buddha is not pure history in any of the forms in which it has come down to us; but there has been tolerable unanimity so far in the attempt to make history out of it, and that by the application of what, for brevity's sake, I may call the *reducing process*. You understand my meaning. For thousands, or in this case millions, units are substituted, obvious exaggerations and embellishments (or what are intended as such) are cut away, the impossible is reduced to the limits of the possible, and what remains is regarded as history. You all know him!— the gifted and privileged prince, who, pierced by the spectacle of the manifold miseries of humanity, forsakes the palace of his father, and tears himself from the arms of his beloved wife, to go and ponder in solitude on the way of redemption! You remember the temptations and the conflict he has to endure, and how at last he awakes to true insight, and goes through the land preaching and converting; how he gradually assembles an ever-increasing band of disciples round him, and at last, in extreme old age, dies in the arms of his faithful ones. Now let us ponder well—far more expressly and seriously than has generally been done—upon the fact that this Buddha, a man of colossal proportions indeed, but yet of like passions and motives with ourselves, is a creation of the European scholars. He is the result of the operation but now described, an operation which has doubtless been successful in many cases, but has quite as often failed. The same criticism which called this human Buddha into existence is within its rights when it attempts to annihilate him again. And it does attempt it. In Senart's "La Légende du Bouddha," it produced a first essay towards explaining the Buddha, not as a historical, but as a mythical being, as the sun-hero, presented, we will not say in human, but in semi-human shape, no more one of ourselves than the Greek Heracles for instance. The same thesis is now defended on a far broader scale and still more thoroughly by Kern. His great work on the History of Buddhism in India[1] is still incomplete, which would be reason enough for my passing no judgment at present on the position he defends in it, even if I were not restrained in any case by the authority of the men who uphold it on the one hand, and by the opposition it has provoked on the other. When the masters are in the lists, the becoming attitude of the uninitiated is that of the

---

[1] Geschiedenis van het Buddhisme in Indië. Haarlem, 1881, &c.

interested spectator rather than the judge of the combat. Carefully abstaining from anything that would presuppose the decision of the conflict in either sense, I can only allow myself at most to express a modest opinion as to its probable issue.

What, then, is the position in which we stand at this moment? If others feel as I do, they will declare themselves definitely cut off from the right to borrow any hypothesis as to the origin of Buddhism directly from the legend, and specifically from the personality depicted in it. Hitherto it has been assumed that two factors combined to produce this legend, viz. history and inventive imagination. You are still under the fresh impression of the light which was thrown by my immediate predecessor upon the part played by the last-named factor, when he sketched the two ideals that stood before the minds of Gautama's disciples and were applied by them to their lord — the ideal namely of the "Chakka-vatti" or "King of kings," formed or transformed under the influence of the altered political condition of India, and the ideal of "the Buddha" or "Sage" born in the speculative schools.[1] Perhaps, as you heard, and still more as you thought over these most significant communications, the idea may have already suggested itself that these materials were amply sufficient to overwhelm and shatter the historical reality altogether, or, otherwise expressed,

---

[1] Rhys Davids, Lectures, &c., pp. 130 sqq., 141 sqq.

that the latter must have been mighty and strongly marked indeed to enable it to resist and survive such an influx of conceptions foreign to itself, which "might have been equally well applied to any other person in India."[1] But to all this we have now to add the sun-myth—as far as it is an addition, I might almost add; for it is the kernel, if not the beginning and end, of the "Chakka-Vatti" himself.[2] In assuming this third factor I am by no means deserting the modest position which I promised to retain. Whether Buddha is the transformed sun-hero I do not attempt to decide. But that purely mythical touches appear in his legend, no unprejudiced reader of Senart and Kern can doubt. Out of a number of examples, permit me at any rate to select one. We heard but now of the contest with the six false teachers. Now one of the miracles by which Buddha put his rivals to shame was this: "he made an immeasurable path on the vault of heaven, stretching from the Eastern to the Western horizon, and whilst he traversed this path, fire shot out from his right eye and streams of water from his left; his hair shone and rays darted forth from his body."[3] So

---

[1] L.c. 129. The words I have quoted are immediately followed by the qualification, "if he had only excited the same feelings." No doubt there must have been some cause for the application, but there was no need that it should lie in any similarity between the special man and the ideals transferred to him.

[2] L.c. pp. 131 sqq.; Kern, l.c. I. 267 v. (where "Cakrawartin" is explained as "ruler of the world," "wheel-turner").

[3] Kern, l.c. I. 145.

runs the story amongst the Southern Buddhists. In the tradition of their Northern brethren it is said that when the time came for the Lord to repair to the abode designed for him, and to take his seat in it, then "rays shot out from his body, and covered the whole building with tints as of gold." After this he performed such dazzling miracles that he could say to his disciples at the close:

"The fire-fly shines so long as the sun appears not, but no sooner is the great light risen, than the insect falls back before the rays of the sun and shines no more."

"Even so these false teachers held men's ears so long as the Tathâgata spoke not, but now that the perfect Buddha has spoken, the heretical teacher has no word to say, and his followers are silent even as he."[1]

Comment seems superfluous. If the Buddha were only compared to the sun, we should never think of a mythical interpretation. But in this case, though such a comparison is doubtless instituted, there is much more besides. What the sun does, that the Buddha does;—both in this story and in many more! In the genesis of the legend, then, ample allowance must be made for the mythical factor. It is obvious what is involved. It is easier to keep this guest on the other side of the threshold than to control his action when once he is admitted! At every moment we have to face the question whether the touch that seemed to reveal

[1] Ibid. iii. 151.

the man Gautama is not really the more or less disguised description of some natural phenomenon. Such being the state of the case, must we not confess that immediate inferences from the legend can no longer be regarded as legitimate? In other words, we are not free to explain Buddhism from the person of the Founder. On the contrary, if we are to have any right to speak of a founder at all, we must win that right independently of the tradition. Is Buddhism or is it not "une œuvre impersonnelle"? This appears to me to be the real question. If we find good reason to answer it in the negative, and must therefore admit the necessity of a founder, then, but then only, shall we be justified in turning to the legend and drawing together its scattered strokes into the image of a personal founder. This method may be rejected as over-cautious, but we can console ourselves under such a reproach better than under the accusation of having failed to reckon with the difficulties, and having thoughtlessly accepted what really offered no certainty.

But I ought not to express myself as though I had any intention of attempting to solve this question myself. My ambition does not aspire to such an epitaph as Phaëton's. True to my first intention, I shall limit myself to such surmises as the present state of the investigations seems to me to justify.

"I take refuge with the Buddha, the doctrine ('dharma') and the community ('sangha')." Such, we may remember, is the formula of adhesion to Buddhism which constantly appears in the sacred books,[1] and is doubtless borrowed from the reality. It is the unanimous opinion, so far as I know, of the scholars who have interpreted this formula, that "sangha," the community, does not mean the whole circle of the faithful, but *the order of mendicants*. It certainly needs no further proof, after this, that the order in question occupies a very high position in Buddhism. To be placed with the Buddha and "the dharma," even as third in the series, is the highest honour that could well be paid it. But how did it reach this position? Two answers are conceivable. Either it rose out of the whole Buddhistic Church, in the longer or shorter lapse of time, to the eminence it ultimately occupied, or it was from the beginning the third member of the triad, and in that case is chronologically antecedent to the Church. The alternative may be expressed still more briefly thus: the "sangha" is either the *fruit* or the *germ* of Buddhism. I do not find the alternative so sharply formulated by all the authorities; but wherever it does appear, there I find the preference invariably given to the second hypothesis: the order of monks is the "prius," the proper and original Buddhism. Nothing, as it seems to me, could be more natural or legitimate than this decision. In the sacred books it is the "bhikshus" or mendicants to whom

---

[1] Even in Açoka's inscription at Babhra mention is already made of "the three that are called Buddha, dharma, sangha." See Kern, Over de jaartelling enz, bl. 37.

the Buddha submits his teaching. The difference between them and "the adherents" is far more than is involved in a different mode of life and the duties connected with it. Beyond all that, there is a genuine distinction in rights and privileges. To convince ourselves of this, we have but to open any one of the sacred books. Let me at any rate take a few examples from the Sutta-nipâta in Dr. Fausböll's translation.[1] The "Ratamasutta" alone would be enough to decide the matter.[2] It is devoted to describing and glorifying the triad mentioned above. Out of the seventeen verses, no less than eight are devoted to the "sangha." In it, as in the Buddha and the "dharma," may be found the "excellent jewels" which the writer extols, and by which he hopes there "may be salvation." Finally, he turns to the spirits, whom he supposes to be his hearers, with this exhortation: "Whatever spirits have come together here, either belonging to the earth or living in the air, let us worship the perfect (tathâgata [one of the epithets of honour bestowed on the Buddha also]) Sangha, revered by gods and men; may there be salvation!"[3] This "sangha" is not the flower or the representative of a greater whole, without which it would be incomplete; it is, in a single word, Buddhism itself. But let us listen to another sutta. Sabhiya, dissatisfied with the answers given to his

---

[1] The Sacred Books of the East, Vol. X. Part ii.
[2] Op. cit. pp. 37—40.   [3] Ibid. v. 17 (pp. 39 sq.).

questions by the six false teachers, turns to Bhagavat, the Buddha, and finds in him what he seeks. Accordingly he becomes his disciple, and expresses his determination thus: "I take refuge in the venerable Gotama, in the Dhamma, and in the Assembly of Bhikkhus; I wish to receive the robe and the orders from the venerable Bhagavat." He is told in answer that he must first go through a period of four months' probation, then "Bhikkhus who have appeased their thoughts will give him the robe and the orders." Sabhiya submits to the conditions, and in due time is received into the order, "having in a short time in this existence by his own understanding ascertained and possessed himself of that highest perfection of a religious life for the sake of which men of good family rightly wander away from their houses to a houseless state. '[The germ of a new] Birth had been destroyed, a religious life had been led, what was to be done had been done, there was nothing else (to be done) for this existence,' so he perceived, and the venerable Sabhiya became one of the saints."[1] It was only thus that he could reach the final goal. For, as it is put elsewhere, "Two whose mode of life and occupation are quite different, are not equal: a householder maintaining a wife, and an unselfish virtuous man. A householder (is intent) upon the destruction of other living creatures, being

---

[1] L.c. pp. 85—95. The passage between inverted commas is repeated on p. 105.

unrestrained; but a Muni always protects living creatures, being restrained. As the crested bird with the blue neck (the peacock) never attains the swiftness of the swan, even so a householder does not equal a Bhikkhu, a secluded Muni meditating in the wood."[1] We do not overlook the fact that between the "bhikshu" and the "adherent" no impassable wall of partition is raised. The latter may become a monk, and conversely a monk, since he is not bound by a vow for life, may cease to belong to the order without necessarily falling away from Buddha. Nor must we forget that the "adherents," too, have their duties to fulfil, and that great privileges are accorded to them. But, as we read in the very Sutta that lays such stress on all this,[2] the "complete Bhikkhu-dhamma cannot be carried out by one who is taken up by (worldly) occupations." It is the monks alone who tread "the noble path."

There is but one satisfactory explanation of all this. In the Buddhistic Church the congregation of monks is not only the supreme and ruling body, but it is the true kernel—in a word, the *community* itself, of which the innumerable believers form a colossal adjunct. *A monastic order with its lay associates:* such is Buddhism. Is it not uniformly so represented in the legend of the Founder? The crowds which he gathers round

---

[1] L.c. pp. 35 sq. (Munisutta, vv. 14, 15).

[2] L.c. pp. 62—66 (Dhammakisutta, v. 18, p. 65).

him might make us forget it; but he himself remains a monk, and they who follow him on his journeys, the disciples in the full sense of the word, are monks likewise. Why should we not accept this representation as it stands?

We have now learned the terms in which to put the question as to the origin of Buddhism. For it still remains a question even when duly formulated. It is not the point of departure, the order of the Bhikshus itself, that we have to account for, for we have already seen that it rose quite naturally out of Brahmanism, and was not the only one of its kind.[1] Nor is it the emancipation from the authority of the Vedas (which doubtless characterized it from the first), for in this too it has been shown[2] to have followed existing analogy. Even the spread of the Buddhistic order beyond the boundaries of Magadha, with its continued existence long after its first formation, however remarkable, is by no means inexplicable. Why should we not suppose,[3] in accordance with the indications of the sacred books themselves, that, in distinction from other ascetic unions which remained dependent upon their teacher and his presence with them, the Buddhistic order extended itself more freely and took up fresh members wherever it had established its branches? But now, if I am not mistaken, we have reached the point at which

---

[1] Vid. sup. pp. 249 sqq.   [2] Vid. sup. pp. 252 sq.
[3] With Rhys Davids, Lectures, &c., pp. 156 sq.

analogy fails us. For Buddhism was not content with this freer and wider extension of its borders. Without ceasing to be a monastic order, it becomes a church. It takes up into itself a countless host of lay brothers and sisters. Presently it oversteps the boundaries not only of its fatherland in the narrower sense, but even of India itself. It establishes itself in Ceylon, and in every region to which its missionaries can penetrate. Whence is this? we ask. How did a religion of the world spring out of a monastic order?

We will not exaggerate the difficulty. We may reflect that up to a certain point such an extension is not unnatural. The householder looks up to the ascetic with reverence and admiration, while the ascetic on his side depends on the laymen for his daily subsistence, and is thus naturally led to show them good-will, and to give them his attention when they come to him with their questions and difficulties. And when during the rainy season the ascetics relinquished for a time their wandering life, a closer connection would establish itself between them and the people of the district in which they sojourned. Without deserting the realm of fact, we can readily conceive that here and there, under special circumstances, this bond might be drawn still closer. But in Buddhism we have something more than an altogether voluntary and, by its very nature, loose connection between the monks and the laymen. For the "upâsakas," the "adherents," though they do not withdraw from social life, yet renounce the laws and usages that prevail in society. And the monks on their side *go out* to preach and to convert. Though we cannot follow the detailed course of their propaganda, it admits of no doubt that they early devoted themselves to missionary enterprize, and ere long organized it systematically. This, then, is the fact of which we are seeking the explanation. May we suppose that *the Founder* of the Buddhistic conventual order consciously lowered the partition-wall between it and the world, and stretched out a rescuing hand across it to the brothers and sisters beyond?

We reserve our answer to this question yet a moment longer. The field of possibility is so wide, that we dare not say it does not hold concealed the materials for some hypothesis that will satisfy our demands still better. Meanwhile, let us look about us for any analogous phenomena which may throw light on our problem. We need not go far in our search; for the history of Christianity furnishes us with a truly striking analogy—indeed I might say more than one. As contemplative asceticism prepared the way in India for the rejection of the authority of the Vedas, so does the ecclesiastical Reformation of the sixteenth century find its antecedents in the medieval mysticism, and in the cloisters where it was most sedulously fostered.[1] But this is not the point to which I now wish to refer.

---

[1] O. Pfleiderer, die Religion, ihr Wesen und ihre Geschichte (Leipzig, 1869), II. 204 f.

The Western no less than the Eastern world has its mendicant orders, though ours differ from those of India in being a later development as well as a radical modification of the original monachism. The monk and the hermit withdraw from society to live to God and so to save their own souls. Their object, in principle at least, and subject to the happy inconsistencies of practice, is selfish. On the contrary, the rise of the mendicant orders is "the practical declaration that even the monks had not acquitted themselves of their task until, while remaining true to their fundamental positions, they had ceased to live for themselves, and after the manner of the Apostles had striven to labour in the world for the purposes of the gospel."[1] This applies as much to the Dominicans as to the Franciscans, but not in the same way. The former, intent on combating heresy, and soon active as judges of the faith, were distinguished by a more aristocratic spirit. The Franciscans, on the other hand, mingled with the common people, and soon entered into the most intimate relations with them. Ere long they found other means of extending their borders besides the influx of fresh mendicant brothers. To the second order, that of the Clarissines, was soon added the "*tertius ordo de pœnitentia*," or the order of the "*fratres conversi.*" Baur describes the latter as "a union in which the

---

[1] F. C. Baur, die christ. Kirche des Mittelalters in den Hauptmomenten ihrer Entwickelung (Tübingen, 1861), S. 467.

layman conformed as nearly to the practice of the monks as was possible to him while still layman. Though the tertiares were united by an intimate bond to the Order, they formed an association in which participation in that Order approximated to the ordinary relations of life, and its rule only regulated the lives of the brothers, positively and negatively, in a lower degree."[1] Gradually the numbers joining this third order grew enormously. .... What say you? Is not this a wonderful counterpart of what must have taken place centuries before in India? The extension of the Franciscans could not of course pass certain barriers. It took place in a well-organized Church under a strong central authority. Even as it was, the creation of an intermediary state such as that of the tertiares excited suspicion and jealousy. If the Order had attempted to go still further, it must unquestionably have come into conflict with the ecclesiastical authorities. But suppose for a moment these barriers removed. In the place of the disciplined West, put such a land as India, where the most unbounded freedom and toleration reign. Will it not follow of itself that from the Christian mendicant orders there will grow up a community similar to the Buddhistic Church?

But it will not have escaped your notice that in drawing this parallel I have been obliged to confine myself to one of the two mendicant orders, that of

---

[1] L.c. S. 487.

the Franciscans. The same expansive power did not lie in the institution of St. Dominic, though in other respects there was so strong a resemblance between the two orders. The contrast in this particular is obviously connected with the different directions, to which I have already referred, taken by their respective activities. But whence does this difference in its turn spring? So much at least is certain, that it fully corresponds to the difference of character of the two founders. His naïve simplicity and unbounded tenderness made Francis of Assisi a man of the people, whilst Dominic's stern intensity of character and deep reverence for ecclesiastical learning seemed to predestinate him for Grand Inquisitor. Nothing is more natural, therefore, than to suppose that each of the founders left his own spirit stamped upon the order he founded, and thus, as it were, prescribed and determined the course of its future development; and in this view accordingly Hase[1] and Baur,[2] not to mention others, unite. I repeat the question, then, with increased confidence: must we not call in the person of the founder in the case of Buddhism likewise to explain what we have observed? Can we suppose that the features which characterize his order, in distinction from the other ascetic unions, are anything else than the impress of his individuality?

---

[1] Franz von Assisi. Ein Heiligenbild (Leipzig, 1856), S. 69 ff.
[2] L.c. S. 169 f.

The temptation is great to go a step further. When we remember that Dante could say of Francis and Dominic, "He tells of both, who one commendeth, which of them soe'er,"[1] we may surely venture to compare St. Francis with the Buddha of the legend. But, after all, the points of difference are too numerous. And yet Francis and the Buddha have in common this one thing: a tender compassion that embraces every creature, not forgetting "our brothers, the birds," and "our sisters, the swallows," but turning above all to suffering man. And this one thing—is it not much? nay, is it not all?

You will more fully understand the bearing of the question I have ventured to ask as to the Founder's personality, if I cite for contrast a few sentences from Dr. Oldenberg: "If it was usual formerly," he writes,[2] "to describe Buddha as the religious re-creator of India, as the one great champion in the great struggle of his time, henceforth as research advances we shall find ourselves more and more distinctly compelled to regard him as simply one of the many contemporary heads of ascetic unions,—one concerning whom it is not and cannot be in any way shown that he excelled his rivals in profundity of thought or force of will even in any approach to the same proportion in which, perhaps by nothing but *a chain of purely accidental*

---

[1] Paradiso, xi. 40, 41.

[2] Zeitschr. d. d. morgenl. Gesellschaft, Band XXXIV. 748 f.

circumstances, he has come to transcend them in actual renown. . . . . From the *multitudinous saviours of the world* who were traversing India in every direction about the year 500 B.C., a second figure has already issued into distinct recognition." This refers, as you will at once suppose, to the founder of the Jaina order, of whom we have already heard, and to whom I will not now return. What we are concerned with at present is the estimate of the Buddha and his historical significance expressed in the passage cited. Elsewhere Oldenberg speaks in the same sense. The " many saviours of the world " appear again in his admirable work on Buddha,[1] and there too we meet with the assertion that " the triumph of his doctrine over that of his contemporary rivals, centuries after they had all died, was decided *by an accident,*" though a certain qualification follows in the admission that possibly " the more rays of light fall into the darkness, the more this play of fortune may be seen to resemble the revelation of an internal necessity."[2] Why only *resemble* it? I would ask. Is it decreed for ever that it must really be an accident? " Saviour of the world " is not such a commonplace title that we can afford to bestow it carelessly; and before we give it to all manner of contemporaries of Çâkya-Muni, we demand the proof not only that they were teachers and heads of ascetic unions, but also that, like their rival, they conceived

---

[1] S. 5, 68.   [2] S. 179.

and began to execute the plan of extending the fruits of their deeper insight even to those who stood outside the circle of their disciples. For this is the point on which all turns. And this, unless everything deceives me, is a *personal* conception, not the outcome of this or that philosophical or unphilosophical system, but one of those "great thoughts" which, to use Vauvenargue's celebrated phrase, "spring from the heart." Only to the man in whom that conception rose can we allow the title of "saviour of the world;" and in explaining the grand result that crowned his effort, we need not reckon with his rivals, and need make no appeal to chance. Let us be on our guard against exaggerated hero-worship, and, above all, against admiration of fictitious heroes, but no less against any semblance of neglecting the full significance of *personality*. The temptation to fall into this latter mistake rises, I think, from a dislike of mystery. But mystery there is and must remain; nor can it be diminished by the facile process of substituting plurals for singulars!

We must regard Buddhism, then, as a turning-point in the religious development of India. What asceticism was in those regions before the rise of Çâkya-Muni, we may learn from one who knows both the land and its literature well, and we shall thus escape all danger of being carried away by the sound and missing the reality. "The motives which led so many Indians to bid farewell to the life of society were, from the nature of the case, very varied. One fell into despair because his fairest expectations had failed him, his friend had betrayed or his beloved deceived him. Another, who in the wantonness of youth had drunk too deeply of the cup of pleasure, came to perceive that sensual indulgence may for a moment intoxicate the spirit, but that the momentary appeasing of a passion brings no true satisfaction, and does but stimulate desires all the more. He perceives that he has been like one who should drink salt water to appease his thirst, and, far from being refreshed, should but increase his pangs. A third, of quiet and retiring nature, feels himself misplaced in the press and turmoil of this world. He sees how men, in base self-seeking, embitter one another's life, and he loses sight ever more and more completely of all the fair and noble traits of humanity that redeem the emptiness and commonplaceness of social life, and so he determines to forsake the evil world, and rather to live in the wilderness with the beasts, than in the courts of kings and in the turmoil of cities. There is yet another who has fulfilled his duties as a man, as a father, as a citizen, and who now longs for rest. The world retains no charm for him, and in his old age he would fain withdraw from the vain engrossments of daily life and give himself up to still reflection on the deep questions of man's destiny here and hereafter."[1] To these special causes are added

---

[1] Kern, het Indische kluizenaars- en monnikenleven (Mededeelingen vanwege het Nederl. Zendelinggenootschap, Deel XXV.), bl. 138 v.

the general influences of the climate of India, which greatly alleviates the privations of life in solitude, and the system of education, so eminently calculated to stimulate the love of a speculative life.[1] Now, easy as all this is to understand, it does not modify the judgment I have already pronounced, that the ascetic's effort is a selfish one. But it need not necessarily remain so. It may be consecrated and transfigured by the spirit of love. The ascetic may strive to make others share the salvation which he himself has gained by withdrawal from the world. In full measure, indeed, it is within the reach of those only who follow him on the path which he has chosen. So it is, and so it must remain. Without renouncing asceticism itself, it is impossible to make any change in this. But the attempt may be made to bring within the reach of those who have not bid farewell to social life such measure of salvation as is possible for them. Now in Buddhism this change of conception was accomplished, and it is this which, as it seems to me, we must derive from the personal initiative of the Founder.

But I press this point no further. Even those who question our right thus to argue from the work to the work-master, will readily allow that the thought I have ascribed to the Founder did actually become a power in the order founded, and takes a prominent place, if not the first, amongst the causes which led to

---

[1] Ibid. bl. 139—141.

its amazing extension. As we like to picture him in history, such in thought and deed does the Buddha appear in the legend. For there it is tender pity for suffering humanity that makes him the saviour of the world; and what but this same feeling could the promulgation of the legend itself rouse and stimulate in others? It is true that this legendary Buddha is more than human, and this weakens in no small degree the impression which his image would otherwise produce. But we are free to believe that the gigantesque proportions which repel us are less offensive to the Asiatic, and, above all, that the deepest impression must be produced upon the minds of the faithful, as upon our own, by those purely human touches which the miracles have neither smothered nor altogether disguised. In this case, it is the spirit of compassion which the legend must quicken, it is the longing to redeem and bless that must be the fruit of pondering over it. From the moment when its main lines were fixed—and no one denies that this was comparatively early—it became the Buddhist's sacred duty to propagate the faith. And who shall tell us how many have been awakened, how many have been sustained in their work, by the example of the Master?

And now, at the close of the whole review, what have we gained that will bring us nearer our goal? This: that we have learned *how* Hinduism became international in Buddhism, and in this knowledge have found the key to explain the character of the latter. "Buddhism sprang from an Indian monastic order. Asceticism—more specifically the Brahmanic, contemplative asceticism—was the connecting link between the national and the universal religion." Such are the results that we must keep steadily in view. I have no need to sound the praises of the Buddhistic ethics, as though any one thought of disparaging them; nor need I expatiate on the beneficent influence which they have exercised in more lands than one. And yet even here we are forced at once to insist on a needful qualification. Buddhism has succeeded in taming barbarians, and still shows itself admirably calculated to assist in maintaining order and discipline; but has it ever supported a people in its endeavours after progress, in its recuperative efforts when smitten by disaster, in its struggle against despotism? No such instances are known. And indeed we had no right to expect them. Buddhism does not measure itself against this or that abuse, does not further the development or reformation of society either directly or indirectly, for the very simple reason that it *turns away* from the world on principle. Let us reckon fully with the meaning and the ultimate consequences of this principle. It must and it does result in absolute quietism—nay, even indifferentism. You do well to protest against any semblance of an attempt to push to extremes the principles adopted by others; and your suspicions might be roused were I to seek out here and there a few strong expressions, in order to show that the Buddhistic ethics are really characterized by the tendency I have attributed to them. But in truth we have not to make any search at all. The same Sutta-nipâta from which I have already quoted places the justness of our inference in the clearest light. It is there said in praise of the Buddha: "As a beautiful lotus does not adhere to the water,[1] so thou dost not cling to good and evil, to either."[2] And so must it be with his faithful disciples also, if they obey his word: "Not by (any philosophical) opinion, not by tradition, not by knowledge, not by virtue and (holy) works, can any one say that purity exists; nor by absence of (philosophical) opinion, by absence of tradition, by absence of knowledge, by absence of virtue and (holy) works either; having abandoned these without adopting (anything else), let him, calm and independent, not desire existence."[3] Elsewhere we are told of men "who consider virtue the highest of all, say that purity is associated with restraint; having taken upon themselves a (holy) work they serve."[4] If one who is such, it is said, "falls off from virtue and (holy) works, he trembles, having missed (his) work; he laments, he prays for purity in this world, as one

---

[1] The same image, but in a better form, appears in v. 812: "As a drop of water does not stick to a lotus."

[2] v. 547 (Sabhiyasutta, v. 38, p. 94).

[3] v. 839 (Mâgandiyasutta, v. 5, p. 160).

[4] v. 898 (Mahâviyûhasutta, v. 4, p. 171).

who has lost his caravan or wandered away from his house."[1] Such a one you might expect would receive praise for his earnest view of life. Not at all! In the judgment of the Master he has not yet reached the ideal state. He still desires something, and fears when it is taken from him or threatens to fail him. Infinitely above him stands the muni, who "having abandoned his former passions, not contracting new ones, not wandering according to his wishes, being no dogmatist, is delivered from the (philosophical) views, being wise, and does not cling to the world, *neither does he blame himself.*"[2]

You observe that here, philosophical investigations and opinions are, to say the least of it, spoken of with scant sympathy. And the truth is, that a strong conviction with the resultant zeal to propagate it is hardly consistent with the quietism commended by the Buddha. We are not left to draw this inference for ourselves, however. A good part of the Sutta-nipâta is devoted to combating dogmatism, which latter is taken in so wide an acceptation as not essentially to differ from making any single assertion and denying its opposite. "The Brâhmaṇa"—here, as elsewhere, the true disciple of the Buddha—"for whom (the notions) 'equal' and 'unequal' do not exist, would he say, 'This is true'? Or with whom should he dispute, saying, 'This is false'? With whom should he enter into

---

[1] *v.* 899 (ibid. *v.* 5, pp. 171 sq.).
[2] *v.* 913 (ibid. *v.* 19, p. 174).

dispute?"[1] This sentiment is not inspired, as one might readily suppose it to be, by an overmastering though transient revulsion from the endless war of words. No; Buddhism raises the rejection of every affirmation to the rank of a principle.[2] Naturally this, like all other quietism, has its limits. It is compelled to turn round upon any one who attempts to undermine the basis on which it rests, just as the sceptic must have an opinion against him who declares that knowledge is attainable. It cannot really avoid either asserting or denying. But the very attempt is a clear testimony to its origin. Vigorous affirmations are characteristic of youth. Long must the conflict of the schools have lasted before it can be commended as the topmost point of wisdom to refrain from forming an opinion! Wearied of life and of barren conflict, Buddhism goes on its way, and takes up the task of rescuing humanity from the vain efforts that lead to nothing.

And, accordingly, the Buddhist propaganda seems to me to bear a peculiar character of its own. Its mission is not to root out what it holds to be deadly errors or to proclaim precious truths, nor, in the first instance, to contend against moral evil or to build up a society in which righteousness and peace shall dwell.

---

[1] v. 843 (Mâgandiyasutta, c. 9, p. 161).

[2] Cf. what Kern—following Koeppen and Burnouf—says on this subject, Gesch. van het Buddhisme in Indië, I. 276 v.; and Rhys Davids, Lectures, &c., p. 155.

It seeks not to convert, but to *rescue*,—to rescue from delusion and desire. The moral life is not its end, but its means. The reality was (happily!) too strong for it, and compelled it to recognize and respect as an independent magnitude that to which in principle it could assign no such lofty place. But its want of a positive ideal avenges itself. It cannot have a future unless it has and gives a prospect in the future. It is not the present inactivity of Buddhism, but its devoted zeal in earlier times, that astonishes us. We gratefully observe that at first compassion overbore quietism. But that quietism, in its turn, has at last maimed compassion, who shall wonder?[1]

It will not have escaped your observation that in speaking of the limits of Buddhism I have had Christianity in my mind. Nor is there the smallest reason why I should not name it. Our judgment of the two religions can only gain in value by our placing them side by side, and letting the light fall both on their resemblances and their differences. No comparison could suggest itself more naturally. This would, indeed, be far otherwise if the doctrine of God adopted by each religion formed its kernel and determined its character. In that case, Christianity would have nothing in common with Buddhism; for it has been said of the latter, not without reason, that if it is a

---

[1] Cf. E. von Hartmann, op. cit. S. 338 ff.

religion at all, it is at any rate a religion without God. But for more reasons than one, no such standard of comparison can be accepted, or, at any rate in this special case, applied without extremely important qualifications. Although theological conviction is far from being a matter of indifference, yet in religion still more stress must be laid upon the disposition of the affections, upon the tone of mind, upon the consecration of heart and life. We must remember also that the denial of God's existence rested in the original Buddhism upon a purely philosophical basis, and left the popular belief in the Devas undisturbed; while in the later development, with its deification of the Buddha, scarcely any trace of it is left. In spite of this difference, then, the resemblance between Buddhism and Christianity retains its high significance and importance. In the one, as in the other, the idea of redemption is the central point. In both religions, the ideal of self-renunciation, purity and devotion, is realized by the Founder himself. The moral requirements of the two coincide in some of their main features and in many details. Nor is this all. By the side of the Buddhistic we have the Christian monachism. How striking the resemblance between them I need not remind you. The danger of actually confounding them is by no means imaginary. But not even this resemblance strikes us so much as the fact that a whole section of the Christian Church recognizes life in the cloister as the complete realization of the demands of

Christianity. "Religio," in the Middle Ages, meant separation from the world; and to the present day the "religious" are the members of the spiritual orders. With this usage, the doctrine of the Catholic Church, as expounded by Thomas Aquinas for instance, is in perfect harmony.[1] How it stands in this respect with Buddhism we have just seen. Could a more striking agreement be conceived?

And yet it is at this very point that the deeper, nay the fundamental, difference between the two religions is revealed. In Buddhism there is monasticism from the first. In Christianity it appears later on; and only gradually, and in the face of opposition, wins the place which it occupies in Catholicism. And this is no mere chronological difference. There could be no Buddhism without "bhikshus"—there is a Christianity without monks. In other words, that which in one case constitutes the very essence of the religion, and cannot be removed even in thought without annulling the system itself, is in the other case no more than one of the many forms under which the idea of the religion reveals itself, or rather—may I not say, without fearing contradiction on your part?—is the natural but one-sided development of certain elements in the original movement, coupled with gross neglect of others which have equal or still higher right to assert themselves.

And, in point of fact, what is more natural than that

---

[1] Cf. J. J. Baumann, die klassische Moral des Katholicismus (Philos. Monatshefte, Band XV., 1879, S. 449—466).

precisely here, in the closer inspection of the place which asceticism takes and the honour in which it is held in the two religions, a clear light should fall on the character of each? Nowhere does the essential nature of a religion reveal itself more distinctly than in its attitude towards asceticism, in the grounds on which, in greater or smaller measure, it commends or discountenances it. We are therefore perfectly justified in following back this special line as far as possible— that is to say, to the very origin of the two religions. Indeed, it may well be said that in this case their diverse origin spontaneously offers, nay forces, itself upon us as the explanation of the difference between them. The conditions under which Buddhism arose are still clearly before our minds. What a contrast to the genesis of Christianity! Born out of the national life of the Jews, Christianity stands in immediate connection with the political pressure of those days that revived the expectations and stirred the aspirations which had grown in the course of ages out of the national religion. Accordingly it was at first intimately bound up with the Jewish nationality. The first Christians never dreamed of withdrawing from the communion of their people. When, after a time, their religion revealed in action the universalism which from the first had belonged to it in principle, the inevitable result of the circumstances was, that a great part of Israelitism accompanied the world-religion on its march through the Roman empire; but of course this could not obviate the necessity, wherever it established itself, of its taking count of the prevailing needs and adapting itself to the existing stage of civilization, and so applying its principles and developing its new forms. In a word, Christianity was calculated, by virtue of its origin, and found itself compelled by its resultant nature, to enter into ever fresh combinations with the national life of its confessors. It could not help *nationalizing* itself, nor does it cease throughout the centuries actually to do so. Its history is that of the mutual reactions of the Christian principles, in the narrower sense, and the national development of the Christian peoples. In such a history, how could monachism, or any other one-sided phenomenon whatever, possibly be more than one of the many shoots of the wide-spreading tree?

But it is not only as regards its *form* that the special characteristic of Christianity is explained by its origin. To its birth from the *Jewish*, in distinction to every other nationality, it owes an essential portion of the *content* to which it has never been untrue amidst all the changes which it has undergone. I speak of it now with exclusive reference to the contrast with Buddhism; for, if I am not mistaken, the difference between the latter and Christianity is closely connected with the respective absence and presence in the two cases of these specifically Jewish elements. Buddhism, in the first place, misses the aggressive character which Christianity has always displayed—outwards towards the unbelievers, and inwards towards the heretics. Why so? Whence comes it that Christianity, in contradiction to Buddhism, has too often been promulgated by force, and has failed to characterize itself, like the other, by unlimited toleration? Because the Christians' God was Israel's Yahweh, "compassionate, gracious, long-suffering and plenteous in mercy," aye! the Father in heaven, but yet "a jealous God," who will endure "no other gods before his face," is "of purer eyes than to behold iniquity," and still from time to time "a consuming fire." The violence committed in the name and to the glory of this God in the course of the ages, not one of us will undertake to defend; for who are we that we should put ourselves in the place of the All-knowing and the Holy One, and identify our fallible opinions with the truth itself? And yet, on the other hand, we cannot regard the combative character of Christianity as a simple defect and disaster. Let us reflect that Buddhism would never have been, as it was, toleration itself, had it been any less sceptical and quietistic. The persecution of those who hold other opinions may start from the vain supposition of the persecutor that he is in possession of the absolute truth; yet at any rate it presupposes the belief in truth, and confirms the sense of its absolutely supreme importance.[1] But whatever difference of feeling may

---

[1] "C'est aux excès du fanatisme religieux que l'on doit l'importance extrême attachée depuis lors à la question de vérité sur tous les domaines." .... "On peut à bon droit se demander si l'amour

remain as to this point, we shall all be at one with respect to the second inheritance from Israelitism. It is the belief in the triumph of Yahweh over everything that opposes him, the expectation of the kingdom of God, the confident trust in the realization of the moral ideal. This is what Buddhism does not possess,[1] and therefore cannot give. It is a blank which cannot be filled, and which nothing can compensate! The conception of the kingdom of God, one of the chief factors in the genesis of Christianity, remains through all the ages its best recommendation and its greatest might. Through this conception it joins in every legitimate effort of the individuals or the peoples who profess it; with this conception it strikes right into the course of their development, and gives it the true direction, the genuine inspiration, the higher consecration. On each new field this one ideal takes a special form. Each of the subordinate branches into which it parts itself is

---

passionné du vrai en toute chose, qui a fait la science moderne, eût été possible ou du moins fût devenu très commun, si l'Europe n'avait pas traversé des siècles d'intolérance. Le fait est que l'antiquité connut cette noble passion à un bien moindre degré que nous." .... "C'est l'intolérance orthodoxe de l'Eglise au moyen-âge qui a imprimé à la société chrétienne cette disposition à chercher à tout prix le vrai, dont l'esprit scientifique moderne n'est que l'application. .... Comment expliquer autrement que la grande science ne se soit développée, n'ait été poursuivie avec constance qu'au sein des sociétés chrétiennes?" (A. Réville, Prolégomènes de l'histoire des religions, pp. 234, 314.)

[1] Read, for example, the strikingly beautiful but comfortless meditation on the fleeting life of man, in Sutta-nipâta, vv. 574—593 (Sallasutta, pp. 106—108 of Dr. Fausböll's translation).

gradually modified under the influence of the never-resting life of humanity. But in the idea of the kingdom of God there is room for them all, and all experience its regenerating power. If it be true that Christianity bears this idea within it in virtue of its origin, may we not find in this connection with the Israelite nationality the secret of its power and the pledge of its endurance?

We stand at the end of the path we had marked out to tread together. Pardon the hope that no justification of the thesis with which I began is now necessary: "The connection of the universal with the national religions furnishes the explanation and the measure of their universalism." Indeed, if the facts which we have observed have not already substantiated it, it would be mere lost labour to attempt to prove it now. I must therefore confine myself to a few hints; and I trust that nothing more is needed.

"Universalism as a fact and as a quality:"—if we bear this distinction in mind, and proceed to review the three religions of the world, noting not their extension and the number of their confessors, but their character, we can have no hesitation in pronouncing Christianity the most universal of religions; and that because it is the best qualified for its moral task—to inspire and consecrate the personal and the national life.

Islam and Buddhism alike fail to acquit themselves of their task beyond a certain point. There they find a line drawn which they cannot pass, because their origin forbids it.

Islam, reared by the genius of one man out of materials imported from elsewhere, enters the world as a rounded system, seems at first completely to answer to the wants of those to the level of whose capacity it was framed, shows itself even afterwards and up to the present time suited to the peoples and the individuals who have not risen above the standpoint of legalism, but misses the power so to. transform itself as to meet the requirements of a higher type of life which in its present form it cannot satisfy. At a given period, it becomes a hindrance to that development of the spirit which it must actually choke if it be not strong enough to cast it off.

Buddhism seems, at a first glance, to possess, in marked distinction from Islam, an astounding power of adaptation. What a difference we note between the Northern and the Southern Buddhists, and, again, within the groups themselves which we so designate! But yet, in the midst of all this variety, there is everywhere the same monstrous onesidedness, the ineffaceable stamp of an origin, not from life, but from the speculation that has turned away from life and is blind to its significance and its worth. They are indeed genuine and not imagined needs to which Buddhism ministers;[1] but are there not other and no less essential demands to which it remains deaf, and in the face of which it is powerless? Even in India, its fatherland, these wants are too deeply felt to allow of its maintaining itself there. How much more must it fall short of its task elsewhere!

And now the third religion of the world! Richard Rothe has said: "Christianity is the most mutable of all things. That is its special glory."[2] The statement will meet with opposition on every side. It will be allowed that Christianity is, alas! capable of being deformed and corrupted, but not that it is mutable in itself. It has been fixed once for all—in the life-image and the teaching of its Founder, thinks one; in the New Testament, says another; in the Church which was founded by Christ and is guided by his spirit, cries a third; in the symbols of this or that Protestant communion, suggest others as an emendation. But Rothe was right. The historical view refuses to be silenced by this "concordia discors," nay, rather finds in it the confirmation of its own position. Not refusing to see Christianity in all these forms—more in some, less in others, but Christianity in all—it will reject as wholly illegitimate the claim of any one of them to *be* Chris-

---

[1] Rhys Davids, Lectures, &c., pp. 157 sqq.

[2] "Das Christenthum ist das allerveränderlichste; das ist sein besonderer Ruhm" (Stille Stunden. Aphorismen aus R. R.'s handschriftlichem Nachlasz (Wittenberg, 1872), S. 357).

tianity itself. It recognizes—how can it do otherwise?—the great difference between the three main types: the earliest confessors of Jesus' name, the Catholics, and the Protestants; between the withdrawal from the world of the first Messianic communities, the Church's struggle for dominion over the world, and the gradual and progressive penetration of the world by the Christlike spirit.[1] But in all these, and in all their countless shades and subdivisions, it sees the Christian principle translated, with varying measure of purity and completeness, into fact. What is the sum of them, then, but "Christianity," and how can we do otherwise than call it "the most mutable of all things"? This character must be recognized, and it can also be understood and explained. For it has its ground in that same close connection between Christianity and Israelitism to which I need not now revert. To this connection it was due that Christianity entered the world without being rounded off or closed as a system. No religious founder ever left more for his followers to do than Jesus. It was his to utter the great principles and to reveal them in his life and death. It was theirs to seek the formula of the Christian life of faith, to think and work out the theory that corresponds to it; not only to realize the idea, but to track out the paths that lead to it. In all this, it need hardly be said, men have gone countless times astray. Above all,

---

[1] R. A. Lipsius, Lehrb. der evang. prot. Dogmatik, 2o Aufl. (Braunschweig, 1879), S. 123 f.

much has been and still is regarded as the sole means of salvation and as eternally valid, which is really no more than one out of many forms, and has none but temporary value. And yet this mutability of Christianity remains an inestimable blessing. Starting from the conviction that religion must be the all-ruling power in the life of peoples and of individuals, we might easily be led to suppose that the completest must likewise be the best religion. Tried by this standard, Christianity must yield to Islam, which gives its confessor a rounded code, and to Buddhism, which offers him an elaborated system of conventual discipline, of rules for life, and of metaphysics. But truly we have no cause to envy the Moslem his Qorán and Sunna, or the Buddhist his "three baskets." That which is no longer susceptible of change may continue to exist, but it has ceased to live. And religion must live, must enter into new combinations and bear fresh fruits, if it is to answer to its destiny, if, refusing to crystallize into formulæ and usages, it is to work like the leaven, is to console, to inspire and to strengthen.[1]

These Lectures deal with the past, not with the future, of religion. But I may be permitted, in conclusion, from the point of view we now occupy, to cast a single glance forward. As long as nations remain approximately on the same level of social and

---

[1] Cf. with the above J. Happel, die Anlage des Menschen zur Religion, vom gegenw. Standpunkte der Völkerkunde aus betrachtet und untersucht (Haarlem, 1877), especially S. 219 ff., 373 ff.

spiritual development, so long the continued existence of their religions, if not absolutely assured, is at least highly probable. This is the very reason why the problem as to the future of Christianity is so much more serious than that which concerns either Islam or Buddhism. This is why it is so specially serious now, when so much is being superseded and is passing away, when a new conception of the world is spreading in ever-wider circles, when new social conditions are in the very process of birth. What Paul writes of himself and his contemporaries,[1] we may, in a somewhat modified sense, apply to ourselves; for in us too "the ends of the ages meet," the ends of the old and of the new. What has Christianity to expect from this revolution? The need of it is keen as ever. It is not for less but for more Christianity that our age cries out. The question only is, whether it will be able to take it to itself, and find in it a power for life, unbroken yet. For those who identify Christianity with the ecclesiastical form in which they themselves profess it, this question can hardly be said to exist. They expect the world to conform to them. They have no need to be reassured or encouraged. But those too—and they are many—who have no such confidence, may be none the less at peace. The universalism of Christianity is the sheet-anchor of their hope. A history of eighteen centuries bears mighty witness to it; and the contents

---

[1] 1 Cor. x. 11.

of its evidence and the high significance they possess are brought into the clearest light by the comparison with other religions. We have good courage, then. Not yet is the vital power exhausted which manifested itself so clearly in the rise of the Catholic Church and again at the Reformation of the sixteenth century. To this our own experience bears witness, and this the future will proclaim!

NOTES.

Note I. (P. 16, n. 4.)

"The Rolls of Abraham and Moses" and "the Fables of the Ancients" in the Qorán.

Sprenger puts forward his conjectures as to "the Çohof" or "rolls of Abraham and Moses" with some hesitation (Das Leben u. die Lehre des Mohammad, II. 348 ff., 363 ff., cf. I. 45 ff.). Their substance is as follows: Bahír or Bahíra, also called Nestor, a ráhib or ascetic, of Israelitish extraction and of Jewish-Christian belief, was residing at Mecca about the time when Mohammed's mission began, and exercised a marked influence upon him. He himself had composed a book for which he claimed a high antiquity, and which he called "The Çohof of Abraham and Moses;" and besides this he was the possessor of yet other apocryphal writings (of which more anon). Mohammed accepted the "Çohof" as authentic, and made them the foundation of his preaching. The substance of their contents may be learnt with fair certainty from Sura liii. 37—55, from which we may also perceive that they were in reality of very recent date, for they placed the destruction of the tribes of Ad and Thamúd (vv. 51—53) in a hoary antiquity, which contradicts the well-authenticated history (Sprenger, I. 62 ff., 505 ff., 518 ff.). It did not escape notice at Mecca that Mohammed had put himself under Bahíra as a teacher, and reference is made to the accusations brought against him in consequence in Sura xlvi. 9—11; xliv. 13; xvi. 105, and also more especially in xi. 20, where Mohammed ascribes divine enlightenment or inspiration to his "souffleur," and appeals to his evidence in support of the Qorán. Nevertheless, he found himself compelled at last to allow that the "Çohof" were spurious. In 616 A.D., when certain Christians of Abyssinia accompanied his own followers who had previously fled thither, back to Mecca, this spuriousness was placed beyond a doubt; and accordingly he does not mention the "Çohof" again after that year, although at first he had been so thoroughly convinced of their genuineness that he had even appealed to the learned amongst the sons of Israel in its support (Sura xxvi. 197). But in spite of his thus renouncing the "Çohof," Mohammed still remained dependent upon Bahíra, and especially upon the use of the apocryphal writings which the latter had, not indeed composed, but brought with him. It is to these that Mohammed's enemies referred when, as the Qorán itself testifies, they reproached him with producing "asátír al-awwalín," i.e. "stories" or "fables of the ancients" (Sura vi. 25; viii. 31; xvi. 26; xxiii. 85; xxv. 6; xxvii. 70; xlvi. 16; lxviii. 15; lxxxiii. 13, cf. xxvi. 137; "holoq al-awwalín," i.e. "inventions of the ancients"). What these writings were cannot be ascertained with certainty; but Sprenger is not disinclined to believe that they were identical with one of the sacred books of the Abrahamic Çabians, which—like Bahíra's forgery—was called "Çohof of Abraham," and, according to Kitáb al Fihrist (ed. Fluegel, I. 21 f.), was translated into Arabic by Ahmed b. Abdallah b. Salám, a client of Harûn ar-Raschid. (Ibid. II. 390—397.)

The respect we owe to Sprenger's learning and acumen must not prevent our roundly declaring that a more arbitrary tissue of false or uncertain surmises has seldom been put forward as history. From whatever side we approach it, it collapses at the first touch. Bahíra's presence at Mecca at any time rests upon weak evidence, which is refuted by Ibn Ishaq, Mohammed's earliest biographer (cf. Nöldeke in Z. d. d. M. G. XII. 704 ff.); and there is no evidence at all that he was there before the year 616 A.D. The name of this supposed Mentor, however, is of comparatively little consequence, if it can be shown that the rôle assigned to him was really played by some one. But it is not so. Sprenger makes all manner of texts refer to this Mentor that cannot possibly apply to any *one* person—still less to such an one: Sura xlvi. 9—11 (where "a witness of the children of Israel" who vouches for the harmony between Qorán and Law must be one who could inspire even Mohammed's opponents with respect); xvi. 105 (where the reproach that "a certain person taught" Mohammed is met by the declaration that the "person" referred to spoke a barbarian language, whereas the Qorán was in Arabic); xxv. 5, 6 (where Mohammed's helpers are mentioned in the plural, as dictating to him "morn and even" what he afterwards proclaimed). Special importance is attached by Sprenger to Sura xi. 20, which he paraphrases thus (II. 366 f.) : "Ist nicht Derjenige, welcher im Besitze einer von seinem Herrn ausgehenden Bayyina [Erleuchtung] war und ihn [den Korân] liest, ein Zeuge für dessen Wahrheit? Und vor dem Korân wurde das Buch des Moses geoffenbart als ein Vorbild und Gnadenausfluss [auch die Uebereinstimmung mit diesem Vorbilde ist ein Zeugniss für die Wahrheit des Korâns]. Diejenigen, für welche das Buch Moses geoffenbart ist, glauben an den Korân u. s. w." Here Mohammed is supposed by Sprenger to ascribe divine inspiration to his Mentor, and indirectly to declare that it was in this way, and not by study, that he had come to know the contents of the "Çohof;" and thus, when this Mentor commends the Qorán, he is an authoritative witness instead of a "souffleur." No doubt it is a clever stroke with which Sprenger credits Mohammed! But now let the text itself be read. It certainly is not very clear. The traditional explanation opposes *v.* 20 to *v.* 19, and supplies at the beginning of the former, "with such (the unbelievers) can he be compared, who," &c.; but this seems arbitrary.[1] It must be clear, however, to all competent judges that Sprenger's interpretation is impossible. "Wayatlûho" is not the continuation of "kána;" "sháhidon minho" (a witness from him or on his part) does not mean "a witness for him;" and the phrase,

---

[1] See the Commentary of al-Beidháwí (ed. Fleischer, I. 341), which takes "yatlûho" as "follows thereon," and therefore as opposed to "min qablihi." Should we not make the suffix in "yatlûho" refer to "man," the subject of the sentence?

"kána alá bayyinatin min rabbihi," though applied to prophets amongst others, does *not* refer specifically to the "Erleuchtung" in which they rejoiced, but rather to the reliance which they (and their followers) placed on the clear proofs of Allah's revelation. Cf. Sura vi. 57; xi. 30, 66, 90; xxxv. 38; xlvii. 15; especially the two last-named passages.

Of course we shall not deny that Mohammed had his trusted friends, who were rightly or wrongly regarded as his teachers. But it is quite another question whether the "Çohof" and the "asátír al-awwalín" were furnished him by these people. (1st.) As to the "Çohof," if we consider all the texts in which they appear (Sura xx. 133; liii. 37; lxxiv. 52; lxxx. 30; lxxxvii. 18, 19; xcviii. 2), it is impossible for us to regard them as one definite book which Mohammed accepted and made use of as authentic. Sura liii. 39—55 cannot be regarded as a table of contents of "the Çohof of Moses and Abraham." It is a résumé of Mohammed's own preaching which he commends to his hearers because of its agreement with the "Çohof." The word does not represent any sharply-defined idea, any more than "Zobor" does (Sura iii. 181; xvi. 46; xxvi. 196; xxxv. 23; liv. 43, 52). The supposed subsequent renunciation of the "Çohof" is in any case a fiction; and, moreover, if Sprenger's interpretation of Sura xi. 20 were correct, this renunciation would be quite superfluous, or rather highly unreasonable. But, I shall be told, it appears from Ahmed ben Abdallah that the Çábians actually possessed "Çohof" of Abraham (see p. 300). My answer is, that we have no knowledge whatever of the character of this writing; that the "Çohof" of the Qorán are spoken of as "Çohof of Abraham and Moses" or "of the elders;" and that Sprenger himself does not identify the Çábian "Çohof" with those of the Qorán. (2nd.) On the other hand, he discovers this Çábian production in the "asátír al-awwalín." But even before the appearance of "Das Leben und die Lehre des Mohammad," his views on this latter subject had already been adequately refuted by Nöldeke (Gesch. des Qoráns, 1860, S. 12 f.). Sprenger is really asking too much when he would have us believe that Mohammed—whom he makes out acute enough in other respects—himself proclaimed the title of the book he had plundered.[1] And now let the passages cited above (p. 301) be read. Even if we start from Sura xxv. 5, 6, we cannot possibly find in "asátír al-awwalín" the title of a book. What in that case would be the meaning of the opponents saying, "that is *mere* asátír al-awwalín"? And how could we explain Sura xxvi. 137, where the Adites say to Húd, "these are but inventions ('holoq') of the ancients"? The formula cannot really be translated otherwise than it is by Nöldeke (S. 13): "das Geschreibsel" or "die Fabeln der Alten, Ammenmährchen." If certain Moslem expounders of the Qorán have found something more in it (Sprenger, II. 393 ff.), it is because of their desire to bring the texts, whenever possible, into connection with special persons and incidents.

Note II. (P. 21, n. 1.)

The Hanyfs.

To what has been said on pp. 19—22 as to the use of the word "hanyf" in the Qorán, we must add that the plural ("honafáo") is connected in one passage with "lilláhi," i.e. "towards Allah," Sura xxii. 32 (this verse, at any rate, was composed at Medina). This is further evidence of the appellative signification of the word, and pleads against the idea that it was established even before Mohammed's time as the proper name of a sect. Indeed, the signification of the Hebrew, Aramaic and Arabic derivatives from *hnf* is completely explained if we follow Fleischer, who (Neuhebr. u. Chald. Wörterbuch von Levy, II. 207) assigns to the root the fundamental meaning, "*des Beugens*, sowohl *Zu-* als *Abbeugens, Krümmens*, wie Dietrich richtig, gegen Gesenius, erkannt hat." Geiger's opinion

---

[1] "Die heimlich benutzten Asátyr" (II. 397). Yet, in the Qorán, Mohammed introduces his opponents as many as nine times, mentioning the book by name!

(Zeitschrift f. jüd. Wissenschaft u. jüd. Leben, I. 185 ff.),[1] that "to be clean" was the primitive signification, has nothing to support it; for the idea that *haf*, Job xxxiii. 9, has risen out of *hanf*, will not readily commend itself to any one who remembers the Old Testament use of *hnf*. If we were to start from this usage, we should naturally be brought to the conclusion that the unfavourable meaning was the original one (Sprenger, I. 67; Dozy, de Israëlieten te Mekka, bl. 206). But can we suppose that in that case it would have been unknown to Mohammed? And if he knew it, how are we to explain the use of the word in the Qorán?

Now, alike in the passage referred to but now (p. 300) from al-Fihrist,[2] and in the traditions concerning Mohammed's predecessors, *passim*, "hanyf" means one who confesses the religion of Abraham. From Sprenger's rich collection (I. 110 ff.) I borrow a few examples. Omayya ben Abi-ç-Çalt was one of those who spoke concerning Abraham, Ishmael, and the faith of the hanyfs (S. 111). Zaid ibn 'Amr openly declares that he professes the religion of Abraham (S. 120). He is advised by a rabbi to become a "hanyf." "But what does 'hanyf' mean?" asks Zaid. The rabbi answers, "The religion of Abraham; he was neither Jew nor Christian, and he worshipped Allah alone." Zaid next turns to a Christian, receives from him the same advice and the same explanation of "hanyf," on which he exclaims, "O God, I take thee to witness that I follow the religion of Abraham" (S. 120). Here, as we see, the characteristic expression found in the Qorán, "neither Jew nor Christian," is put into the mouth of a pre-Mohammedan. In the further traditions about Zaid (S. 121—123) the same features constantly recur, and the religion of Abraham, as well as the consecration of the Ka'ba by him and Ishmael, plays a conspicuous part.

Sprenger (I. 122 f.; III. 159, n. 1, and elsewhere) is not blind to the "tendency" of all these passages, and admits, for example,

---

[1] Afterwards adopted by Sprenger, l.c. III. 8 f.

[2] "I have," writes Ahmed ibn Addallah, "translated this book out of the book of the Hanyfs, that is to say the Abrahamic Çábians, who believe in Abraham," &c.

that the prophecies of Mohammed's appearance which they contain are not historical. But he condemns the practice of rejecting them "without sufficient grounds," and so resolving the biography of Mohammed into mist. "Der Bericht, dass die Lehre des Propheten von Zayd und anderen in ihren wesentlichen Bestandtheilen verkündigt wurde, also schon vor ihm vorhanden war, hätte nur von seinen Feinden und nicht von seinen Freunden erdichtet werden Können"—and must therefore, it is implied, be historical. Unquestionably we must refrain from deciding "without sufficient grounds." But Sprenger does not consider the facts, 1st, that if the traditions represented the truth, it would follow that Mohammed must *from the first* have come forward as the preacher of Abraham's religion, which he did not; and 2nd, that when once Mohammed had identified his religion with that of Abraham, the inference would be drawn that even before his time his spiritual kindred *must* have preached and recommended this very religion, and *could not* have done otherwise. For the rest, when we find that so keen a critic as Sprenger believes that Zaid really did teach all that is assigned to him by the tradition, we can but join with Nöldeke (l. c. S. 14) in expressing our amazement. "Ueberhaupt," writes the latter, "wäre es höchst wunderbar, wenn nicht allein Mohammed die Reden Zaid's so wörtlich auswendig gelernt hätte, dass er sie nacher in den Qorân hätte hineinsetzen können, sondern auch daneben noch ein anderer dieselben Reden in ihrer Urgestalt auf die Nachwelt gebracht hätte."

I repeat what I have said in the text (p. 21): We need not deny that Mohammed had predecessors; but we must deny that the tradition gives us a faithful representation of them, or is correct in calling them hanyfs. In explaining their views we can get no help from this name,—always supposing that the ideas as to "the milla of Ibrahím" which (following Dr. Snouck Hurgronje) I have put forward in the text, are correct.

Note III. (P. 32, n. 1.)

Did Mohammed place the Hajj amongst the Duties of the Moslem?

The Mohammedan theologians are unanimous in answering this question in the affirmative. They refer in support of their opinion to Sura iii. 91 b.: "And the hajj to the house is a service due to Allah from men, in so far as they are able to journey thither." In the text (pp. 32 sq.) I have simply accepted their opinion, for it has been taken up into Islam, and has formed a part of it as it has now existed for more than twelve centuries. Dr. Snouck Hurgronje, however (l. c. bl. 42 vv.), has urged weighty considerations, not indeed against the approval and recommendation of the hajj by Mohammed, but against the thesis that he enjoined it upon all the faithful. His observations must be read in their entirety before a really adequate estimate can be made of their value; but I must nevertheless attempt to summarize them here.

Before the flight, Mohammed, very naturally, says nothing about the hajj. At that time it was still an entirely heathen festival that had no attractions for him and his followers, and for the present no modification of its character could be so much as thought of. After the battle of Badr (Anno H. 2, A.D. 624), his eye was unceasingly fixed upon Mecca, and the return thither was the goal of his efforts. Not long after comes the revelation of Sura iii. 89—92, in which Mohammed, so to speak, appropriates the Ka'ba and the pilgrimage thither, and claims them for Islam by referring their origin to Allah, and in which he exhorts the faithful, "so far as they are able to perform the journey," not to hold aloof. Abraham, who is brought into connection with the Ka'ba in these verses, comes decidedly into the foreground in the somewhat later passage, Sura xxii. 25—39. Here a threatening tone is assumed towards those who exclude the Moslems from the holy places. Abraham, at the command of Allah, had instituted the hajj. His ordinances are taken up and explained by Mohammed, especially those concerning the sacrifice of the camels and the distribution of their flesh. A warning against idolatry is added (*vv.* 31 sq.), and finally the truth is enforced that "the flesh of the sacrificial beasts can by no means reach unto God, neither their blood; but piety on the part of the faithful reacheth Him" (*v.* 38). Provisionally, however, these lessons could not be put into practice. Mecca was still inaccessible to the Moslems. Perhaps the pericope, Sura ii. 185—199, contains precepts dating from the year 6 A.H. (628 A.D.), when Mohammed and his disciples set out for Mecca, but halted at Hodaibiya, and there made a treaty in virtue of which the Moslems were to be allowed to visit the Ka'ba in the following year, which, accordingly, they did ("Omra of the completion," A. H. 7, A. D. 629). But with these ordinances of A. H. 6 others are united, dating from the year of Mohammed's hajj (A.H. 10). After Mecca was conquered (A.H. 8, A.D. 630), Mohammed still let a year pass without taking any part in the pilgrimage, being too fully occupied with the subjection of Arabia and with his military expeditions. But in that year Ali, in his name, read out to the assembled pilgrims Sura ix. 1—12 (perhaps also *vv.* 36, 37), in which the treaties with the heathen are declared void (A.H. 9, A.D. 631). Thus everything was prepared for the observance of the hajj in complete Moslem fashion the following year. This observance, accordingly, took place, and what Mohammed and his followers did on that occasion, taken in connection with the distinct injunctions of Sura ii. 185—199, was erected into the rule which remains in force to this day.

The course of these events does not support the view that Mohammed imposed the hajj as a duty upon all men without distinction. He quietly abides his time, and does not seem to have any idea that the Moslems who deferred the hajj were guilty of a trespass against Allah's commandment. And to this we must add, that "neither in the treaties which he concludes with converted tribes, nor in the numerous verses of the Qorán in which the duties of the faithful are summed up, is there any mention made of the hajj" (l. c. bl. 43).

I think it can hardly be denied that these considerations seriously shake the traditional acceptation of Sura iii. 91 b. And yet, on the other hand, the utterances in the Qorán concerning the hajj, thus chronologically arranged and placed in their historical framework, seem to me to show that this traditional acceptation is far from being unnatural. The limited sense in which Mohammed speaks of "men" in Sura iii. 91, must almost have vanished when, in Sura xxii. 25—39, he had represented the hajj as an ordinance of Allah, proclaimed by Abraham. The terms which he uses in this passage are extremely general. Allah has "appointed (ordained) the holy place of worship for all men, alike for those who abide therein, and for the stranger" (v. 25). Abraham is to proclaim the hajj "amongst the peoples," and they are to "come to him on foot and on fleet camels, by every deep ravine" (v. 28). And to him—so the prophet adds—who shall honour the sacred ordinances of Allah, it shall be well with his Lord (v. 31). He reveals the piety of his heart therein (v. 33). To every people—he continues—Allah has made it a sacred institution that they should thankfully praise the name of Allah over the cattle that he gives them, and to this the sacrifice at the hajj corresponds (v. 35, cf. 37). All this, taken together, does not indeed bring us to the position taken by the Moslem theologians, but it explains how they themselves came to take it. The observance of solemnities to which the prophet attached such great significance and value, could not be left to the free option of the faithful, and the theologians eagerly caught at an expression which, like Sura iii. 91, might be taken without violence as a commandment addressed to every individual.

NOTE IV. (P. 57, n. 1.)

The Pronunciation of the Divine Name "Yahweh."

By declaring, as soon as I had occasion to use it, that we have good grounds for pronouncing the name of the god of Israel "Yahweh," I implied that the objections which have been urged against this pronunciation—most recently by Friedrich Delitzsch (Wo lag das Paradies? Eine biblisch-assyriologische Studie, S. 158—166) and von Hartmann (Das relig. Bewusstsein u. s. w. S. 370 f.)—have not convinced me. I must now briefly explain the reason of this. On the derivation and significance of the name I will not now touch, but will confine myself exclusively to the anterior question of how it was pronounced.

First of all we must define the point under discussion. The four letters Yhwh, which stand for the god of Israel in the ordinary text of the Old Testament, must be vocalized Yahweh (or Yahaweh). So far there is—or at any rate there ought to be—no difference of opinion. No one who wrote down these four letters can have meant to indicate any other pronunciation. If he had intended his readers to say Yahu or Yaho, for instance, he would have omitted the fourth letter.[1]

If we reject the pronunciation "Yahweh," therefore, we must begin by rejecting the spelling "Yhwh." This is what Delitzsch actually does; and von Hartmann, too, considers it not improbable that this spelling was devised in order to bring the divine name into connection with the verb *hwh* (hawah), "to be" (cf. Exod. iii. 14). According to this, the national deity was called Yah, or Yaho, Yahu, Yehu, by the people. The first of these forms, it will be remembered, occurs repeatedly in the Old Testament;[2] Yaho and Yahu are also very frequent, but only in compounds, especially in proper names which begin with Yeho (yo), or end in Yahu (yah); Yehu, finally, seems to be discovered by von Hartmann in the name of the well-known king (S. 371), which Delitzsch prefers to regard as a compound (Yah-hû = "Yahweh is he," or "Yahweh is it"). This latter view is at any rate possible, which is more than can be said for von Hartmann's. As witnesses that these shorter forms are the original ones, Philo Byblius, Clemens Alexandrinus and Origen are summoned. They

---

[1] The pronunciation "Yahwah" is now generally abandoned. Yahwoh would, in the abstract, be conceivable, but—very naturally—has never yet been supported by any one, and need not be further noticed.

[2] Exod. xv. 2; xvii. 16; Isaiah xii. 2; xxvi. 4; xxxviii. 11; Song of Sol. viii. 6; twenty times in the Psalms, exclusive of a good twenty more in the formula "Hallelû-yah."

support the pronunciation Yeuô, Yaô, Yoû (but Origen Yaè also). Chief stress, however, is laid on non-Israelitish proper names compounded with Yaho, Yahu, which are said to show that this divine name was also in use amongst other Semitic nations, and especially amongst the Babylonians, the teachers of them all. Originally, then, the god Yaho or Yahu was worshipped by other related tribes in common with Israel; and it was in opposition to them that the more highly cultivated Israelites afterwards called this deity Yahweh. In speaking of the popular religion, therefore (pp. 61 sqq.), I ought, according to this view, to have used the name Yaho or Yahu.

The opposite theory finds in "Yahweh" the original form and pronunciation, and in Yah, Yahu, &c., abridged derivatives from it. There are no grammatical objections to this. On the contrary, it is strictly consonant with analogy that a verbal form in *-èh* should lose its final syllable. *Yahwèh* would thus become *Yahw*, and this last, again, would pass quite regularly into *Yaho* (*yo*). Equally natural is the transition into *Yahu* (*yah*), when the divine name comes at the end of the compound. Nor is the monosyllable *yah* by any means strange as an abridged form of Yahweh. It is found especially in poetry, and almost always in expressions in which the divine name is so closely connected with the verb that it may be said to form a quasi compound with it. But what are we to say, in this case, to the witnesses for the pronunciation Yaô or Yaû? Origen (ed. De la Rue, II. 539), as I have already pointed out, is also acquainted with the form Yaè (i.e. Yahwèh); and in support of this latter pronunciation we may further appeal to Theodoret, Epiphanius and the Samaritan tradition (cf. Baudissin, Studien zur semit. Religionsgeschichte, I. 183 ff.). The authorities for the two views are therefore pretty evenly balanced.

This being so, the choice, as it seems to me, cannot be doubtful for a moment. The shortening of proper names—especially the names of deities taken up into compounds—as the natural result of rapid pronunciation, is quite accordant with analogy. On the contrary, I am not aware of any other instance of such a lengthening or expansion as is assumed by Delitzsch and von Hartmann. This anomaly, however, we might admit, if we could lay it to the account of the theologizing Scribes. But the writing *Yhwh*—and consequently the pronunciation *Yahweh*—appears as early as ± 900 B.C. on the stone of Mesha (line 18), where it must surely have been borrowed from the popular usage of Israel. And it is on this pronunciation, too, that the etymology in Exod. iii. 14 rests; for, whatever we may think of its correctness or incorrectness, it is almost impossible that it could have so much as suggested itself if the name of Israel's god had been not Yahweh, but (for instance) Yaho or Yahu. Mesha's inscription and Exodus iii. 14 (certainly later than 900 B.C.!), when taken together, lead to a decision from which there is no appeal.

Even the alleged use of Yaho or Yahu amongst other Semitic peoples cannot alter the verdict. The evidence produced in favour of it turns out, point by point, either to break down completely or at least to be very defective. Cf. Baudissin, l. c. S. 220—227. I cannot allow the validity of the considerations urged on the other side by Delitzsch (S. 163 f.). That the Philistine royal names Mitinti, Zidqâ, Padi, are compounded with Yahu, and therefore correspond exactly to the Hebrew names Mattityah, Zidqyah, Pedayah, is by no means apparent; for what distinguishes the latter series of names from the former, is the very syllable which raises the composition with Yahu above all doubt. It is further maintained by Delitzsch—in conflict with his former communication to Baudissin (S. 226, n. 6)—that the simple sound *I* signified in Accadian "god" and "the supreme god," just as *ili*, *ilâ* (Hebrew *êl*) did; that the Assyrians pronounced this *I* with the nominative termination *ia-u*; that accordingly the character for *I* was called by the Assyrians *ia-u*; and that it can only be regarded as an accident that hitherto *Ya-u*, as the name of the deity, has not been met with in any Assyrian inscription. If this is really "an accident," then the name will sooner or later be discovered. But after weighing the objections urged against Delitzsch by Tiele (Theologisch Tijdschrift, Deel XVI. (1882), bl. 262 vv.), I regard it as more than doubtful whether this discovery will ever take place.

Note V. (P. 64, n. 1.)

Interpretation of Hosea ix. 3—5.

It will be observed that in translating Hosea ix. 3, 4, I have allowed myself a departure from the Masoretic text, and that departure must here be justified. Israel has fallen away from his god and has worshipped other gods at the harvest-feasts, as if it were they who had given him this abundance (cf. chap. ii. 10). There is, in truth, no reason why the people should rejoice and exult like the heathens (v. 1).[1] This will soon appear, when "threshing-floor and wine-press shall not feed them, and the must shall fail them" (v. 2).[2] For—so the prophet continues—"they shall not remain in the land of Yahweh, but Ephraim shall return to Egypt, and they shall eat unclean food in Assyria" (v. 3). The foreign land itself is unclean (Amos vii. 17), and so likewise is the food that is eaten there. Now this is the conception which is more fully worked out in v. 4. As that verse now reads, it is in contradiction with itself and with chap. iii. 4. For whether we follow the accents and connect *zibchêhêm* with the words that follow, or whether (as is unquestionably better) we take it as subject of the preceding "*welô ye'erebû-lô*," in any case it implies that, even in the foreign land, Israel makes sacrifices to Yahweh. Now this may be reconciled, in a fashion, with the end of the verse ("it—i.e. their food—comes not into the house of Yahweh"), but not with the beginning "they shall pour no libations of wine to Yahweh;" for if they offered sacrifices, then *a fortiori* they could make their ordinary libations. Still less can this sacrificing in a foreign land be reconciled with chap. iii. 4, where sitting down "without sacrifice" (the same word as in chap. ix. 4!) is one of the marks of life in exile. The contra-

---

[1] The reading, *el-gîl*, has been justified by reference to Job iii. 22. But it is not at all surprising that the old translators read *al*, which cannot be adopted, however, unless we change *gîl* into *tagîl*. Is it possible that *tagîl* is the true reading?

[2] For *bah* read *bâm*, or—simply changing the vowel—*bôh*.

diction cannot be removed by a changed interpretation of the text; for "their sacrifices are not acceptable to him (Yahweh)," still implies that sacrifices are made.[1] There is only one escape, but that is a very simple one. For *ye'erebû* read *ye'erekû*. The verb *'arak* signifies "to lay in order," "to arrange," "to prepare," and is used in Gen. xxii. 9, Leviticus i. 7, 1 Kings xviii. 33, of laying wood upon the altar, and in Lev. i. 8, 12—exactly as in our passage—of placing the sacrificial parts on the wood. There is no change of subject, therefore; and the meaning is this: "They shall pour no libation of wine to Yahweh, and shall not lay out their sacrifices before him (upon the altar)." This conjecture finds no support in the old translations. The mistake, then, must be a very old one, and it would escape notice all the more easily because it brings v. 4*a* into correspondence with Jer. vi. 20*b*.

An error has also crept into the words that immediately follow. *lahém* must be changed into *lahmâm*, or else followed by it. The change or omission is easily explained by the great similarity of the two words. The meaning then becomes, "as food eaten in mourning is their food (to them); all who eat thereof make themselves unclean; for (there in the foreign land) their food serves (only) for (stilling) their desire (hunger); it comes not into the house of Yahweh (and so remains unconsecrated)." If such is their plight in ordinary seasons, how much more painfully must they feel on the feast days their absence from the holy land and the loss of those religious solemnities which cannot be celebrated in any other country (*v.* 5)!

With the exception of these minor points of difference, my view of Hos. ix. 3—5 agrees with that of Wellhausen (Gesch. Israels, I. 22 n.) and Robertson Smith (The Old Testament in the Jewish Church, p. 237).

---

[1] Wellhausen's translation, "Sie spenden Yahve keinen Wein und keine Opfer die ihm munden," is too free, and only conceals the difficulty without removing it. For the rest, Wellhausen allows (Gesch. Israels, I. 83, n. 1) that Hos. ix. 4 and iii. 4 belong together.

Note VI. (P. 80, n. 2).

The Egyptian Origin of Levi.

De Lagarde, in his treatise "Erklärung hebräischer Wörter" (Abhandlungen der kön. Ges. der Wissenschaften zu Göttingen, Band XXVI. and Orientalia, Heft II.), S. 20 f., puts forward the conjecture that the Levites were the Egyptians, who—according to Exod. xii. 38, Num. xi. 4—joined on to the departing Israelites. "Levi" is not an ordinary proper name, and is accordingly used for "Levite, Levitical," as well as for the (supposed) ancestor of the Levites. That "Levi" was no inappropriate name for the strangers that "joined themselves on," may be seen from Isaiah xiv. 1; lvi. 3 (cf. supra, pp. 185 sq.). According to Exodus ii. 1—10, Moses was of unmixed Israelite descent; but what is more natural than that Israel should have concealed the Egyptian origin of its deliverer from the house of bondage, and made him one of its own children? "War Moses nicht israelitischer, sondern aegyptischer Herkunft, so erklärte sich, warum er in den Leviten, seinen mit ihm gewanderten Stammesgenossen, vozugsweise seine Stütze suchte und fand: es erklärte sich, warum die Leviten die geistige Leitung der israelitischen Nation übernehmen konnten—sie waren eben als Aegypter im Besitze einer höheren Kultur als diejenigen, mit denen sie ausgezogen waren: es erklärte sich, warum die Leviten im gelobten Lande nicht als wirklicher Stamm auftraten: es erklärte sich endlich was die aegyptischen Quellen über den Auszug der Israeliten aus Aegypten aussagen" (S. 21).

When Dr. Maybaum (Die Entwickelung des altisr. Priesterthums, S. iii.—vi.), had combated this hypothesis, de Lagarde declared (Gött. gel. Anz. 1881, S. 38—40) that he had not made himself responsible for it, but had thrown it out as a suggestion, and commended it to the attention of scholars. Let us see to what results a closer examination, such as he desires, will lead us.

If we could accept as purely historical the accounts given in the Pentateuch of Levi (Gen. xxix. 34) and his posterity (Gen. xlvi. 11;

Exod. vi. 16—27), or at any rate the statements about Moses and his descent, then there would be no "Levi question" at all. But it is well known that even the narratives concerning Moses, and *a fortiori* those relating to the patriarchal period, fail to offer us any certainty, and that in consequence we cannot dispose of such a conjecture as de Lagarde's by a simple appeal to the Israelite tradition. His point of departure, however, is not happily chosen. In the Hebrew "lawah" (in Niph'al "to hang on, to join oneself to") there is not even a side hint of what he finds in it, viz., the joining on *of foreigners to Israel*. Nor can it be made out from Exod. xii. 38, Numbers xi. 4, that any *Egyptians* accompanied the Israelites at the exodus. But may there not be other facts, not mentioned by de Lagarde, that make the connection between Levi and Egypt probable? Attention may be called, for instance, to several Levitical proper names. To begin with, there is Phinehas (the son of Eleazar b. Aäron, and the son of Eli), which cannot be explained from Hebrew, but which actually appears in Egyptian documents and can also be provided with an Egyptian etymon. Cf. Dillmann, Exodus und Leviticus, S. 60,—who, nevertheless, very properly rejects the most usual explanation (= "the negro") as not being consonant with the Old Testament usage. Again, the grandfather of the elder Phinehas, on the mother's side, bears an Egyptian name, *Putiël* (Exod. vi. 25), related to "*Potiphar*," "*Potiphera*." The Egyptian origin of the name Moses—questioned by Land, Theol. Tijdschr. III. 362 n.—is admitted by a very great majority of the commentators. Cf. Dillmann, l.c. S. 15 f., and Rev. F. C. Cook in the Speaker's Commentary, Vol. I. pp. 482 sqq. Neither has any Hebrew etymon been found as yet for "Aaron" (against Redslob, see Theol. Tijdschr. VI. 648); and it would not be at all surprising if the Egyptologists, who have not at present been any more successful, should hereafter have better fortune. On the other hand, I cannot think that Cook (l.c. p. 488) is correct in deriving "Gersôm" from the Egyptian; for the connection of this name (and the almost identical "Gersôn") with the Hebrew *grsh*, "to drive out," seems unmistakable, and is not invalidated by Exod. ii. 22. But, *per contra*, I must refer, in this connection, to 1 Sam. ii. 27, where it is said of Eli's family that they "had been *servants* (LXX.) in Egypt, *to the house of Pharaoh*"—an expression which is not used of Israel as a whole,[1] and which might be taken as a reminiscence of the closer connection in which this family had stood to the royal house of Egypt.[2]

It will be seen that these traces are few and weak, and—be it specially observed—detected exclusively in the family of Amram, to which Eli also belonged. Now we are not in the least justified in extending to other Levitical clans anything that may be true of this one family, or in drawing inferences therefrom with respect to the whole tribe. The names of the clans themselves (Gen. xlvi. 11; Exod. vi. 16 sqq.; Numbers iii.; xxvi.) do not lend the least support to the hypothesis we are discussing; and in some cases they distinctly point to a different origin (Qorah, Hebron, Yizhar, &c.). Still less can the name Levi itself be taken, as de Lagarde suggests, as a side reference to Egypt. If the name were to be taken appellatively at all, it would be far more obvious to connect it with the tribe's joining on to, or dependence on, the sanctuary of Yahweh, than with its foreign origin and its joining on to Israel. But even this supposition cannot be admitted. The tribe of Levi, as Gen. xlix. 5—7 shows indisputably, existed before it had consecrated itself to the divine service, and therefore cannot have derived its name from that consecration itself. According to Kohler (Der Segen Jacob's, Berlin, 1867, S. 34), "Levi" means "turning," "twisting" (cf. liwyah and liwyathán), and was therefore originally the mythic serpent or dragon which fights against the sun. Other tribal names are connected with mythology (cf. Theol. Tijdschrift, V. 290 vv.), and this explanation may therefore be regarded as not improbable. But however this may be, in no case can we allow any weight to the considerations by which de Lagarde seeks to support the supposed Egyptian descent. There is not the least

---

[1] Once, in Deut. vi. 21, spoken of as "servants of Pharaoh."

[2] The fantastic combinations of Prof. Lauth, in his "Moses der Ebräer, nach zwei ägyptischen Papyrus-Urkunden" (1868), and "Moses-Hosarsyphos-Salichus, Levites-Aharon frater, &c." (1879), cf. Z. d. d. M. G. XXV. 139—148, I prefer to pass over in silence.

necessity to suppose that Levi's origin had anything to do with its failure to obtain a special territory (cf. Theol. Tijdschr. VI. 653 v.). We shall do better to connect this phenomenon with the anti-Canaanite disposition of the Levites, to which testimony is borne by Gen. xlix. 5—7; xxxiv. These passages likewise show how little right de Lagarde has to contrast Levi and Israel. They present Levi as ultra-Israelitish, as the upholder *quand même* of Israel's unadulterated nationality. Add to this, finally, that it is an exaggeration, at any rate, to ascribe to Levi "die geistige Leitung der israelitischen Nation."

Note VII. (P. 119, n. 1.)

The Antiquity of Israelitish Monotheism.

In the essay above referred to (p. 119, n. 1), I have treated this subject with special reference to Prof. H. Schultz's Alttestamentliche Theologie. Die Offenbarungsreligion auf ihrer vorchristlichen Entwicklungsstufe (1869), I. 95—123, 259—270; II. 84—88. Contemporaneously with my essay appeared Graf Baudissin's Die Anschauung des A. T. von den Göttern des Heidenthums (Studien zur semit. Religionsgeschichte, I. 47—178). We reviewed each other's work in the Theol. Tijdschrift, X. (1876), bl. 631—648, and in Schürer's Theol. Literaturzeitung, I. (1876), S. 661—664, respectively. Cf. further Rösch in Theol. Stud. u. Kritiken, 1877, S. 739 ff. Schultz's epicrisis may be found in the second edition of his Alttest. Theologie (1878), S. 440—457.

The difference between Baudissin and myself, though not without significance, concerns subordinate questions only. We agree that the sole existence of Yahweh, with the converse doctrine of the absolute non-existence of "the other gods," is not expressly taught before Deuteronomy and Jeremiah. Baudissin maintains, however, that there was an antecedent period, from Amos to Isaiah, in which Yahweh was regarded as the god of Israel, but in which his relation to the heathen world was not expressly dwelt upon, so that the question whether "the other gods" existed *for the heathen*, was not entered upon; but, nevertheless, predications were made of Yahweh which, if the prophets had given themselves a clear account of what they involved, must have led to the recognition of Yahweh as the absolutely only One, and to the denial of all reality to the gods of the heathens. This position, according to him, is a "Zwischenstufe" between the older monolatry and the absolute and fully self-conscious monotheism of Deuteronomy, or, in other words, "ein Monotheismus, dessen Consequenzen mit Bezug auf die Heidenwelt noch nicht gezogen waren." I maintain, on the other hand, that the very fact that the prophets of the eighth century did not draw these consequences—which were surely sufficiently simple—proves that they had not yet reached the true monotheistic position. If, in spite of this, they use expressions concerning Yahweh's supremacy over the heathen world as well as Israel, and concerning the gods of the heathens, which practically amount to a denial of the existence of the latter and leave no room for other gods by the side of Yahweh, this shows that they belong to the period of transition, or of *nascent monotheism*. Traces of this—exactly as we should expect on my hypothesis—are still distinctly to be found in Deuteronomy itself (cf. Theol. Review, l. c. pp. 347—351). What Baudissin calls "eine Zwischenstufe" is not really a "Stufe" at all, but should rather be characterized as the very natural struggle between the old conception and the new and higher one that is in the very act of disengaging itself from it.

I gladly leave to the reader the choice between these two views, which are very closely related to each other. More importance must be attached to the difference between my own view and that which is now supported by Schultz. It is brought out especially in § 6 (S. 451—453) and § 7 (S. 453—455) of the chapter on the unity of God already referred to. In the former passage, Schultz maintains that the prophets had already preached monotheism before the time of Jeremiah; and in the latter, while acknowledging the difficulties inseparable from any solution, he maintains that this monotheism was nothing new, but had been established in Israel from the time of Moses downwards. On this I would remark,

1. That, as indicated just now, I myself acknowledge the monotheism of the prophets of the eighth century,—as a *nascent* monotheism, consisting in the repeated overstepping of the line between monolatry and the recognition of one only God. Schultz himself would not have ascribed any more than this to the earlier prophets, had he considered their monotheistic utterances (given in § 6) in connection with the texts that he himself has collected (§ 3, S. 444 —447), as containing the antique conception and nothing more. He will not hear of the other gods being non-existent simply with reference to Israel. "Alsob"—he says—" die antike polytheistische Denkweise einen Gott, den man nicht verehrte, der aber als wirklicher Gott *seines Volkes* anerkannt ward, mit solchen Namen (viz. no-god, vanity, lie, abomination) hätte bezeichnen können!" All this is perfectly just; only what is here attacked is not "die Meinung der Gegner." It is not Baudissin's, for he very clearly distinguishes the conviction of Amos *cum suis* from "die antike polytheistische Denkweise," and even calls it "Monotheismus." It is not mine, for I recognize monotheism *de facto* in these strong expressions of the prophets, and only deny that they had acquired it as a permanent possession. Now and then they rise to the recognition of the sole existence of Yahweh and the denial of "the other gods," but generally they do not get beyond the monolatry in which they, or at any rate the earlier ones amongst them, had been brought up. It will readily be seen from this,

2. That, in my opinion, the still older monotheism of the period before the prophets has no existence. Schultz admits that *the people* were not monotheistic, and that the priestly narratives and laws of the Pentateuch cannot be taken as evidence concerning the times anterior to the eighth century B.C. (S. 453 f.). Nevertheless he still ascribes monotheism to the more advanced Israelites of this period on the ground of Ps. xviii. 32 (31); 1 Sam. ii. 2; Ps. viii.; xxix.; utterances of the prophetic writers in the Pentateuch, such as Gen. ii. 4 sqq.; iv. 3, 26; xii. 17; xxiv. 31, 50; xxvi. 29; Num. xvi. 22; xxvii. 16; Exod. xv. 2; Num. xiv. 21; and the blessings pronounced upon the patriarchs in Gen. xii.; xviii.; xxii.; xxvi.; xxviii. Two of these texts (Num. xvi. 22; xxvii. 16) are from the

hand of the priestly author. With all the rest I have dealt in the Theological Review, l.c. pp. 352—358 (with which cf. Baudissin, S. 161 ff.). I have nothing to add, unless it be that I ought to have expressed myself even more strongly. It would need the clearest evidence to justify the thesis adopted by Schultz, for it clashes with what we know for certain concerning Solomon, for instance, (and I for my part would add David also,) and with what flows by legitimate inference from the prophetic literature. The texts to which he appeals do not even approximately meet the requirements of the case.

Completely parallel with the view here defended is that of Duhm, die Theol. der Propheten (S. 92 ff. and *passim*), and Wellhausen (Encycl. Brit. art. Israel).

Note VIII. (Pp. 135, n. 1; 136, n. 1.)

Inferences from the Inscription of Cyrus.

The reasons why I cannot assent to some of the inferences that have been drawn from the inscription of Cyrus have been touched upon in the text (pp. 135 sq.). What follows may serve to illustrate them.

1. From the inscription of Darius at Behistun we may gather, as it seems to me, that there was no difference of religion between this monarch and the Achæmenian line to which Cyrus and Cambyses belonged. When Darius has narrated how, with the help of Ahuramazda, he has defeated the Magian Gaumatâ, he proceeds thus (col. i. 14): "The empire that had been wrested from our race, that I recovered, I established it in its place; as in the days of old; thus I did. The temples which Gomátes the Magian had destroyed, I rebuilt; I reinstituted for the state the sacred chaunts and (sacrificial) worship, and confided them to the families which Gomátes the Magian had deprived of those offices."[1] Darius could hardly

---

[1] The translation is Sir H. Rawlinson's, in Records of the Past, Vol. I. p. 113. For comparison, I give Prof. Oppert's translation of the Median

NOTE VIII.

have expressed himself thus if Ahuramazda, whose servant he declares himself to be, had not been reverenced by Cyrus and Cambyses.

2. And, again, the splitting up of the Achæmenians into two branches, as conceived, for instance, by Halévy,[1] appears to me irreconcilable with the inscription of Behistun. Of course I do not speak of the division itself. The pedigree of Darius (son of Hystaspes, of Ariaramnes, of Teïspes, of Achæmenes; Behistun, col. i. 2) and that of Cyrus (son of Cambyses, of Cyrus, of Teïspes; Babyl. Inscrip. r. 21, 22) harmonize admirably. The latter supplies a correction to Herodotus (vi. 11). But if we are to suppose that the two sons of Teïspes (Cyrus, the grandfather of Cyrus the Great, and Ariaramnes) parted from each other, and each ruled over a kingdom or special province of his own, then it seems very strange that Darius should make no mention of the fact, but on the contrary should put the unity of the whole Achæmenian family in the foreground. "On that account," he says, Behistun, col. i. 3, 4, "we are called Achæmenians; from antiquity we have descended; from antiquity those of our race have been kings. There are eight of my race who have been kings before me; I am the ninth; for a very long time[2] we have been kings." If the royalty of which Darius

---

text (l.c. VII. 91): "The kingdom which had been robbed from our race, I restored it, I put again in its place. As it had been before me, thus I did. I reestablished the temples of the gods which Gomates the Magian had destroyed, and I reinstituted, in favour of the people, the calendar and the holy language, and I gave back to the families what Gomates the Magian had taken away."

[1] Cyrus et le retour de l'exil (Revue des Études juives, I. 9 svv., especially p. 14 svv.).

[2] According to others, "in a double line" [i.e. the line of Cyrus and that of Darius himself]; and according to yet others, twice, viz. first in the early times, when the ancestors up to Achæmenes (inclusive) were independent kings, and then again from Cyrus the Great onwards. Cf. Oppert, l.c. p. 88, n. 1.—M. Büdinger, in the Sitzungsberichte der phil. hist. Classe der Kais. Akad. der Wissensch. zu Wien, Band XCVII. S. 713 ff., prefers the first-mentioned interpretation, and with respect to the royal forefathers defends another hypothesis which at any rate deserves a further consideration.

speaks in such lofty terms had been exercised in two kingdoms or provinces, I do not see how he could possibly have failed to mention the fact here. How can we help regarding his silence as a confirmation of the accounts of the Greeks, who, however much they differ in other respects, agree in stating that Cambyses, the father of Cyrus, held sway in Persia?

3. In spite of these considerations, we should be obliged to recognize as a fact the dominion of Cyrus and his forefathers in Susiana, if the Babylonian cylinder bore unequivocal witness to it. But this is not the case. These forefathers are called upon the cylinder (r. 22), "sar al An-za-an," "king of the city of An-za-an," and Cyrus himself is called, in the annals of Nabonedus, "sar An-za-an."[1] Now this "An-za-an" is identified either with the first word in the formula "Anzan Susunqu" of the Susianic inscriptions, or with "An-du-an," which is explained, in the only place where it occurs, by "Elamtu" (Elam). But is not this very hasty, or at any rate extremely unsafe? We cannot wonder that both identifications are rejected by Oppert (Gött. gel. Anzeigen, 1881, S. 1254 ff.). He thinks it is still uncertain what city is indicated by "An-za-an," and even whether the name should be so pronounced; but he is inclined to regard it as a designation of the residential city of the Persian princes, be it Pasargadæ or Marrhasion or Persepolis. The fact that Cyrus is first called "king of An-za-an" and then "king of Persia" in one and the same document, strongly confirms this view, even if it cannot be taken as a proof that "An-za-an" is either an ideogram or a synonym for Persia itself. However this may be, the way in which Halévy (l.c. pp. 14 svv.) romances about the supposed "roi de Susiane," and sacrifices to this fiction both the accounts of the ancients and the evidence of Darius himself, cannot be too strongly condemned.

---

[1] Cf. Th. G. Pinches, in Transactions of the Society of Bibl. Archæology, VII. 151, 155. Further on (p. 159), Cyrus is called, "sar mat Parsu," king of Persia.

NOTE IX. (P. 156, n. 4.)

Ezra and the Establishment of Judaism.

The "Revue de l'histoire des religions" contains (Tom. IV. 22—45) an essay on "Esdras et le code sacerdotal," which might be passed over in silence were it not from the hand of a scholar such as Joseph Halévy. The conception of Ezra's person and work supported by E. Reuss, Graf, Wellhausen and others, has not impressed Halévy at all favourably. He regards it as in part exaggerated, and in part wholly mistaken. This impression should have led him to a comprehensive study of the entire question, which would include the criticism of the books of Ezra and Nehemia, and a running comparison of "le code sacerdotal" with the other collections of laws and with Ezekiel. But it does not appear that Halévy has undertaken any such labour. As for Ezra and Nehemia, he is not even acquainted with the contents of the books, far less with their composition. As to the antiquity of the priestly laws, he offers us nothing but a few detached remarks, which even if they were just would be in no way conclusive. Such demonstrations as this will certainly never convert the upholders of Graf's hypothesis.

Halévy provisionally assumes the trustworthiness of the accounts of Ezra, especially including Neh. viii.—x. In these accounts he fails to recognize the Ezra of the newer criticism, the father of Judaism, the author of the priestly laws, the redactor of the Pentateuch. Ezra, he finds, like the poet of Psalm li., is a man dependent on the Thorah, and inspired with a zeal to support the observance of its long neglected precepts. From Ezra ix. x. he gathers that he was without energy and especially without initiative. The abuses which he finds at Jerusalem grieve him to the quick. He mourns and weeps over them; but he has to be stirred up to action by others. Nehemia is quite another man. Compared with him, Ezra appears insignificant to the last degree. The supposition (Wellhausen, Gesch. Israels, I. 423) that the former lent himself to the accomplishment of the latter's plans, is not only unproved, but in the highest degree improbable. It is quite a mistake, says Halévy, to find the proclamation of a new code of law in Neh. viii.—x.; and the appeal to 2 Kings xxii. xxiii. breaks down; for the very thing which the comparison really proves is, that the two events were *not* parallel. Nor will he admit that Neh. viii. 14—17 proves what has been deduced from it; for although the account in question refers to Lev. xxiii. 40, yet Ezra iii. 4 (where not only Lev. xxiii. 39—44, but Num. xxix. 12—39 also, is presupposed) forbids us to take the passage as implying that Lev. xxiii. 40 was carried out for the first time on this occasion, and had been previously unknown. It is absurd, he continues, to infer from Ezra vii. 12, 21; 14, 25 (Wellhausen, I. 422), that Ezra brought a new book of law with him from Babylonia; for, to say nothing of the fact that these verses 14, 25, belong to a spurious document, they imply no more than that Ezra knew and loved the Thorah, and betook himself to Judæa in order to further the subjection of the people to it.

The weakness of the argument is obvious. Ezra's lamentations in Ezra ix. certainly prove that he was in thorough earnest with his devotion to the Thorah (Deut. xxiii. 2—9) and his pain at its being neglected by the people; but how any one who has read Ezra x. can deny that these feelings were coupled with drastic energy and a zeal that nothing could appal, is almost inexplicable. Nehemia too was full of energy—who will question it?—but (as appears especially from Neh. xiii.) his ideas completely coincided with Ezra's. It is this, and this alone, that explains the opposition he had instantly to face when he undertook the rebuilding of the walls of Jerusalem (Neh. iii.—vi.).[1] There is nothing unnatural, therefore, in the supposition that he co-operated with Ezra. But in what did they co-operate? Neh. viii.—x. gives us the answer. One is almost tempted to ask whether Halévy has read these chapters, and especially chap. x. If he has, how can he write (pp. 34, 35), "qu'après la lecture aucune mesure n'a été prise pour introduire dans la pratique les prescriptions propres au code sacerdotal, comme par

---

[1] Graetz, Gesch. der Juden, II. 2, S. 139 ff.

exemple la célébration du jour de pardon que ce code regarde comme le plus saint de l'année"? Whether Lev. xvi. was already taken up into the priestly code at that time is indeed questionable.[1] But it is untrue that this code itself was not practically introduced. See Neh. viii. 18; x. 33—40 (32—39); and compare my Religion of Israel, Vol. II. pp. 227, 229 sqq. To attempt to put aside the evidence of Neh. viii. 17 by an appeal to Ezra iii. 4, is superficial in the extreme. In the latter passage it is the Chronicler himself who is speaking, in his well-known style, but Neh. viii.—x. he has taken from elsewhere, and these chapters have far higher historical worth. Cf. my Religion of Israel, Vol. II. pp. 286—291, and Wellhausen in Bleek's Einleitung in das A. T. 4te Aufl. S. 268, n. 1. Finally, no one will wonder, after all that has been said, at the high significance which we attach to those texts which bring Ezra and the Law into so close a connection with each other. They give us exactly what we require to explain Neh. viii.—x., if only we refrain from watering them down, and accept them as meaning that Ezra brought with him out of Babylonia something which at that time was not known, much less adopted, in Judæa.

In conclusion, Halévy declares (pp. 37, 38) that he entertains serious doubts as to the truth of the narrative of the Chronicler (Ezra vii.—x.), which represents Ezra as having arrived in Judæa and attempted a reformation there thirteen years before Nehemia. This, he says, is contradicted by Neh. vii. 7, where Ezra, there called Azariah, follows Nehemia—"ce qui fait penser que la tentative de réforme qui fait l'objet des chapitres ix. et x. du livre d'Esdras est identique à celle qui a été exécutée sous Néhémie." It is quite in harmony with this view, he urges, that Ezra should never have been regarded as a great man, or been specially exalted as such, till a far later time: Jesus Sirach (chap. xlix. 13) only mentions Nehemia, and the ancient haggada, 2 Makk. i. 10—ii. 18, gives to the latter the honour which Pharisaism ascribes to Ezra.

Against such reckless criticism we cannot protest too earnestly.

---

[1] Cf. Reuss, in the introduction to his translation of "L'histoire sainte et la loi," p. 260.

The writer overlooks the fact that Ezra vii.—x. is borrowed in part from Ezra's own memoirs. He takes no notice of Neh. xii. 36, where Nehemia himself tells us that Ezra, the sophér, led a band of singers on occasion of the consecration of the walls of Jerusalem, which is surely proof enough that at that time he was no obscure or insignificant individual, but had already won his spurs. The appeal to Neh. vii. 7 is unpardonable. Neh. vii. is the catalogue of the exiles who returned with Zerubbabel and Joshua (v. 5), a duplicate of Ezra ii. If Nehemia and Ezra had appeared there, they would have been about a hundred and twenty years old in 445 B.C.! But, besides this, Nehemia tells us himself (chap. i.) that he was an officer in the Persian court in the twentieth year of Artaxerxes I., and (chap. vii. 4, 5) that the catalogue in question contained the names of those who had gone to Judæa "at the first." As to Ezra, he is mentioned neither in Neh. vii. 7 (where Azariah stands), nor in Ezra ii. 2 (where we find Seraiah). "Azariah" is a very common name, borne by about twenty-five different individuals in the Old Testament. What right can we have to alter it into "Ezra"? But the appeal to Neh. vii. 7 really does not deserve the attention we have given it. As for Sirach xlix. 13, compare my Religion of Israel, Vol. III. pp. 87—89. The account of Nehemia in 2 Makk. i. 10—ii. 18, proves nothing either for or against Ezra, unless one first takes the liberty of crediting Ezra with the collection of "the Prophets and the Writings," and then takes 2 Makk. ii. 13 as evidence that it was not he, but Nehemia, that accomplished it!

To the question of the antiquity of the priestly laws, Halévy only devotes a few pages (pp. 38—44), and there he confines himself to the comparison of Lev. xxiii. 40 and Neh. viii. 15, a comparison intended to prove that, when Neh. viii. 15 was written, an exegesis was already current which expanded and modified the commandment in question. I consider this extremely doubtful. But if it were so, what then? No one says that Neh. viii. 15 was written by Ezra. For the rest, the defenders of the post-exilian origin of the priestly thorah will gladly answer Halévy if he will but set out his objections. But as long as he thinks he can settle the question by a few quotations, he has not earned a refutation. Does he think his few lines on Ezekiel xx. (p. 39) can draw the sinews of R. Smend's commentary on that prophet?

Compare, further, M. Vernes in the Revue de l'histoire des rel. Tom. IV. pp. 373—377, who appears to me to assign more than its true merit to his contributor's article, but insists, at the same time, with the fullest justice, on the distinction between the two questions: Is the priestly thorah later than Deuteronomy, exilian or post-exilian? and, What is the true relation in which Ezra stands to this thorah? On the last point opinions may differ, and in fact the "Grafianer" are not unanimous. But this is a matter of subordinate consequence, concerning which, in the very natural absence of historical data, we shall perhaps never arrive at certainty. The affirmative answer to the former question, on the other hand, is as firmly established as could possibly be desired.

Note X. (P. 186, n. 2.)

Explanation of Leviticus xxii. 25.

Wellhausen (Gesch. Israels, I. 390) finds in the earlier priestly legislation, from which Leviticus xvii. sqq. is largely drawn, a spirit of hostility towards the heathen, which was the consequence of the demand for holiness. He speaks of "der schroffen Ausschliessung heidnischer Ausländer vom Gottesdienst, von denen nach Lev. xxii. 25 nicht einmal Opfer angenommen werden dürfen." Dillmann (Exod. und Levit. S. 574) reads in Lev. xxii. 25 the very opposite of what Wellhausen "makes the writer say," for according to him the supposition underlies this text, "dass auch Fremde dem Jahve für sich opfern lassen dürfen." Which of the two is right?

$V.$ 24a forbids the sacrifice of castrated animals to Yahweh. The lawgiver might indeed have been content with the simple prohibition, without thinking it necessary to add that such beasts were not pleasing to Yahweh and would not be accepted by him. But the analogy of $vv.$ 19, 20, 21, 23, would lead us to expect that the author

—who prefers saying too much rather than too little—would not withhold some such further explanation. The exegesis of vv. 24 b, 25, must not lose sight of this. According to the Jewish tradition, v. 24 b forbids the castration of bulls, &c., and must be translated, "and in your land ye shall not make (them)," (i.e. shall not bring them into the condition indicated by the participles in v. 24 a). Knobel and Dillmann object to this interpretation, which seems to them to attach a meaning to the Hebrew verb "make" or "do" which it cannot bear. There can be no doubt that such a use of the verb is unusual and forced, but what else can it mean in this passage? Knobel interprets: "and in your land ye shall not prepare (such sacrificial beasts);" whatever the heathen may do, in your land nothing of the kind shall happen. Dillmann thinks that the meaning is: "(not only here, in the desert, but) in your own land too, ye shall refrain from doing it" (i.e. what is forbidden in v. 24 a). But neither the contrast between the Israelitish and the heathen usage, nor the contrast between the desert and Canaan, is to the purpose here. The latter is especially inapposite, since all the sacrificial laws are given for Canaan. In my opinion, v. 24 b must be closely connected with 25 a, and together they express the thought that the Israelites are no more at liberty to assign to the altar these castrated animals in their own land, than they are to receive or buy them "from the hand of a foreigner," in order "to bring the meat-offering of their god from one of all these (i.e. of all these kinds of castrated animals)." By uniting vv. 24 b, 25 a, the expression in v. 24 b is made tolerable, if not altogether defensible. But this way of taking the passage is chiefly recommended by v. 25 b, which has reference not only to v. 25 a, but also to v. 24 a, to which it adds the very supplement which we missed but now in v. 24: "for their mutilation, their defect, is in them (i.e. for they, these sacrificial beasts, are mutilated and defective); they will not be acceptable for you (i.e. will not be received in grace for you)." "For you" implies that it is Israelites who offer the sacrifices in v. 25 as well as in v. 24, and hence that "the foreigner" does not appear in this passage either as the sacrificer or as the person on whose behalf the sacrifice is made, but exclusively as the provider of the castrated sacrificial beasts. To explain the expression, "*from the hand* of a foreigner," reference is usually made to Num. v. 25; Isaiah i. 12. But in these passages it is the priest or Yahweh himself who accepts or demands the offering from the offerer, whereas in Levit. xxii. 25 it is the Israelites who receive the sacrificial beast " from the hand" of a third party, though offering it themselves and on their own behalf. Dillmann was close upon giving the explanation here supported, but allowed himself to be drawn away from it by his objections to the traditional acceptation of *v.* 24 *b*, objections which, as it seems to me, are in a great measure met by the close union of *vv.* 24 *b* and 25 *a*.

The question we have asked must therefore be answered by the assertion that the sacrifice of a foreigner is neither forbidden nor assumed in this passage. It is simply not referred to. This is by no means surprising. In the priestly legislation the "ben-nécár" (unless he serves the Israelite as a slave [Gen. xvii. 12, 27], which is of course out of the question here) as definitely stands outside the community, as the "gér" (according to this very thorah, Lev. xxii. 18) takes his place within it. The sacrifice of a "ben-nécár" therefore must be regarded as lying quite outside the lawgiver's field of vision; it did not need to be forbidden and it could not be assumed.

NOTE XI. (P. 192, n. 1.)

Bruno Bauer and Ernest Havet.

The principal objections to B. Bauer's "Christus und die Cäsaren" are touched upon on pp. 191 sq. Here I may add a few references and remarks to show that his main thesis (of which his reader is often allowed completely to lose sight) has been correctly represented, and that the considerations which must lead to its rejection might have been expressed far more strongly yet.

B. Bauer is perfectly serious in his denial of the Jewish origin of Christianity. See S. 300—301. The Jewish element is simply the framework (S. 302). The content, "das Gemüth," comes from

Rome, especially from the further development of the Stoic philosophy which took place there (S. 302—305, cf. 47—61 on Seneca), and from Alexandria, especially from Philo, the disciple of Heraclitus (S. 305—308). This of course involves the thesis that the supposed founders of Christianity are not historical personages. Bruno Bauer accepts this consequence without reserve, as appears especially from S. 298 ff. (on the creative "Urevangelium," about 115—140 A.D.) and from S. 345 ff. (on the rise of the New Testament literature and the symbolical significance of the figures of Peter and Paul).

I will not now argue against B. Bauer from the New Testament, which is the very matter in dispute; but I cannot refrain from calling attention to the fact that his hypotheses concerning the origin of some of the books frequently overstep all legitimate bounds. When a man places the Apocalypse, as our author does (S. 171 ff.), about the middle of the reign of Marcus Aurelius (i.e. 170 A.D.), without so much as mentioning the external and internal objections to such a date, has he not really forfeited his right to a voice in the matter? But quite apart from the evidence of the New Testament, B. Bauer's thesis is condemned:

1. By the truly reckless distortion of Judaism which it necessarily involves. I refer not only to S. 300 f. (on "der angebliche Hillel"), but also and especially to S. 293 ff. (on Bar-Cochba, R. Akiba and the very late origin of the Jewish Messianic expectation); and, further, to the utter failure to appreciate the significance of Essenism, which is all the more surprising since the Egyptian Therapeutæ are recognized as historical (S. 306—308), and the authenticity of Philo "de vita contemplativa" is expressly taken under protection.

2. By the slovenly style in which the dependence of the New Testament upon Seneca is worked out, though B. Bauer's whole system must stand or fall with it. From the "de Providentia," cap. i. 2, he cites (S. 52) these words: "Gott hege gegen die Guten einen väterlichen Sinn und übe sie, die er gern kräftig hat, durch Schmerzen und Schaden. Gott prüft (experitur) den Guten, härtet ihn ab und bereitet ihn für sich zu." As parallels to this, bor-

rowed from it, he then quotes Rom. ix. 18 ("so God shows mercy on whom he will, and *whom he will he hardeneth;*" but according to B. Bauer, "wen Gott lieb hat, härtet er ab"!) and Hebrews xii. 6, 7 (N.B. a literal citation of Prov. iii. 11, 12!). A few pages further on (S. 57), the parallel passages in Seneca and Paul concerning slaves are mentioned; but Job xxxi. 13—15, with which Paul coincides in substance, is passed by in silence. But enough! In his work, "Das Urevangelium u. s. w." (vid. sup. p. 191, n. 1), B. Bauer indignantly repudiates the charge of having failed to appreciate F. C. Baur's classical treatise on Seneca and Paul (S. 39 ff.). If he had been able to read it in an unprejudiced spirit, his whole book would have remained unwritten.

"Le Christianisme et ses origines," by Ernest Havet, is a far superior work. The First Part (Tom. I. II. L'Hellénisme) retains its value even for those who cannot accept its positions. Certain expressions make one think that B. Bauer might have claimed Havet as his precursor. The latter, for instance, declares his intention (I. Préface, p. v) of studying Christianity "dans ses sources premières et plus profondes, celles de l'antiquité hellénique, dont il est sorti presque tout entier," and thinks (ibid. p. xix) that the first two Gospels are still more Greek than the Epistles of Paul. But, after all, that "presque tout entier" implies some limitation. It is true that everything in "L'Hellénisme" that has even a distant resemblance to Christianity is carefully searched out, and throughout this process, as well as in the summary of the conclusions (T. II. 311 svv.), the resemblances are placed, in a one-sided manner, in the foreground, and the differences, which are sometimes quite as essential, are disguised or passed by in silence. But in spite of all this, there is no intention of excluding Judaism, or of denying its contribution to the genesis of Christianity. On the contrary, this Judaic influence is recognized from the first (e.g. T. I. Préf. p. xiv, &c.), and is therefore expressly illustrated in a Second Part ("Le Judaisme"). With this Second Part itself I have no intention of dealing here. Even M. Vernes' very friendly criticism (Mélanges de critique religieuse pp. 181—217), though in my opinion it yields too much to Havet, nevertheless makes it abundantly evident that he has gone on a false track in "Le Judaisme," and was mistaken in thinking that he could transform the history of the Old Testament literature without any knowledge of the language in which it is written. The fact is, then, that of the two factors which have to be taken into consideration in explaining the origin of Christianity, one is unknown, or at any rate very imperfectly known, to Havet. Of course this fact could not be without its influence upon his solution of the problem;—a problem to which it is by no means immaterial whether one gives their true place, for instance, to prophetism and to Deuteronomy, or whether, with Havet, one brings them down from the pre-exilian era to the Greek or even the Maccabæan period. But it would be a mistake to suppose that the one-sidedness of Havet's solution could be deduced simply from this perverse conception of Judaism. To convince ourselves of this, we may read, more especially, T. II. 319 svv., III. 485 svv., where the position is defended that "L'Hellénisme" was already well on the way towards reforming itself in the same direction as that in which Christianity actually led the world, and might have reached the goal without Christianity, and perhaps even better than with it. Havet is indeed quite aware that he is dealing in mere fancies when he asks, and tries to answer the question, What would have happened if the impulse from Judæa had not been given? (T. II. 321 sv.). But involuntarily he allows what appears to him the most reasonable answer to this imaginary question, to exercise an influence on his solution of the historical question that he has undertaken to consider. Hellenism as, in his opinion, it *would have become*,—having risen in its entirety from the polytheistic, the national and the æsthetic position, to monotheism, universalism and an ethical conception of life,—is constantly placing itself, as it were, between his eyes and the actual Hellenism, and making the latter play a part which it never really assumed. Any one is at liberty—strange as the fancy may be—to regard the impulse from Judæa as superfluous, and to regret its having been given; but it remains a fact that it was given, and that the new world owes its rise to it. And this being so, it must not be denied that the movement of Hellenism towards monotheism, universalism and humanity, which Havet describes with so much talent, however valuable as an ally of Christianity and as a main cause of its triumph, cannot be regarded as the spring whence Christianity flowed—either altogether, or, as Havet expresses it, "*presque* tout entier."

NOTE XII. (P. 227, n. 3.)

Explanation of Matthew xxiii. 15.

The taunt cast upon the Scribes and Pharisees in Matt. xxiii. 15 ("Ye compass sea and land to make one proselyte,"), is certainly not free from exaggeration.[1] But it is highly probable that it rests upon a basis of fact. How could the Evangelist have written such words if the Scribes and Pharisees had in reality been indifferent to the accession of proselytes, or had even opposed it? At present, however, we are not in a position to decide exactly what is meant by their "compassing sea and land" to gain proselytes, or whence such attempts really emanated. It would be far from strange if, after the fall of the Jewish state in 70 A.D., and still more after the events under Trajan and Hadrian, the sentiments of the authorities at Jerusalem had undergone a change with respect to proselytism. Such a change, we know, took place with regard to the translation of the Holy Scriptures into Greek; for the favour with which it was at first regarded passed, after the events just referred to, into the strongest condemnation. Cf. Dr. M. Joël, Blicke in die Religionsgeschichte zu Anfang des zweiten christl. Jahrh. I. 6 ff. The author does not succeed in proving that it was the Christians who caused Hadrian to withdraw his permission to rebuild the temple of Jerusalem; but neither was any such special occasion needed to make the leaders of the Jews distrustful of heathens and Gentile-Christians alike, and to set them at work

---

[1] The older apologetic will not allow this; but the consequence is, that it has to conceal the weakness of its case behind mere assertion. See especially Danz, in Meuschen N. T. ex Talm. illustr. pp. 649—666.

to devise means for protecting their fellow-believers from the temptation to apostasy to which they stood exposed. Cf. Hausrath, Neutest. Zeitgeschichte, IV. 341. In the first century of our era they were far more free, and at any rate some of them, especially "the house of Hillel," may very well have yielded to the drift towards the extension of their faith which may be deemed inseparable from the belief that that faith was revealed by God. Cf. Geiger, das Judenthum und seine Geschichte, I. 88 f.; Dérenbourg, Hist. de la Palestine d'après les Thalmuds, pp. 222—229.

NOTE XIII. (P. 236, n. 2.)

The Buddha-Legend and the Gospels.

Prof. Seydel treats of the intercourse between India and the West, op. cit. S. 305 ff.; gives the "Buddhistisch-christliche Evangelienharmonie," S. 105—293; and points out the inferences that may be thence deduced, S. 294 ff. The parallels that have been detailed are divided into three classes. The first class includes those which offer no such resemblances as to warrant the inference of a historical connection. They may be merely accidental, involuntary parallels. To the second class belong those parallels which point directly to the dependence either of the Buddhists on the Gospels or of Gospels on the Buddha-legend; and, finally, the third class contains those which can only be explained on the hypothesis of Buddhistic influence on the origin of the Gospels. These last (S. 296 f.) are five in number, and the writer assigns all the more weight to them because there is not a single case which gives even the smallest probability to the opposite hypothesis of the dependence of the Buddhists on the Gospels. If these parallels of the third class have once proved the influence of Buddhism, then of course those of the second class gain increased importance. Seydel divides them into two groups, of twelve and eleven respectively; the former appear to him to testify more clearly than the latter to an acquaintance with the Buddha-saga (S. 298 ff.). And, lastly, fifteen parallels may be found, even in the first class, which are not wholly without significance (S. 300 f.).

While awaiting the verdict upon Seydel's book which a careful and impartial weighing of all the details may warrant, I confine myself here to a very brief defence of the *prognosis* I have ventured upon on p. 236. In the first place, we must admit that the decision on the point at issue is likely to remain to some extent subjective. The *possibility* of the influence of the Buddha-legend must be admitted or denied on strictly objective grounds, and, in my opinion, Seydel has established it; but the recognition of this influence as *actual* must depend upon the impression produced on the investigator by the consideration of the parallels, and this impression will not be the same in every mind. In the second place, it seems to me that Seydel has not paid enough attention to the standing contrast of conception and character between the Buddha-legend and the Gospels, which accompanies their resemblance—often striking enough—in special points. Compared with the Lalita Vistara, the Gospels, especially the first three, are eminently sober and simple. There is not any trace of an attempt to make the Christ vie with the Buddha in supernatural power, in the homage received from the dwellers in heaven and earth, and so on. Yet the Evangelists unquestionably placed the Christ above the Buddha, whose legend they or their predecessors *ex hypothesi* knew and made use of to embellish their story. Is this the natural relation? Should we not rather expect that they would, at any rate here and there, leave their model far behind them? In the third place, we must remember that mutual independence, even where there is real and great agreement, must always be recognized as a possibility. The parallel to Solomon's first judgment (1 Kings iii. 16—28) in the Jâtakas[1] is well known. Borrowing on either side, though not absolutely inconceivable, is in the highest degree improbable here. Why may not either narrative alike rest upon a fact? There is nothing against, but everything in favour of, the supposition that more than one trait in which the narratives concerning the two Founders coincide, should be explained

---

[1] Rhys Davids, Buddhist Birth Stories, I. pp. xiv—xvi, cf. xliv—xlvii.

from the existence of similar motives and conditions in either case. This must not be regarded as a subterfuge, but, on the contrary, must be allowed its full claim to consideration as in itself highly probable.

Lastly, and chiefly, we must never forget that the derivation of this or that detail from a foreign "Sagenkreis"—acquaintance with which is not proved already, but is the very point to be established—can only be allowed when it is clearly shown that the circle of ideas in which the writer unquestionably moved does not itself offer anything, or at least does not offer enough, to explain the details in question. This rule Prof. Seydel appears not to recognize, or at least not always to observe. The fast ascribed to Jesus before beginning his work (Matt. iv. 2; Luke iv. 2), which conflicts with his own custom (cf. Matt. ix. 14—17; xi. 7—19, and the parallel passages), was borrowed, according to Seydel, from the Buddha-legend (S. 154 f.). But ought we not to refer, in this connection, to Exod. xxxiv. 28; Deut. ix. 9? The question of the apostles concerning the man born blind: "Who did sin, this man or his parents?" (John ix. 2), has no meaning, he thinks, unless we interpret it by the Buddhistic doctrine of re-birth, according to which a man endures in his present life the penalty for what he has done amiss in a previous existence (S. 232 f.). One might ask whether this doctrine is specifically Buddhistic, and whether it is not possible that a sin committed in the womb may have been in the mind of the speakers (cf. Meyer's Commentary)? But in any case nothing can be more obvious in connection with this passage than the comparison of the Judæo-Alexandrine doctrine of pre-existence (e.g. Sap. Sal. viii. 20), which renders the Buddhistic parallel quite superfluous. Now these two parallels are amongst the five to which Seydel ascribes the highest degree of evidential value. A third (S. 166 ff.)—the pre-existence alike of the Buddha and of the Johannine Christ—he himself does not regard as conclusive. In the two that remain, referring to the presentation in the temple (Luke ii. 22 sqq.; S. 146 f.) and the sitting "under the fig-tree" (John i. 46 sqq.; S. 168 ff.), the difference appears to me far to overbalance the resemblance, and to throw it altogether into the shade. The simple scene in the temple at Jerusalem is really no parallel at all to the homage rendered to the Buddha-child, and in John i. it is Nathanael, and not the Christ, who sits under the fig-tree, as the Buddha sits under the Tree of Knowledge. In my opinion, then, these parallels of the third class completely fail to give us that firm basis which we should require to enable us confidently to go on further. And when it appears—as it actually does —that the details in the second group find their origin explained, so far as any explanation is needed, in the Old Testament, then to me at least the alleged Buddhistic influence becomes in the highest degree questionable.

Note XIV. (P. 253, n. 3).

The Founder of Jainism in the Buddha-Legend.

Dr. Bühler was the first to identify the founder of Jainism with one of the six false teachers put to shame by Buddha, Nâtaputta the Nirgrantha (Indian Antiquary, VII. (1878), p. 143). He was soon followed by Jacobi, who, in the Introduction to his edition of "The Kalpasûtra of Bhadrabâhu" (Abhandlungen für die Kunde des Morgenlandes, VII. No. 1), p. 1 sqq., not only based the identification on the similarity of the names and of certain details in the lives, but endeavoured further to support it by proofs drawn from the chronology of the Buddhists and the Jainas. Kern (vid. sup. 253, n. 4), Oldenberg (Z. d. d. M. G. XXXIV. 748 ff.; Buddha, sein Leben u. s. w. S. 67, 78) and others gave in their adhesion. Oldenberg's scruples with regard to the hypotheses by which Jacobi endeavours to explain the difference between the chronological systems of the two sects (Z. d. d. M. G. l. c.), are acknowledged by the latter as having a relative importance, but not as being insurmountable (ib. XXXV. 667—674).

Reference must likewise be made to an essay of Jacobi's, "On Mahâvira and his Predecessors" (Ind. Antiq. IX. 158—163). Starting from the Buddhistic accounts of the opinions of the false teachers (ib. VIII. 311—314), especially those of Nâtaputta, he points out the agreement between them and the doctrine of the Jainas, thus strengthening the proof already given of the connection between Nâtaputta and Jainism. But at the same time he so far modifies his former opinion as to accept the belief of the Jainas themselves that Mahâvira-Nâtaputta was not the founder of a new sect, but the reformer of a doctrine which had long existed. Twenty-three Jainas are made to precede him in the tradition. How we are to judge of them in general, may be gathered from the statement that the first of them, Rishabha, lived 840,000 great years, and died 300,000,000 oceans of years before the death of Mahâvira! But the immediate predecessor of the latter, Pârsva, is only separated from him by a space of 250 years, and may therefore be a historical personage. Jacobi endeavours to make it probable, by a variety of considerations, that he really was so. He calls attention, amongst other things, to the fact that the Buddhists ascribe an idea to Nâtaputta which the Jainas themselves say he combated, though his predecessor Pârsva adopted it. Jacobi takes this as an indication that the Buddhists, very naturally, failed to distinguish between the shades of opinion amongst their opponents. He further reminds us that, although the Buddhists mention the contest between the Buddha and the founder or reformer of Jainism, the Jainas, on the other hand, never mention the Buddha. This, too, appears to him very natural, inasmuch as, on his hypothesis, the Buddha departed from an age-old system, and must therefore have felt the necessity of justifying himself for so doing; whereas the Jainas were already in possession, so to speak, and might think it beneath them to enter upon any discussion with an innovator like the Buddha. For the further elaboration of all this I must refer to the essay itself (pp. 160—163).[1]

Jacobi does not conceal from himself the hazardous nature of his

---

[1] When Jacobi (l.c.) shows that the other five false teachers likewise "betray the influence of Jainism in doctrine or practice," he unintentionally weakens his proof of the identity of Mahâvira and Nâtaputta very materially. In the further discussion of this question, it will be necessary closely to define the meaning of the term "Jainism," or misconception and confusion will be the result.

hypothesis. "All these arguments are open to one fatal objection, viz., that they are taken from the Jaina literature, which was reduced to writing so late as the fifth century A.D." (p. 161). This is indeed no small difficulty. And a second objection of no less weight may be found in the fact that Nâtaputta's immediate predecessor, whom Jacobi recognizes as historical, is incorporated in an utterly absurd theory in which we should look for anything rather than history. It appears to me very comprehensible that such scholars as Barth (l.c. pp. 150 sq.) and Rhys Davids (Lectures, &c. p. 27) do not feel at liberty, for the present, to follow Jacobi on the path he has taken.

www.ingramcontent.com/pod-product-compliance
Lightning Source LLC
Chambersburg PA
CBHW030259240426
43673CB00040B/1004